21 世纪应用型精品规划教材　旅游管理专业

旅　游　英　语

赵海湖　王　宁　主　编
黄晓云　陈　杨　吕　倩　副主编
　　　　李艳丽　刘志霞

清华大学出版社
北　京

内容简介

本书把旅游行业知识和英语语言运用技能作为学习目标，将英语语言技能的学习融合到旅游行业新兴话题中进行编写。全书内容按照从整体到局部的原则，分为旅游服务、酒店行业、旅游景区、会展服务和中国传统文化5个模块12个单元，内容涵盖旅游行业、旅行社、酒店行业、"互联网+旅游"、邮轮业、旅游景区、会展业和"一带一路"旅游文化等知识。

同时，本书在内容编排上以企业的需求和高职高专学生为目标对象。此外，在国家"一带一路"倡议背景下，广州作为海上丝绸之路的起点，故而本书又结合了地方旅游特色以及"一带一路"沿线的旅游文化，使得书中内容能够与时俱进，更符合为培养地方经济服务的旅游英语人才之所需。

本书封面贴有清华大学出版社防伪标签，无标签者不得销售。
版权所有，侵权必究。举报：010-62782989，beiqinquan@tup.tsinghua.edu.cn。

图书在版编目(CIP)数据

旅游英语/赵海湖，王宁主编. —北京：清华大学出版社，2020.3(2024.7重印)
21世纪应用型精品规划教材. 旅游管理专业
ISBN 978-7-302-54960-4

Ⅰ.①旅… Ⅱ.①赵… ②王… Ⅲ.①旅游—英语—高等学校—教材 Ⅳ.①F59

中国版本图书馆 CIP 数据核字(2020)第 029788 号

责任编辑：孟　攀
装帧设计：杨玉兰
责任校对：谢若冰
责任印制：刘　菲

出版发行：清华大学出版社
　　网　　址：https://www.tup.com.cn，https://www.wqxuetang.com
　　地　　址：北京清华大学学研大厦A座　　邮　　编：100084
　　社　总　机：010-83470000　　邮　　购：010-62786544
　　投稿与读者服务：010-62776969，c-service@tup.tsinghua.edu.cn
　　质量反馈：010-62772015，zhiliang@tup.tsinghua.edu.cn
　　课件下载：https://www.tup.com.cn，010-62791865

印　装　者：北京嘉实印刷有限公司
经　　销：全国新华书店
开　　本：185mm×230mm　　印　张：14.75　　字　数：358千字
版　　次：2020年4月第1版　　印　次：2024年7月第7次印刷
定　　价：39.80元

产品编号：082880-01

前　　言

　　世界经济的不断发展，全球一体化进程的加速，国与国之间及各个地区间的交流日益频繁，促进了我国出入境旅游业的蓬勃发展。2017 年我国入境旅游人数 13,948 万人次，比上年同期增长 0.8%；国际旅游收入 1,234 亿美元，比上年同期增长 2.9%；中国公民出境旅游人数 13,051 万人次，比上年同期增长 7.0%。在"一带一路"倡议背景下，"一带一路"沿线国家在我国入境旅游市场中的活跃度持续上升。根据《文化部"十三五"时期文化发展改革规划》，我国要加强与"一带一路"沿线国家的文化交流与合作。

　　据世界旅游组织预测，到 2020 年中国将成为世界上第四大国际旅游客源地和最大的国际旅游目的地。我国《旅游质量发展纲要(2013—2020 年)》提到，旅游发展的总体目标是"到 2020 年，旅游质量基础进一步坚实，旅游市场秩序明显改善，旅游服务水平显著提升，旅游质量体系更加完善，游客满意度居服务业前列，在国际上树立'美丽中国之旅'品牌，旅游业为全面建成小康社会做出更大贡献"。

　　随着我国出入境旅游的快速发展，旅游英语人才的需求越趋广泛，高职旅游英语教学日益受到人们的重视，而旅游英语教材是教学活动得以顺利进行的重要载体，缺乏优秀的教材，教学质量和教学效率就得不到保证。根据多年教学实践以及对旅游英语教材的市场调查，编写组发现当前的旅游英语教材存在以下问题。

　　(1) 教材的内容和素材滞后过时。许多旅游英语教材选取的内容和素材不能体现旅游产业更新和社会发展的现状。比如，现在旅游行业发展的态势有"互联网+旅游、乡村旅游、邮轮旅游、会展旅游、'一带一路'旅游文化"等，但这些素材在现有的旅游英语教材中较少体现。如今随着智能手机、在线支付的普及，教材很多内容也需要更新。

　　(2) 体现中国本土特色的教材不多，和具体省市当地特色相结合更是少之又少。例如，书中的旅游出行习惯都是按照西方的行为习惯来安排，缺少与中国具体省市相结合的内容，对于接待来中国旅游的外宾也缺少中国的特色。此外，某个地区使用的教材不能很好地与当地的特色相结合，地区培养的高职旅游英语人才毕业后大部分都服务于当地的旅游业，但学生在学习使用旅游英语教材时没有加深和强化对当地旅游的了解。

　　(3) 教材配套产品不足，质量不高。当前的教材主要以纸质书面材料为主，局限于课堂教学，未能开发教材媒介的多元化潜质。现行的旅游英语教材大部分只包括教科书、教学参考书，配套产品局限在音频和磁带，没有配套的视频材料等。

　　(4) 语言难易程度与高职学生英语水平不一致。现有的教材都是面对国内所有高职院校的普适类教材，编写教材前没有对使用教材的学生的英语水平进行深入的了解，教材难度与学生的实际英语水平不匹配，未能遵守循序渐进的阶段性原则，内容编排的随意性较大，语言与专业知识结构没有呈递进性结构编排。

(5) 内容的编排不利于具有高职学生特点的教学方法的实施。很多阅读教材只是给出阅读的文章和知识点，导致课堂上教师"满堂灌"，不能发挥学生的主体作用。

因此，为了更科学更合理地培养国际旅游人才，编者进行了本书的编写。

首先，本教材以旅游行业内容为依托，教学内容与旅游学科、职业和活动密切相关，旨在扩大学生的知识面，最大限度地向学习者提供有意义的、真实的语言和语言学习环境，激发学生的兴趣和创造力，引导学生在运用语言的同时，拓宽对旅游行业的了解。

其次，本教材把旅游行业知识和英语语言运用技能作为学习目标，将英语语言技能的学习融合到旅游行业新兴话题中进行编写。教材内容按照从整体到局部的原则，分为旅游服务、酒店行业、旅游景区、会展服务和中国传统文化 5 个模块 12 个单元，内容涵盖旅游行业、旅行社、酒店行业、互联网+旅游、邮轮业、旅游景区、会展业、"一带一路"旅游文化等知识。在英语语言技能方面，本教材侧重的是旅游英语阅读、写作和翻译能力的培养，同时可与旅游英语听说教材配合使用，以提高学生在旅游真实工作场景中的读写译能力。

最后，在素材选取方面，本教材的英语阅读素材均选自旅游业中各类实用性材料，包括景区宣传册，国内英文旅游期刊，国外旅游网站，英文原版文献等，确保内容的真实性和时效性；同时选择适合高职旅游专业或者旅游类学生英语水平的素材，以提高学生学习的兴趣和效果。

每单元的内容如下。

(1) 本单元主题相关的信息搜索(学生课前完成)：学生课前通过提供的二维码，搜索查找与本单元旅游主题相关的信息，并通过移动学习平台(如微信群、雨课堂等)与其他同学进行分享，了解每单元的背景知识，教师课堂点评总结。

(2) Passage A 及配套练习：学生阅读文章完成规定的阅读练习，以及针对 Passage A 的语言知识点，设计了相应的课后练习，如词汇填空、句子翻译等，来巩固所学语言知识。

(3) Passage B 及配套练习：学生阅读文章完成规定的阅读练习，以及针对 Passage B 的语言知识点，设计了相应的课后练习，如词汇填空、句子翻译等，来巩固所学语言知识。

(4) 中译英段落翻译：每单元设有中译英段落翻译练习，该练习内容均与各单元主题内容相关，既可逐渐提高学生的翻译能力，又可让学生了解更多与单元主题相关的文化知识。

(5) 工作场景项目任务：在每个单元设计了与单元主题相关的工作场景中需要完成的任务，如菜单设计、旅游线路设计、会议安排等，学生模拟真实工作场景，使用英语语言进行实践。

(6) 旅游英语应用文写作：该部分按照难易程度循序渐进的原则，设计了旅游行业中常见的应用文写作，如简历、导游词、签证申请表、旅游调查问卷等，满足旅游业中实际工作的需求。

(7) 补充阅读(学生可课后完成，或者可作为每单元阅读课的阅读素材)：每单元最后附上 1 篇与本单元主题相关的英语新闻材料或者旅游真实工作场景的阅读材料，提高学生学习的主动性，拓宽学生的视野。

此外，本教材还提供配套教学和学习资源。具体配有电子课件、导游技能大赛获奖导游词电子版、中国主要景点英文介绍电子版、与每单元主题相关的视频、旅游英语词汇扩展等，可从清华大学出版社网站下载。

在"互联网+"时代下，本教材编写中倡导使用多媒体、网络、视频等教学手段；在学生学习方面，引导学生使用微信群、公众号、app 等移动学习平台进行学习。

本书编者的分工如下(按姓氏首字母顺序)：陈杨执笔第 7、8 单元，以及写作部分；黄晓云执笔第 4、9、10 单元；李艳丽执笔第 6、11、12 单元；吕倩执笔第 5 单元；王宁执笔第 3 单元；赵海湖执笔第 1、2 单元。

本书在编写过程中得到了教学同行、业内人士以及清华大学出版社的大力支持，在此一并致谢。因多方面原因，书中难免有错误和不足之处，恳请广大读者批评指正，提出宝贵意见。

编　者

目 录

Module One　Travel Services 1

Unit 1　Tourism and Tourism Industry 3
　　Passage A　Tourism Industry 4
　　Passage B　Tourism in China 8
　　Writing: Resume 简历 13
　　Supplementary Reading 16

Unit 2　Travel Agency 19
　　Passage A　Travel Agency 20
　　Passage B　Tour Guide 25
　　Writing: Welcome Speech 欢迎词 30
　　Supplementary Reading 32

Unit 3　Online Travel Service 35
　　Passage A　Booming Time for Online
　　　　　　　Travel Services 36
　　Passage B　How is Technology
　　　　　　　Transforming Chinese
　　　　　　　Tourism 41
　　Writing: Visa Application and Invitation
　　　　　　签证的申请与邀请 47
　　Supplementary Reading 54

Module Two　Hospitality 57

Unit 4　Hospitality Industry 59
　　Passage A　The Hospitality Industry 60
　　Passage B　Club Med 65
　　Writing: Reservation Letter 预订信 69
　　Supplementary Reading 72

Unit 5　Food and Beverage Services 75
　　Passage A　Chinese Cuisine 76
　　Passage B　Western Cuisine 82
　　Writing: Menu 菜单 87
　　Supplementary Reading 90

Module Three　Tourist Attractions 93

Unit 6　Tourism Product 95
　　Passage A　Types of Tourism 96
　　Passage B　Customized Tour 101
　　Writing: Tourism Advertisement and
　　　　　　Brochure 旅游广告与
　　　　　　宣传册 107
　　Supplementary Reading 109

Unit 7　Tourist Attractions 112
　　Passage A　World Heritage 113
　　Passage B　Mount Huangshan 118
　　Writing: Tour Commentary 导游词 123
　　Supplementary Reading 126

Unit 8　Cruising 128
　　Passage A　An Introduction of
　　　　　　　Cruising 129
　　Passage B　Carnival Cruise 134
　　Writing: Tour Itinerary 旅游线路 138
　　Supplementary Reading 143

Module Four　MICE 145

Unit 9　Introduction to MICE 147
　　Passage A　MICE 148
　　Passage B　Incentive Travel 153
　　Writing: Other forms in Tourism 旅游
　　　　　　其他相关表格 158
　　Supplementary Reading 161

Unit 10　Canton Fair 164

Passage A　Canton Fair 165
Passage B　Travel Services for MICE 170
Writing: Tour Contract 旅游合同 175
Supplementary Reading 182

Module Five　Traditional Chinese Culture 185

Unit 11　Traditional Chinese Culture and Festivals 187
Passage A　A Glimpse of Traditional Chinese Culture 188

Passage B　A Brief Introduction to Traditional Chinese Festivals 195
Writing: Farewell Speech　欢送词 202
Supplementary Reading 204

Unit 12　Chinese Arts 207
Passage A　Peking Opera 208
Passage B　Chinese Calligraphy 213
Writing: Tourism Questionnaire 旅游调查问卷 219
Supplementary Reading 223

参考文献 227

Unit 1   Tourism and Tourism Industry

Learning Objective

After learning this unit, you should:
- Acquire the knowledge and information of tourism industry all over the world, especially in China.
- Grasp professional English words and expressions for tourism industry.
- Get some cultural knowledge about tourism industry in China.
- Find ways to improve your writing skills about resume.

Keywords

tourism industry, domestic tourism, outbound tourism, inbound tourism

Information search

Please search some information about the topic of this unit by scanning the QR codes: (Travel Column of *China Daily*), (China Plus), (World Tourism Organization), (Travelogue of CCTV), (Ministry of Culture and Tourism of the People's Republic of China). After reading the information, please share with your classmates some information about the topic of this unit.

Warm-up:

Task 1: Please match the pictures with the words related to tourism industry.

A. accommodation B. food service C. touring
D. entertainment E. transportation F. shopping

Task 2: Please visit the website *http://www2.unwto.org/*, and try to find out as much information about tourism industry as possible, and share your information with your partner.

Passage A   Tourism Industry

The history of tourism began with the tavern and inn of early days. They offered food and shelter to travelers. The food was usually simple and travelers had to share beds with each other. The service was friendly, but the accommodations lacked the comfort and convenience travelers expect today.

Mass tourism is a product of the late 1960s and early 1970s. It is a type of human planned activities mainly for people's motivation of sightseeing, entertainment, curiosity or knowledge. Exactly, tourism consists of several key elements—food service, accommodation, transportation, touring, shopping and entertainment. Travel has always been considered to help to increase one's knowledge and broaden one's mind.

Nowadays, the tourism industry has been one of the fastest growing industries. According to UNWTO, international tourist arrivals grew by 7% to 1,323 million and international tourism generated US$1.6 trillion in export earnings in 2017. UNWTO also forecast a growth in international tourist arrivals between 4% and 5% in 2018. By 2030, UNWTO forecast that international tourist arrivals will reach 1.8 billion.

Actually, the growth of tourism has generally exceeded the growth of the worldwide economy. Already, in terms of direct and indirect employment opportunities, tourism is the largest industry in the world, and could become the largest sector of world trade. For many countries, tourism has become an important way to promote economic development and a major source of foreign currency. Sometimes it seems as if a new area springs up every day wherever there are sun and sea.

This global spread of tourism has produced economic and employment benefits in many related areas for lots of countries. It benefits not only airlines, hotels, restaurants, and taxi drivers, but also many commercial items, such as sunglasses, cameras, film and sports clothing. That's one of the important reasons for encouraging tourism industry in many countries.

There are many factors contributing to the rapid development of tourism industry. First, it depends on modern, rapid and inexpensive transportation. Tourism involves the movement of people. Therefore, transportation and tourism are closely related to each other. For example, the fastest growth of international tourism took place at the same time as the growth of air transportation, which is a post Second World War phenomenon. Second, creation of more and more disposable income for many people is necessary for tourism. With such income, people can travel wherever they want. Another important factor is urbanization. Generally speaking, residents of the big population cities take more holiday trips than those of rural areas. Besides, long weekends and paid vacations are one of the most important conditions for the development of modern tourism. In some countries, the cost of the holiday for employees is subsidized by government or employers.

Though tourism produces positive effects on economic growth, and we should try our best to promote tourism, we must be aware that tourism may bring about a terrible impact on our environment if it develops improperly. Firstly, scenic spots are exploited incorrectly. In order to attract tourists, a lot of artificial facilities have been built, which have certain negative impact on the environment. Secondly, some tourists don't have the awareness to protect the environment, and throw their garbage here and there. Some people even kill the local wildlife to eat, which badly damages the balance of the natural environment. It is wrong to sacrifice the environment for the growth of tourism. We need to find a balance between increasing needs of tourists and healthy development of tourism industry.

New words and expressions

lack [læk] *vt.* 缺乏，缺少
curiosity [ˌkjʊəriˈɒsəti] *n.* 好奇心
accommodation [əˌkɒməˈdeɪʃn] *n.* 住处
export [ˈekspɔːt] *vt./n.* 出口，输出
forecast [ˈfɔːkɑːst] *vt.* 预报，预测
exceed [ɪkˈsiːd] *vt.* 超过；超越；胜过
benefit [ˈbenɪfɪt] *n.* 利益，好处　*vt.* 使受益，有助于
involve [ɪnˈvɒlv] *vt.* 包含，使参与
disposable [dɪˈspəʊzəbl] *adj.* 可支配的，可任意处理的
urbanization [ˌɜːbənaɪˈzeɪʃn] *n.* 城市化，都市化
rural [ˈrʊərəl] *adj.* 乡下的，农村的
subsidize [ˈsʌbsɪdaɪz] *vt.* 补助，给……发津贴

aware [əˈweə(r)] *adj.* 意识到的

exploit [ɪkˈsplɔɪt] *vt.* 开发，开采

artificial [ˌɑːtɪˈfɪʃl] *adj.* 人工的，人造的

wildlife [ˈwaɪldlaɪf] *n.* 野生动物

sacrifice [ˈsækrɪfaɪs] *vt.* 牺牲

balance [ˈbæləns] *n.* 平衡

broaden one's mind 扩大视野，开阔眼界

Notes

1. mass tourism: 大众旅游。首先是指旅游活动参加者的范围已扩展到普通的劳动大众。大众旅游的另外一层含意则是现代旅游活动开始形成以有组织的团体包价旅游为代表的大众型旅游模式，并且形成广大民众中占支配地位的旅游形式。二战后，由于交通快速发展，尤其是航空业，大大促进了大众旅游的发展。

2. UNWTO：全称 United Nations World Tourism Organization，联合国世界旅游组织，总部设在西班牙马德里。它是联合国系统的政府间国际组织，是旅游领域的领导性国际组织，有 156 个正式会员国和 6 个联系成员。其宗旨是促进和发展旅游事业，使之有利于经济发展、国家间相互了解以及世界的和平与繁荣。

3. disposable income: 可支配收入，指拿到手的收入，即收入中扣除掉基本养老保险、基本医疗保险、失业保险、公积金、个人所得税等剩下的那部分，居民家庭获得并且可以用来自由支配的收入。

4. paid vacation: 带薪假期。在中国，带薪假期包括国家法定假日(如春节、元旦等)、年休假、产假、婚假、丧假、探亲假等。

5. sacrifice the environment for the growth of tourism: 为了旅游发展，牺牲了环境。sacrifice A for B：为了 B，牺牲 A。

6. find a balance between increasing needs of tourists and healthy development of tourism industry：在游客与日俱增的需求和旅游业的健康发展之间找到平衡。find a balance between A and B：在 A 和 B 之间找到平衡。

7. Sometimes it seems as if a new area springs up every day wherever there are sun and sea. 有时候，(旅游行业)看起来像是只要有太阳和大海的地方，每天就会快速发展的产业。spring up: 迅速成长；突然产生。

8. Exactly, tourism consists of several key elements—food service, accommodation, transportation, touring, shopping and entertainment. 旅游包括几个要素，食、住、行、游、购、娱。

Unit 1 Tourism and Tourism Industry

Exercises

1. Answer the following questions according to the passage.

(1) What is the tourism like in the early days?
_____

(2) What are the key elements of tourism?
_____

(3) According to UNWTO, what is the forecast for tourism industry?
_____

(4) Why is tourism encouraged in many countries?
_____

(5) Why is tourism industry developing so rapidly?
_____

(6) What are the terrible impacts of tourism on the environment?
_____

2. Fill in the blanks with the appropriate form of the words or phrases given below in the box.

lack	broaden one's mind	export	forecast	exceed
involve	be subsidized by	aware	wildlife	be related to

(1) In my free time, I like reading to _____.
(2) We are making a film about _____.
(3) He _____ that average salary increases will remain around 4%.
(4) Our travel expenses _____ the college.
(5) Despite his _____ of experience, he got the job.
(6) The demand for places at some schools _____ the supply.
(7) Smokers are well _____ of the dangers to their own health.
(8) The nation also _____ beef.
(9) I seem to have _____ myself in something I don't understand.
(10) This heart attack may _____ his overwork.

3. Translate the following expressions into English or Chinese.

(1) mass tourism _____
(2) broaden one's mind _____
(3) increase one's knowledge _____

(4) spring up _____
(5) sports clothing _____
(6) depend on _____
(7) be related to _____
(8) paid vacation _____
(9) 造成，引起(某事) _____
(10) 风景区，名胜 _____
(11) 人工设施 _____
(12) 可支配收入 _____
(13) 农村地区 _____
(14) 游客到达人数 _____
(15) 外汇 _____
(16) 出口收入 _____

4. Translate the following sentences into English with the words or phrases given in the brackets.

(1) 我们应当努力在家庭和工作之间找到平衡，让每个人都开心。(find a balance between A and B)

_____

(2) 地震对这个地区的旅游业造成极大不利影响。(produce/have a negative impact on)

_____

(3) 我们不能够为了工作而牺牲健康。(sacrifice…for…)

_____

(4) 去年，这个城市的旅游收入达 800 亿美元，增长了 6%。(grow by…to…)

_____

(5) 人们的生活越来越好，这是旅游快速发展的一个原因。(contribute to)

_____

(6) 这个公司被认为是这个地区发展最快的企业之一。(be considered to)

_____

Passage B   Tourism in China

Tourism is developing rapidly in China. It is one of the fastest-growing industries in the country. As a result of the reform and opening-up policy, an increasing number of foreigners are swarming into China, eager to see this mysterious land with a splendid culture and a civilized history of more than 5,000 years. With the increase of disposable income and free time among

Chinese, growing numbers of people are participating in tourism home and abroad.

In recent years, investments in tourism industry increasingly become a larger part of the national economy, with higher market share. Tourism industry is fast emerging as China's important economic driving force.

As a future pillar industry, it occupies a very significant position in the national economy. Its annual revenue and employment is among the top few of the industries in China. According to China's Ministry of Culture and Tourism, in 2018, the total revenue of China's tourism industry reached RMB 9.94 trillion, accounting for 11.04% of the GDP in the country, with over 79.91 million people working in tourism and related industries, accounting for 10.29% of the total employment opportunities in China. Tourism industry has become the main source of tax revenue and the key industry for economic development.

Domestic tourism market: In 2018, domestic tourist arrivals reached 5.5 billion and tourism revenue was RMB 5.1 trillion, an increase of 10.8% and 12.3% respectively over 2017. The national holidays and developed transportation have enabled Chinese people to conduct more traveling and led to prosperity in domestic market.

Inbound tourism market: The total number of inbound tourist was 141.2 million in 2018, increasing by 1.2% over 2017, and that of tourists staying overnight was 62.9 million. International tourism receipts were USD 127.1 billion in 2018, increasing by 3.0% over 2017. Foreign tourists made 47.95 million trips among the inbound trips in 2018—76.3 percent from Asia, 7.9 from North and South America, 12.5 percent from Europe, 1.9 percent from Oceania and 1.4 percent from Africa. The top 5 countries supplying China's major sources of inbound tourists in 2018 were Myanmar, Vietnam, South Korea, Japan and the United States. China saw an increasing number of inbound tourists from the Belt and Road countries.

Outbound tourism market: More and more middle class population with strong consumption power is traveling out of China. Chinese tourists made 149.7 million outbound trips in 2018, up14.7% over the previous year. China continues to lead global outbound travel in terms of expenditure. China's outbound tourism market is estimated to increase by 5 percent annually on average in the coming years, bringing the number of outbound tourists to 157 million in 2020, said Dai Bin, the president of China Tourism Academy(CTA).

Tourism brings China a lot of good. It enables the Chinese to know about the outside world and contributes to promoting the international relationship and mutual understanding between countries. More importantly, it is financially beneficial to China, because tourism greatly encourages foreign investment in this country.

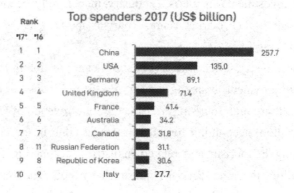

Top spenders 2017

New words and expressions

splendid [ˈsplendɪd] *adj.* 灿烂的，壮观的
civilized [ˈsɪvəlaɪzd] *adj.* 文明的
mysterious [mɪˈstɪəriəs] *adj.* 神秘的
priority [praɪˈɒrəti] *n.* 优先，优先权
pillar [ˈpɪlə(r)] *n.* 柱，支柱
revenue [ˈrevənjuː] *n.* 收入，财政收入
trillion [ˈtrɪljən] *n.* 万亿
domestic [dəˈmestɪk] *adj.* 国内的
prosperity [prɒˈsperəti] *n.* 繁荣，兴旺
inbound [ˈɪnbaʊnd] *adj.* 入境的
Oceania [ˌəʊsiˈɑːniə] *n.* 澳洲，大洋洲
outbound [ˈaʊtbaʊnd] *adj.* 出境的
previous [ˈpriːviəs] *adj.* 以前的，先前的
estimated [ˈestɪmeɪtɪd] *adj.* 估计的，预计的
expenditure [ɪkˈspendɪtʃə(r)] *n.* 花费，支出
mutual [ˈmjuːtʃuəl] *adj.* 相互的，共同的
beneficial [ˌbenɪˈfɪʃl] *adj.* 有利的，有益的
swarm into 涌入，蜂拥而进
driving force 动力
on average 平均

Unit 1 Tourism and Tourism Industry

Notes

1. this mysterious land with a splendid culture and a civilized history of more than 5,000 years: 这块有着灿烂文化和 5,000 年文明历史的神秘土地。中国的历史，从三皇五帝算起（三皇：伏羲、神农、黄帝；五帝：少昊、颛顼、帝喾、尧、舜），起点大约在公元前 3,000 年，先后经历了夏商周秦汉，魏晋南北隋，唐宋元明清，中国近代，中国现代等，至今中国大约五千年历史。

2. China's Ministry of Culture and Tourism: 中华人民共和国文化和旅游部。我国将文化部、国家旅游局的职责整合，组建文化和旅游部，作为国务院组成部门，不再保留文化部、国家旅游局。2018 年 3 月，中华人民共和国文化和旅游部批准设立。

3. GDP: Gross Domestic Product, 国内生产总值，指一个国家(或地区)所有常驻单位，在一定时期内，生产的全部最终产品和服务价值的总和，常被认为是衡量国家(或地区)经济状况的指标。

4. developed transportation: 发达的交通。中国拥有着最发达的交通网络，拥有世界最发达的高速公路网络，每天承担着几千万吨货物的高速运转；中国有全球最大的高速铁路网络，让数百座城市紧密连接在一起；两百多座机场，编织起了庞大的空中运输网络；在广袤的海岸线上，全球前 10 的港口，中国拥有 7 座。

5. the Belt and Road: "一带一路"(缩写 B&R)，是"丝绸之路经济带"和"21 世纪海上丝绸之路"的简称，由中国国家主席习近平于 2013 年 9 月和 10 月分别提出的建设"新丝绸之路经济带"和"21 世纪海上丝绸之路"的合作倡议。在"一带一路"倡议背景下，我国与沿线国家的旅游业将迎来广阔的机遇。

6. China saw an increasing number of inbound tourists from the Belt and Road countries: 来自"一带一路"国家到中国旅游的入境游客大大增加。

7. China Tourism Academy(CTA): 中国旅游研究院

Exercises

1. Reading Comprehension: Choose the best answer for the following questions.

(1) Why did tourism industry develop rapidly in China? ____
  A. Reform and opening-up policy.
  B. The increase of disposable income and free time among Chinese.
  C. The Belt and Road initiative.
  D. All above.

(2) The total revenue of China's tourism in 2018 was ____, accounting for ____ of the GDP in the country.

A. RMB 9.94 trillion, 11.04%   B. USD 9.94 trillion, 11.04%
C. RMB 9.94 million, 10.29%   D. USD 9.94 trillion, 10.29%

(3) International tourism receipts were ____ in 2018, increasing by ____ over 2017.
A. RMB 127.1 billion, 3.0%   B. USD 127.1 billion, 3.0%
C. USD 127.1 billion, 30%   D. RMB 127.1 billion, 30%

(4) Which area has the most foreign tourists for China in 2018? ____
A. Europe.   B. Oceania.   C. Asia.   D. South America.

(5) Chinese tourists made ____ outbound trips in 2018, up ____ over the previous year.
A. 149.7 billion, 14.7%   B. 149.7 million, 1.47%
C. 149.7 million, 14.7%   D. 149.7 billion, 1.47%

2. Fill in the blanks with the appropriate form of the words or phrases given below in the box.

fastest-growing	South America	splendid	mysterious
trillion	prosperity	outbound	on average

(1) Initiated by China's Ministry of Culture and Tourism, the poll reveals the ten most popular _____ destinations with Chinese tourists.

(2) The book includes a wealth of _____ photographs.

(3) China has the _____ robot market.

(4) _____ locates in the Southern Hemisphere.

(5) _____, American shares rose by 38%.

(6) Their wealth totaled $20.1 _____.

(7) It is a strange and _____ creature.

(8) We wish your country _____ and her people happiness.

3. Translate the following expressions into English or Chinese.

(1) reform and opening-up _____

(2) home and abroad _____

(3) national economy _____

(4) market share _____

(5) pillar industry _____

(6) 国内旅游 _____

(7) 入境旅游 _____

(8) 出境旅游 _____

(9) "一带一路" _____

(10) 相互理解_____

4. Translate the following sentences into Chinese.

(1) Many students swarm into the canteen after class.
_____

(2) In China, the minority nationalities account for 6 per cent of the population.
_____

(3) The number of the students in this university has an increase of 10 percent over last year.
_____

(4) In terms of both salary and career success, she is successful, while in terms of family, she failed.
_____

(5) I hope your holiday will be beneficial to you.
_____

(6) China saw an increasing number of inbound tourists from the Belt and Road countries.
_____

5. Translate the following passage into English.

受经济发展的推动，到国外度假已成为中国人的一种休闲方式。去年，中国出境游客(outbound tourist)已高达 8,300 万人次。中国家庭已经逐渐习惯了去国外度假。父母通常在暑期休年假，以便和孩子一同出游。世界旅游组织(World Tourism Organization)的一份分析报告指出，中国游客是最强大的假日消费群体。他们已经成为海外购物的一支重要力量，创造了巨大的消费价值。

6. Activity

Group work: Suppose you are going to invest in tourism industry, which area will you invest? And where will you invest? Why? Discuss with your group mates and each group makes a presentation for about 3 minutes.

Writing: Resume 简历

1. Writing Skills

简历的基本内容包括以下几项。

个人基本信息：姓名、性别、出生年月日、地址、联系方式(包括手机号码、电子邮箱)等。

求职目标：说明求职者想要从事什么样的工作。

教育背景：(1)应届毕业生首先应列出就读学校及院系、起止时间，按照由近至远的时间顺序。其次，参加的培训、学习经历或者实习经历都可以列出。必要时，还可列出在学校的主要课程名称，但所有内容都要选择与所应聘的工作相关。(2)在这部分，非应届毕业生只需注明就读的学校名称、院系专业、起止时间即可。

工作经历：(1)非应届毕业生把与应聘职位相关的经历按时间顺序写出来，工作经历的时间顺序均是由近至远。(2)应届毕业生可以写社会实践，包括兼职工作、项目参与、校园实习等课外实践活动，突出选择与应聘岗位密切联系的实践活动。

获奖及荣誉：(1)应届毕业生按照时间由近至远的原则列出在学校所获得的奖项，包括比赛、奖学金等；(2)非应届毕业生应该重点列出在工作经历中获得的业绩与奖励等。

技能证书：包括外语类水平、计算机能力、各项认证考试证书、与应聘岗位相关的职业资格证等。

业余爱好：写明性格特征和业余爱好。我们写简历往往只罗列自己的优点，显得缺少真实性和诚信度。在陈述完闪光点后，这部分可以婉转表述自己的缺点和不足，增加简历的真实性。

2. Useful Expressions and Sentences

(1) personal data/information: name, sex, height, weight, address, phone number, date of birth, place of birth, marital status etc.

(2) objective/career objective/position wanted/position applied for/job objective: hotel room service supervisor; HR assistant; secretary

(3) academic activities/social activities: won the first place in…; won the champion in…; won the second place in the…competition in 2016; President of College Student Union; Party Secretary of the department student branch; Commissary in charge of class studies.

(4) working experiences: be in charge of…/be responsible for…; worked as sales representative in…; achieved or completed several projects in…; developed or participated in…

(5) awards/honors: won the first scholarship in 2014; won the title of excellent League member in 2015; won the title of "Excellent Student" in 2016

(6) qualifications/certificates: CET-6, Accountant Qualification Certificate

(7) special skills/technical qualification and skills: competent for speaking and writing in Japanese; proficient in Windows 2010; excel in shorthand; fluent in English reading, speaking etc.

(8) hobbies: jogging, hiking, playing the guitar, long distance running, traveling

3. Sample Writing

Resume

Personal Information

Name: Zhang Dan	Sex: Female	Date of birth: 08/13/1992
Place of birth: Shenzhen	Height: 163cm	Nationality: Chinese, Han
E-mail: Zhangdan 0813@163.com		Telephone: 130XXXXXXX

Career Objective: sales representative

Salary desired: negotiable

Education

2010.09-2014.07 B.S. in Marketing, Shenzhen University

2007.09-2010.07 Shenzhen No.16 Middle School

Working Experiences

2016.06—present

Developed and presented hair color market analysis & recommendations to color team, HR. and upper management of Maybelline, Brand Management Intern, L'OREAL-Marketing

2014.10—2016.05

Responsible for sorting orders, shipping arrangements, deliveries, provisional employee of Sales Department at Shenzhen Lijun Medical Instruments & Equipment (Holdings) Company

Qualification and Certificates

College English Band Six, National Computer Band 2

Skills

Excelling in Windows 2010 and XP, Microsoft application, Adobe photoshop

Self-appraisal

Team work spirit, be able to work under great pressure, good presentation and communication skills

4. Writing Practice

As a student majoring in Tourism English, you are going to graduate in July and you want to look for a job in tourism industry. Please prepare a resume for yourself.

旅游英语

Supplementary Reading

Part Ⅰ

Travel Safety

While most trips will be pleasant and without incident, it is a good idea to do some research and be prepared before you leave home. Be attentive to basic preparations, such as copying essential documentation and noting emergency contact information, and ensure that you are aware of any risk of seasonal natural hazards, seismic activity, extreme weather patterns, disease outbreaks or endemic health issues, personal security concerns, or any patterns of socio-political instability in your destination. One good place to start your research is with the websites of government agencies that report safety, security, and health issues related to travel in a foreign country.

Just as we travel to places with different climate and customs, we also travel to locations faced with different types of hazards that could interrupt out trip plans or have a potential impact on your health and security. Consequently, it is as important to familiarize ourselves with basic knowledge about cultural norms in a country as it is to be aware of any risks we may encounter while traveling. There are many sources that can prepare travelers for potential crisis event in a destination. Websites, such as news and weather sites and your country's foreign offices website are good places to start.

If an event hits before you leave for your destination, there could be cancellation or postponement of inbound tourism. Check on the status of the event and if required, find out what the procedures may be in place for altering your schedule.

Useful words and phrases

    hazard [ˈhæzəd] *n.* 危险，危害
    endemic [enˈdemɪk] *adj.* 某地特有的，(尤指疾病)地方性的
    familiarize [fəˈmɪliəraɪz] *v.* 使(某人)熟悉，使通晓
    encounter [ɪnˈkaʊntə(r)] *v.* 遭遇，遇到
    postponement [pəˈspəʊnmənt] *n.* 推迟，延期
    be attentive to 注意，照应

Read the passage and decide whether the following statements are true(T) or false(F).

    1. _____ Basic preparations include copying essential documentation and noting emergency

Unit 1 Tourism and Tourism Industry

contact information.

2. _____ You should try to find out whether there are any patterns of socio-political instability in your destination.

3. _____ The website of government agencies is a good place to find information about safety, security add health issues related to travel in a foreign country.

4. _____ We do not have to know basic knowledge about cultural norms in the destination country.

5. _____ If an event hits before you leave for your destination, you have to cancel your trip.

Part II

Knowledge about Emergency

Survey: Take this fun quiz to test your knowledge about various disasters and emergency preparation items.

1. As long as a thunderstorm is five miles away or farther from you, you are pretty safe from lightning strikes. This statements is ____.

 A. true   B. false

2. When an earthquake strikes, you should ____.

 A. run outside to avoid falling building debris

 B. take cover under a heavy piece of furniture

 C. panic

 D. lean against an inside wall or stand under an inside doorway

3. Which areas of the United States are vulnerable to earthquakes? ____

 A. The West Coast, particularly California.

 B. The Eastern Seaboard.

 C. The central United States.

 D. All 50 states.

4. What's the most common disaster that occurs in the United States? ____

 A. Fire.   B. Flood.   C. Earthquake.   D. Tornado.

5. What's the Number one disaster-related killer in the United States? ____

 A. Fire.   B. Flood.   C. Earthquake.   D. Tornado.

6. If your car stalls while you're evacuating from a flood, you should ____.

 A. stay inside the car until assistance can arrive

 B. leave it

 C. call a towing service

 D. flag someone down to help you start it

7. When treating frostbite, you should _____.
   A. rub the limbs down with snow
   B. give the victim a cup of hot chocolate to warm-up
   C. gradually warm the body by wrapping in dry blankets
   D. plunge the affected areas in hot water
8. The most dangerous part of a hurricane is _____.
   A. the breaking waves
   B. the gale-force winds
   C. the flood-causing rains

Unit 2　Travel Agency

Learning Objectives

After learning this unit, you should:
- Be able to give a full presentation about functions and types of travel agency.
- Get some practical knowledge about being a tour guide.
- Master the basic words and expressions about travel agency and tour guide.
- Find ways to improve your writing skills about welcome speech.

Keywords

functions of travel agency, types of travel agency, being a good tour guide

Information search

Please search some information about the topic of this unit by scanning the QR codes: (Travel Column of *China Daily*), (China Plus), (World Tourism Organization), (Travelogue of CCTV), (Ministry of Culture and Tourism of the People's Republic of China). After reading the information, please share with your classmates some information about the topic of this unit.

Warm-up

Task 1: Please tell the full Chinese names of each travel agency below, and write down their full English names.

1　　　　2　　　　3　　　　4

旅游英语

5　　　　　　　6　　　　　　　7　　　　　　　8

1. _____
2. _____
3. _____
4. _____
5. _____
6. _____
7. _____
8. _____

Task 2: Please visit the website of a travel agency, and try to introduce the travel agency in brief.

Passage A　Travel Agency

Tourists can find many ways available for them to get information about their destinations and make reservations for their trip. A travel agency is a retail business selling travel related products and services to customers.

The British company, Cox&Kings, is said to be the oldest travel agency in the world. Modern travel agencies begin with Thomas Cook in the late 19th century. Brownell Travel established in 1887 is the oldest one in North America. With the development of commercial aviation from the 1920s, travel agencies become more and more popular.

Functions of travel agency

As the name implies, a travel agency's main function is to act as an agent. Its profit is the difference between the advertised price paid by customers and the discounted price provided by suppliers, such as airlines, car rentals, cruise lines, hotels, railways, sightseeing tours and package holidays. This is known as the commission. A British travel agency would consider a 10%～12% commission as a good arrangement. In the USA, most airlines pay no commission at all to travel agencies. Travel agencies, in this case, usually add a service fee to the net price.

In general, a travel agency has the following functions.

1. Provision of travel information

One of the primary functions of a travel agency is to provide necessary information about travel. This information is provided at a convenient location where potential tourists may ask certain questions and seek advice for his proposed travel. A good travel agency is something of a personal counselor who knows all the details about travel and the needs and interests of the intending travelers.

2. Preparation of itineraries

A tourist journey is characterized by an itinerary using various means of transport to link one place with another. Preparation of different types of itineraries is another important function of a travel agency. A travel agency gives advice to potential travelers on the types of programs which they may choose for their travel.

3. Ticketing

Selling tickets to clients using different modes of transports like air, rail and sea is yet another important function of a travel agency. This calls for a thorough knowledge of schedules of various modes of transports. Air carriers, railways, and steamship companies have hundreds of schedules and the men behind the counter should be familiar with all these. Ticketing is however not an easy job as the range and diversity of international transports, e.g. airfares, is very complex and changeable.

4. Insurance

Insurance both for personal accident risks and baggage is another important activity of travel agency.

Types of Travel Agency

To meet different needs of customers, various types of travel agencies offer a variety of travel products and services. There are two main types of travel agencies, namely general travel agency and specialized travel agency.

General agencies are like department stores, with a wide variety of products and services to meet the needs of a variety of customers. They handle all types of travel—airplane, rail, cruise, rental car and all types of accommodation. They offer all kinds of tours, from sightseeing trips through Europe's capital cities to rafting trips on the Snake River. Customers can find products from high-priced to economy. Owners of general travel agencies believe that a diversity of products and services offers a steadier revenue.

Specialized travel agencies are the ones tend to concentrate on one form of travel or on services to a special group of travelers. Some specialty agencies reflect the talents and interests of the owner and staff. These are some specialty agencies, for example, (1)adventure travel, organizing trips to exotic or difficult-to-reach destinations; (2)agencies concentrating on senior citizen; (3)agencies arranging tours exclusively for singles; (4)agencies offering tours specially designed for physically disabled people.

New words and expressions

available [əˈveɪləbl] *adj.* 可获得的，可利用的
retail [ˈriːteɪl] *n.* 零售
aviation [ˌeɪviˈeɪʃn] *n.* 航空
function [ˈfʌŋkʃn] *n.* 功能，作用
discount [ˈdɪskaʊnt] *vt.* 打折扣，减价出售
rental [ˈrentl] *n.* 租费，租金额
cruise [kruːz] *n.* 游览，旅行，周游
commission [kəˈmɪʃn] *n.* 佣金，手续费
provision [prəˈvɪʒn] *n.* 供应，(一批)供应品
potential [pəˈtenʃl] *adj.* 潜在的，有可能的
counselor [ˈkaʊnsələ] *n.* 顾问
itinerary [aɪˈtɪnərəri] *n.* 路线，旅行日程
characterize [ˈkærəktəraɪz] *vt.* 具有……的特征
mode [məʊd] *n.* 方式，状况
complex [ˈkɒmpleks] *adj.* 复杂的
changeable [ˈtʃeɪndʒəbl] *adj.* 易变的，常变化的
specialized [ˈspeʃəlaɪzd] *adj.* 专业的，专门的
specialty [ˈspeʃəlti] *n.* 专业
variety [vəˈraɪəti] *n.* 多样，种类
concentrate [ˈkɒnsntreɪt] *vt.* 集中(注意力)，专心于
exclusively [ɪkˈskluːsɪvli] *adv.* 专门地，特定地

Notes

1. Cox&Kings: Cox&Kings 是世界上最早的旅游企业，其业务经营始于1758年，而且是各大洲领先的休闲游集团之一，也是世界上经验最丰富的旅游企业之一。在过去30年的时间里，Cox&Kings 转型为一家多样化的跨境旅游企业，服务群体主要专注于全球新时代消费者。

2. Thomas Cook: 托马斯·库克，是现代旅游的创始人，有"近代旅游业之父"之称。他是第一个组织团队旅游的人，也组织了世界上第一例环球旅游团。库克编写并出版了世

界上第一本面向团队游客的旅游指南——《利物浦之行指南》。库克组织了欧洲范围内的自助游，向自助旅行的游客提供旅游帮助和酒店住宿服务。19 世纪中期，托马斯·库克创办了世界上第一家旅行社——托马斯·库克旅行社(即现今的托马斯库克集团，中国官方授权的品牌名为"托迈酷客")，标志着近代旅游业的诞生。

3. A good travel agency is something of a personal counselor who knows all the details about travel and the needs and interests of the intending travelers.一个好的旅行社是了解旅游细节以及潜在游客的需求和兴趣的私人顾问。

4. There are two main types of travel agencies, namely general travel agency and specialized travel agency. 旅行社主要有两类：一般旅行社及专业旅行社。

5. Snake River: 蛇河，全长 1670 公里，发源于怀俄明州黄石国家公园地区，流经美国怀俄明州、犹他州、内华达州、爱达荷州、俄勒冈州和华盛顿等州，流域面积达 28.2 万平方公里。为美国西北部一条主要河流，位于哥伦比亚河左岸，是其最大支流，也是美国西北太平洋沿岸地区最重要河流之一，成为爱达荷州与俄勒冈州和华盛顿州的边界。

6. adventure travel: 探险旅游，是旅游者到人迹罕至或险状环生的特殊环境里进行的充满神秘性、危险性和刺激性的旅行考察活动。按旅游项目分为空中、陆地、水上三类。

Exercises

1. Answer the following questions according to the passage.

(1) What is said to be the oldest travel agency in the world?

(2) What is the profit for a travel agency? What profit can a travel agency wake?

(3) What are the main functions for a travel agency?

(4) Why isn't ticketing an easy job for a travel agency?

(5) What are the two main types of travel agencies?

(6) What types of travel does a general travel agency handle?

(7) Please give some examples for specialty agencies.

2. Fill in the blanks with the appropriate form of the words given below in the box.

| available | reservation | function | discount | commission |
| itinerary | complex | changeable | specialize | exclusively |

(1) There are three small boats _____ for hire.

(2) Many students _____ in engineering.

(3) This chair can also _____ as a bed.

(4) He also got a _____ for bringing in new clients.

(5) This project involves a lot of _____ technical problems.

(6) He went to the desk to make a _____.

(7) The weather here is quite _____.

(8) The room is for women _____.

(9) The two sides have agreed on the _____ of the visit.

(10) Tour prices are being _____ as much as 33%.

3. Translate the following expressions into English or Chinese.

(1) travel agency _____

(2) make reservation _____

(3) car rental _____

(4) sightseeing tour _____

(5) net price _____

(6) travel information _____

(7) primary function _____

(8) potential tourist _____

(9) 轮船公司 _____

(10) 国际运输 _____

(11) 一般旅行社 _____

(12) 专业旅行社 _____

(13) 百货商店 _____

(14) 难以到达的目的地 _____

(15) 探险旅游 _____

(16) 老年人 _____

4. Translate the following sentences into English with the words or phrases given in the brackets.

(1) 到了这个时候，你应该熟悉了文章的内容。(be familiar with)

(2) 为了适应旅游需要，北京修了很多旅馆。(meet the needs of)

(3) 这个岛屿拥有丰富多样的景致及种类繁多的野生动植物。(a wide variety of)

(4) 我想到生病的孩子时就无法专心工作。(concentrate on)

(5) 这个景区的特点是空气清新、交通方便。(be characterized by)

(6) 你在手术的问题上需要咨询专业意见。(seek advice for)

Passage B Tour Guide

A tour guide is a person who has acquired a tour guide certificate and is assigned by a travel agency to escort tourists on their travels, providing them with travel services. They are the ones who go between different people and they are the soul of the tourism industry.

According to the working area, tour guides can generally be classified into four kinds: tour escort, national guide, local guide and scenic-spot guide. A tour escort travels with the tourist during the entire trip in outbound area. A national guide travels with tourists around his or her own country from the beginning to the end of their journeys. Local guides accompany tourists in their local region. Scenic-spot guide conducts tours of one or several hours at a specific scenic spot. The tour may be given on foot or in some sort of vehicle.

Here are some important skills for becoming a good tour guide.

Excellent Public Speaking and Narration Skills

You will generally be speaking in front of a huge group of people on most of the tours you lead, so you have to understand the basic principles of public speaking. You should learn how to speak clearly, how to talk calmly and slowly so that tourists can understand you, and also learn how to control your breathing so that you don't get tired. Narration is understood as how to relate a story to someone. Story telling is one of the key elements of guiding tours, especially in historically significant towns or areas where lots of interesting events have taken place.

Excellent Problem Solving Skills

During a trip, problems could arise and range from tour buses breaking down to one of the passengers getting ill and needing to get rushed to the hospital. Problems can also be small ones, like a passenger complaining that they are too hot, or some members of the group arguing. You have to be a good problem solver if you hope to be a good tour guide, and know how to deal with anything that comes to your way quickly and effortlessly.

Good Language Skills

If you can speak a second language you will have a better chance of being hired as a tour guide, and if you speak more languages, then that is even better. Even if you can only speak a little of the language, this is enough for some tour companies, so mention this in your job applications.

Great Organizational and Leadership Skills

Developing this skill is one that will make your job easier and that will stand you in good stead for the rest of your career. Tour companies and escort agencies prefer to hire people who demonstrate excellent organizational skills, as it eliminates problems on the tour, it saves them time and money, and it reduces risk.

For those of you who are interested in the occupation of tour guide, getting a license is just the first step. Once you are determined to make it a career, you should be ready to learn throughout your life through work, experience and study. In addition, another thing that you need to understand beforehand is that a tour guide license is different from a tour escort license. If you hope to take tourists abroad, you will have to take another exam.

New words and expressions

acquire [əˈkwaɪə(r)] *vt.* 获得，取得
assign [əˈsaɪn] *vt.* 分派，分配
escort [ˈeskɔːt] *n.* 陪同，护送
soul [səʊl] *n.* 灵魂
classify [ˈklæsɪfaɪ] *vt.* 分类，归类
accompany [əˈkʌmpəni] *vt.* 陪伴，陪同
specific [spəˈsɪfɪk] *adj.* 具体的，明确的
vehicle [ˈviːəkl] *n.* 车辆，交通工具
narration [nəˈreɪʃn] *n.* 叙述

principle ['prɪnsəpl] *n.* 原则

element ['elɪmənt] *n.* 要素

arise [ə'raɪz] *vi.* 出现，产生

range [reɪndʒ] *n.* 范围

effortlessly ['efətləslɪ] *adv.* 毫不费力地

eliminate [ɪ'lɪmɪneɪt] *vt.* 消除

reduce [rɪ'dju:s] *vt.* 减少，缩小

occupation [ˌɒkju'peɪʃn] *n.* 职业，工作

beforehand [bɪ'fɔ:hænd] *adv.* 提前，预先

tour guide 导游

relate to…… 涉及，联系

break down 损坏，出故障

stand sb. in good stead 给某人好处，对某人有用

Notes

1. tour guide certificate: 导游证。导游证是持证人已依法进行中华人民共和国导游注册、能够从事导游活动的法定证件。《导游人员管理条例》的规定：在中华人民共和国境内从事导游活动，必须取得导游证。目前，我国导游人员资格统一考试每年进行一次。

2. According to the working area, tour guides can generally be classified into four kinds: tour escort, national guide, local guide and scenic-spot guide. 根据工作范围不同，导游大致可以分为四种：领队、全陪、地陪以及景点导游。

3. A tour escort travels with the tourist during the entire trip in outbound area. 领队是全程带领游客出境的导游。在我国，港澳台旅行团导游也是属于出境领队。

4. Excellent Public Speaking and Narration Skills: 优秀的公众演讲和叙述技巧。

5. escort license: 领队证。申请领队证的人员应当符合下列条件：热爱祖国、遵纪守法；有完全民事行为能力的中国公民；可切实负起领队责任的旅行社人员；熟悉掌握旅游目的地国家或地区的有关情况。被取消领队资格的人员，不得再次申请领队证登记。

Exercises

1. Reading Comprehension: Choose the best answer for the following questions.

(1) ____ are the soul of tourism industry.

    A. The operators   B. Manager of travel agencies

    C. Tour guides   D. Tourists

(2) ____ travels with tourists around his or her own country from the beginning to the end of their journeys.

    A. A tour escort   B. A national guide

    C. A local guide   D. A scenic-spot guide

(3) What problems will possibly arise during a trip? ____

    A. Buses break down.

    B. Passengers get ill.

    C. Some members of the group argue.

    D. All above.

(4) Tour companies and escort agencies prefer to hire people who demonstrate ____, as it eliminates problems on the tour, it saves them time and money, and it reduces risk.

    A. excellent organizational skills

    B. excellent problem solving skills

    C. excellent public speaking and narration skills

    D. good language skills

(5) If you hope to take tourists abroad, you will have to take another exam, and get ____.

    A. a tour guide certificate

    B. a tour escort certificate

    C. a foreign language certificate

    D. a scenic-spot tour guide certificate

2. Fill in the blanks with the appropriate form of the words or phrases given below in the box.

assign	classify	specific	relate to
arise	effortlessly	reduce	beforehand

(1) It _____ the risk of heart disease.

(2) All these questions _____ to philosophy.

(3) It is necessary initially to _____ the headaches into certain type.

(4) When teachers _____ homework, students usually feel an obligation to do it.

(5) It had been arranged _____.

(6) I create what I want easily and _____.

(7) There are several _____ problems to be dealt with.

(8) No mistakes could _____.

3. Translate the following expressions into English or Chinese.

(1) 导游证 _____

(2) 领队 _____

(3) 全陪 _____

(4) 地陪 _____

(5) 景点导游 _____

(6) public speaking _____

(7) basic principle _____

(8) problem solving skill _____

(9) job application _____

(10) tour escort license _____

4. Translate the following sentences into Chinese.

(1) Your hard work throughout the year will stand you in good stead for the exams.

(2) It's a skill that will benefit you throughout your life.

(3) If you can control your breathing, you can control anything.

(4) Their car broke down when on the way to Tibet.

(5) Courses range from cookery to computing.

5. Translate the following passage into English.

这个旅行社主要经营(the major business)出境游、国内游、入境游等业务，同时兼营国际国内航空票务代理、景区开发与管理、会展服务、旅游汽车出租(rental)、海外留学咨询(study abroad & consultation service)、信息技术咨询服务、计算机技术开发等业务。目前，该旅行社有将近400家营业厅(sales office)，同时还在马来西亚、香港、澳门、北京、云南、四川、湖南、喀什等地设有分支机构(branch)，业务遍及全球100多个国家和地区。

6. Activity

Group work: In the world, there are many famous travel agencies. Please introduce one of the famous travel agencies with pictures or short videos. Each group makes a presentation for

about 8 minutes.

Writing: Welcome Speech 欢迎词

1. Writing Skills

  导游欢迎词是给客人留下良好的"第一印象"的最佳机会，良好的开端是成功的一半，导游词是客人与导游员的第一次接触，让客人第一时间感受到导游员的专业能力，并树立一个良好形象。导游员也可以借此机会展示自己的风采，给客人们留下深刻的第一印象。规范化的导游词应包括以下内容。

  (1) 表示欢迎。首先代表接待社、组团社向客人表达真挚的欢迎之意，热烈欢迎他们来到目的地城市做客。

  (2) 介绍自己。可以先介绍司机，然后介绍自己、地陪等所有人员，并把大家的联系方式留下，请客人牢记。

  (3) 预告行程安排。在旅游大巴上简单介绍目的地城市的概况和当天安排游览的景点、用餐等情况；行程的详细安排要告知每个客人，细心提示一些注意事项，让客人感受到温馨。

  (4) 表明态度，预祝成功。最后表达良好的祝愿，愿意为大家热情服务，确保大家都能对行程满意，希望得到游客的支持与合作。

2. Useful Expressions and Sentences

  (1) Ladies and gentlemen, welcome to XXXX. My name is XXX, I am your tour guide you can call me XXX, this is our driver XXX.

  (2) Hello, everyone/my dear friends. My name is XXX. On behalf of China International Travel Service, I'd like to welcome you all to XXX. The bus will take you to your hotel about fifteen minutes.

  (3) I am Steve, your tour guide for today. We're going to be pulling up to the hotel in just a few minutes. Please sit back and enjoy the view of the ocean on the left hand side of the bus as we enter the city.

  (4) Right now, I'd like to take a minute to familiarize you with the area and tell a brief safety precaution. You have to fasten safety belts and remain seated until we reach our destination.

  (5) Dear guests, let me introduce myself. My name is XXX. I am your guide and will support you during the tour. I promise you are going to enjoy your stay here in XXX.

  (6) This is a beautiful, quiet city where you can relax, sit by the beach, enjoy great meals and feel very safe. You can walk into town and enjoy the fountains or take a moonlit walk along the water.

(7) After the long flight you must be very tired, so now we are heading to our hotel directly so that you can get settled and have a rest.

(8) I will be your guide during your stay in this city. I am willing to do my best to make your visit a very pleasant one and I do want this to be the most wonderful trip you've never had.

(9) If you have any questions or problems, do not hesitate to ask. It will be my pleasure and honor to be at your service.

(10) As your guide, I highly appreciate your understanding and cooperation.

3. Sample Writing

(Situation: The local guide gives a welcome speech to the guests.)

Good morning, ladies and gentlemen. Welcome to Guangzhou, a beautiful city representing the merits and achievements of modern China after it opened to the outside world some 20 years ago.

After the long flight you must be very tired, so now we are heading to our hotel directly so that you can get settled and have a rest. It takes us about 40 minutes to get to the hotel, first let me introduce my team and our schedule in this city first.

Our driver is Mr. Chen. You can just call him Jack. He has about ten years' driving and working experience in travel industry. So you are in very safe and competent hands. My name is Wong Lily, you can call me Lily.

We are from China International Travel Service. On behalf of my company and my colleagues, I'd like to extend a warm welcome to you. Welcome to Guangzhou.

Perhaps the first thing you need to pay attention to is the coach you're sitting in. Our coach is a blue Benz with CITS painted on both sides, and the number is 0987. It's preferable that you remember the number so that you can identify the coach whenever necessary.

I will be your guide during your stay in this city. I am willing to do my best to make your visit a very pleasant one and I do want this to be the most wonderful trip you've never had. If you have any questions or problems, do not hesitate to ask. It will be my pleasure and honor to be at your service.

Now let me introduce our schedule in Guangzhou.

4. Writing Practice

Work as a tour guide in your hometown and make a welcome speech to a tour group from the USA.

旅游英语

Supplementary Reading

Part Ⅰ

Rise in Globetrotting Chinese Prompts Worldwide Demand for Tour Guides

China's booming tourism industry with its legions of tailored and themed tours, is driving rampant demand for professional tour guides around the world, especially those with creativity, comprehensive knowledge of visit-worthy places and good interpersonal and language skills.

One who knows the career well is Lei Lei, a tour guide from Hubei province, who has been working and living in Paris for 13 years.

In 2006, Lei went to France to do a postgraduate course in international trade. But after graduation, the global financial crisis made it extremely hard for him to find work. A friend persuaded Lei to become a registered tour guide on Ctrip, China's largest online travel agency.

"Starting from picking-up and taking tourists to airports, I began to gradually master multiple skills of being a tour guide. To provide better services, I got a French driver's license and a local tour guide certificate," Lei said.

Each month, he can earn about 3,000 euros ($3,440), much more than he can from other various part-time jobs.

What really helped his career take off, however, was two big shifts in the global tourist market. First, more Chinese tourists began heading to Europe. The number of Chinese tourists to Europe doubled in the second quarter of 2018, compared to the previous year, according to the Ministry of Culture and Tourism.

The second fact is that more Chinese are switching from holidaying as a part of a group tour to traveling independently.

"More and more tourists are not satisfied with glancing over sightseeing spots quickly with a tour group. They want to know more interesting stories and cultures. So more Chinese tourists favor booking a local tour guide and hearing more about local customs and events," Lei said.

As part of his job, Lei helps tourists to book the most exotic hotels and take them to enjoy the best-rated food. He also helps solve tourist's problems like sickness and lost luggage. His professionalism and good reputation has brought more customers, enough for him to establish his own tourism company.

Meanwhile, 23-year-old Liu Mengxia, is another registered tour guide on Ctrip. Having decided she doesn't like jobs with fixed hours, or in one place, she opted for the tourist industry, and gained her tour guide certificate in China in 2015.

After just three years, she has her own tour guide team, including operations and customer service staff. During busy seasons, she can receive 10 orders a day.

Currently, there are more than 5,000 people registered as domestic tour guides on Ctrip in China, and 70 percent of them are located in smaller cities. The average service fees of a tour guide is around 300 yuan ($44.14) to 400 yuan per day, and their average monthly salary is around 8,000 yuan－often higher than average local salaries, Ctrip said.

Useful words and phrases

globetrotting [ˈgləʊbtrɒtɪŋ] *n.* 自助游
rampant [ˈræmpənt] *adj.* 猖獗的，蔓延的
postgraduate [ˌpəʊstˈgrædʒuət] *adj.* 研究生的
registered [ˈredʒɪstəd] *adj.* 注册的，登记过的
switching [swɪtʃɪŋ] *n.* 开关，交换，转换
exotic [ɪgˈzɒtɪk] *adj.* 异国的，外来的
professionalism [prəˈfeʃənəlɪzəm] *n.* 职业化，职业水准或特性
opt [ɒpt] *vi.* 选择，挑选
service fee 服务费，手续费

Read the passage and decide whether the following statements are true (T) or false(F).

1. _____ Lei Lei is a tour guide from Hubei province, who has been working and living in London for 13 years.

2. _____ To provide better services, Lei Lei got a French driver's license and a local tour guide certificate.

3. _____ The number of Chinese tourists to Europe doubled in the first quarter of 2018, compared to the previous year, according to the Ministry of Culture and Tourism.

4. _____ Liu Mengxia doesn't like jobs with fixed hours, or in one place, she opted for the tourist industry, and gained her tour guide certificate in China in 2015.

5. _____ Currently, there are more than 5,000 people registered as domestic tour guides on Ctrip in China, and 70 percent of them are located in smaller cities.

Part Ⅱ Survey

This is a survey of knowledge about Good Service to Customers. Take this fun quiz to find out whether you can offer good services to the customers or not.

1. _____ You should try to memorize tourists' name in the tour.
   A. True   B. False

2. _____ Your clothes matter when dealing face to face with tourists.
   A. True   B. False

3. _____ You should tell the tourist if he/she is at fault.
   A. True   B. False

4. _____ Argue with the tourists. Stand for your right.
   A. True   B. False

5. _____ Apologize to tourists even if the fault was done by another staff.
   A. True   False

6. _____ When shaking hands, your hand should go soft and let the other party squeeze it.
   A. True   B. False

7. _____ Feedback by tourists is not important.
   A. True   B. False

8. _____ We must put ourselves in the tourists' shoes if they lodge a complaint.
   A. True   B. False

9. _____ Repeat tourists' complaint after they have said it to be sure.
   A. True   B. False

10. _____ Give away name cards with only one hand.
    A. True   B. False

Unit 3   Online Travel Service

Learning Objectives

After learning this unit, you should:
- Acquire the knowledge and information of online travel service.
- Get some information about Ctrip.
- Be familiar with the new technologies used in tourism industry.
- Master the basic words and expressions about online travel service and new technologies in tourism industry.
- Find ways to improve your writing skills about visa applications and invitations.

Keywords

online travel service, Ctrip, VR, AR, AI

Information search

Please search some information about the topic of this unit by scanning the QR codes: (Travel Column of *China Daily*), (China Plus), (World Tourism Organization), (Travelogue of CCTV), (Ministry of Culture and Tourism of the People's Republic of China). After reading the information, please share with your classmates some information about the topic of this unit.

Warm-up

Task 1: Look at the pictures below, try to tell what are some of the new technologies in tourism. Match the phrases with the pictures below. Please list as many new technologies as possible in tourism industry at present.

    A. self-service ticket machine   B. electronic ticket business
    C. online touring   D. facial recognition system

旅游英语

Task 2: As for online travel service, what can be learnt from the following chart?

China's online travel booking market

Passage A Booming Time for Online Travel Services

Nowadays, with the development and spreading of Internet, travel industry has seen great changes, and a new form of travel services, called online travel service(OTS), has been prevailing.

Compared with traditional travel services, online travel service has the following features.

(1) Rich in information. Participants can get all types of latest traveling information they need by visiting related websites.

(2) High self-determination. Tourists can travel at an economical cost, decide on certain scenic spots they want, reserve hotels and even only consult those providers when preparation is made and then travel independently.

(3) Quick response. Whenever and wherever tourists want any traveling information, they can surf on the Internet for relevant information. Their needs can always be served very soon.

(4) Latest information. The information tourists can get is always the latest, leading them to go on a most comfortable tour.

(5) Low price. Tourist can always enjoy favorable discount not only in transportation and

accommodation, but also in catering and entertainment.

According to a report, in 2018 the revenue of OTS reached 1.08 trillion *yuan* ($160 billion), increasing 30 percent year on year, and hitting a record high. In recent years, China's online tourism service is witnessing a boom, and firms in the business are growing rapidly. More and more online travel agencies or OTAs are emerging and offering new, customized products and services.

Five OTAs in China hold the key to the fortunes of Chinese tourism as they take up totally 80 percent market share. Ctrip is the big boy of the pack. In October 2015, it swallowed up Qunar. According to a report, the combine of Ctrip and Qunar occupies a more than 60% share of the OTAs market. Fliggy from Alibaba, Tongcheng-Elong Holdings Ltd, which is backed by Tencent, and Tuniu Corp are the other three big players. Ctrip also holds stakes in Tongcheng-Elong and Tuniu.

In 2017, Ctrip further extended its operations and expanded its distribution across the sector. Its total sales revenue jumped 30 percent over 2017 to reach 690 billion yuan. According to Sun Jie, CEO of Ctrip, in the future more offline tourism businesses will turn to online operations, with an aim to achieve better integration and utilization of industry resources, and provide more convenient and efficient services to consumers.

Chinese consumers are spending increasingly more money on services. Tourism is the mainstay of consumption of services. Tourism is becoming a main driver of China's economic growth. More and more Chinese travelers prefer independent and flexible trips instead of traveling with tour groups, and more people are willing to experience local events, food and culture.

This trend, however, has created certain challenges for OTAs. First, rapid growth has led to shortage of skilled manpower. Qualified tourism professionals are few and far between. Travel customizers need to have professional knowledge, foreign language skills and good service ability. At present, professionals with comprehensive abilities are quite scarce in the sector. Besides, OTAs also lack a mature supervision mechanism, which may result in varied service quality. The government has to make relevant laws and regulations for the customized tourism sector.

The birth of online travel service has brought about a revolution in the travel industry. It enables more people to go on a tour more conveniently and comfortably as well as poses greater competition pressure on traditional travel agencies. Certainly, online travel service will dominate the travel market in the future.

(source: http://chinaplus.cri.cn/news/china/9/20180927/188985.html?from=singlemessage&isappinstalled=0)

New words and expressions

booming ['bu:mɪŋ] *adj.* 急速发展的
prevailing [prɪ'veɪlɪŋ] *adj.* 盛行的，普遍的
traditional [trə'dɪʃənl] *adj.* 传统的
economical [ˌi:kə'nɒmɪkl] *adj.* 经济的，节约的
provider [prə'vaɪdə(r)] *n.* 供应者，提供者
independently [ˌɪndɪ'pendəntlɪ] *adv.* 独立地，自立地
response [rɪ'spɒns] *n.* 反应，回答，答复
catering ['keɪtərɪŋ] *n.* 提供饮食及服务
customize ['kʌstəmaɪz] *vt.* 定制，定做
swallow ['swɒləʊ] *vt.* 吞，咽
integration [ˌɪntɪ'greɪʃn] *n.* 整合，一体化
utilization [ˌju:təlaɪ'zeɪʃn] *n.* 利用，使用
efficient [ɪ'fɪʃnt] *adj.* 有效率的
flexible ['fleksəbl] *adj.* 灵活的
professional [prə'feʃənl] *adj.* 专业的，职业的 *n.* 专业人士
scarce [skeəs] *adj.* 缺乏的，罕见的
mature [mə'tʃʊə(r)] *adj.* 成熟的
dominate ['dɒmɪneɪt] *v.* 支配，占有优势
self-determination 自主性
shortage of 缺少……
few and far between 稀少的，罕见的

Notes

1. online travel service(OTS): 在线旅游服务提供商。在"互联网+"的大环境下，出现更加注重服务价值的在线旅游服务提供商的总称。OTS 为消费者提供从设计行程到行程中体验的全程保障。

2. online travel agencies or OTAs: 在线旅行社/在线旅游代理商

3. Ctrip: 携程旅行网，创立于 1999 年，总部设在中国上海，员工超过 30,000 人，是中国领先的在线旅行服务公司，向超过 9,000 万会员提供酒店预订、酒店点评及特价酒店查询、机票预订、飞机票查询、时刻表、票价查询、航班查询和度假预订等服务。

4. Qunar: 去哪儿网，是中国领先的无线和在线旅游平台，其网站上线于 2005 年 5 月，公司总部位于北京。根据 2014 年 9 月艾瑞监测数据，在旅行类网站月度独立访问量统计中，

去哪儿网以 4474 万人名列前茅。截至 2015 年 3 月 31 日，去哪儿网可实时搜索约 9,000 家旅游代理商网站，搜索范围覆盖全球范围内超过 28 万条国内及国际航线、约 103 万家酒店、85 万余条度假线路、近万个旅游景点，并且每日提供超过 20 万种旅游团购产品。

5. Tongcheng-Elong Holdings Ltd: 同程艺龙控股有限公司，是中国在线旅游行业的创新者和市场领导者。公司是同程及艺龙合并而成的企业，合并于 2018 年 3 月完成。同程及艺龙分别创立于 2004 年及 1999 年，在合并前各自取得独立的业务成果，是中国领先的在线旅行平台，拥有创新的业务模式并与众多旅游服务供应商保持长期合作关系。受益于同程及艺龙多年来的经验及技术发展及其互补资源，同程艺龙控股有限公司取得了更大的规模经济效应和巩固市场领先地位，同时增强提供全面旅游产品及服务种类的能力。

6. Tuniu Corp: 途牛旅游网，创立于 2006 年 10 月，并于 2014 年 5 月在纳斯达克成功上市。已在北京、上海和深圳等城市设立了超过 300 家线下门市。

7. tourism professional: 旅游专业人士

Exercises

1. Answer the following questions according to the passage.

(1) What are the features of online travel services?
_____

(2) What is the revenue of OTS in 2018?
_____

(3) What are the five biggest OTAs in China?
_____

(4) Why do more and more offline tourism businesses turn to online operations?
_____

(5) What are the challenges for OTAs?
_____

(6) What revolution does OTS bring about?
_____

2. Fill in the blanks with the appropriate form of the words or phrases given below in the box.

booming	result in	bring about	prevailing	traditional
independently	customized	flexible	scarce	efficient

(1) Based on the requirement, even this service can be _____.

(2) Errors in theory will inevitably _____ failures in practice.

(3) She wears a fashionable hair style _____ in the city.

(4) But this new process has _____ great change.

(5) We need a foreign policy that is more _____.

(6) We can not only be used _____, but also be shared with others.

(7) Jobs are becoming increasingly _____.

(8) China's travel market is _____.

(9) Most Britons want a _____ wedding.

(10) An _____ transport system is critical to the long-term future of London.

3. Translate the following expressions into English or Chinese.

(1) 上网冲浪 _____

(2) 优惠的折扣 _____

(3) 创历史新高 _____

(4) 持有股份 _____

(5) 销售总收入 _____

(6) 线下旅游业务 _____

(7) 产业资源 _____

(8) 旅游专业人士 _____

(9) professional knowledge _____

(10) supervision mechanism _____

(11) make relevant laws and regulations _____

(12) travel customizer _____

(13) competition pressure _____

(14) online travel service(OTS) _____

(15) high self-determination _____

(16) traveling information _____

4. Translate the following sentences into English with the words or phrases given in the brackets.

(1) 过去 40 年，中国发生了翻天覆地的变化。(see/witness)

_____

(2) 我们将尽最大努力，以最少的花费举办这个会议。(at an economical cost)

_____

(3) 20世纪80年代，一些大企业开始吞并一些较小的公司。(swallow up)

(4) 与去年相比，出境游人数上升了很多。(compared with)

(5) "互联网+"给很多老人购票带来了很大挑战。(create challenges for)

(6) 因为没有足够的钱，他决定取消去旅游的计划。(shortage of)

Passage B   How is Technology Transforming Chinese Tourism

September 27th is World Tourism Day, which has been celebrated each year by the United Nations World Tourism Organization(UNWTO) since 1980. The theme of 2018 is "Tourism and the Digital Transformation" as digital technology has greatly affected the tourism industry.

Virtual reality (VR), augmented reality(AR), artificial intelligence (AI), Internet-plus—these terms have gradually become familiar to people traveling in China. A wide range of the newest technologies have been applied in almost every part of China's tourism industry.

Technology used at scenic spots

Technologies such as virtual reality, augmented reality, and artificial intelligence enable tourists to enjoy entertaining and interactive visual experiences. A growing number of China's tourist attractions, including theme parks, museums, and even zoos are applying those technologies to attract visitors.

The Palace Museum is a leader in the use of these technologies. The famous museum, popularly known as the Forbidden City, put on a digital exhibition in October 2017 to make its silent historical relics come alive. By wearing a VR helmet in a moving seat, visitors felt as if they were walking through the famous landmark during ancient times. They were even able to talk with a virtual senior minister with the help of artificial intelligence. In this way, visitors enjoyed a truly immersive experience that combined vision, sound, and movement. The Palace Museum also opened a digital gallery to show images of items which are too old and fragile to put on public display.

In April 2018, an intelligent robot tour guide was put to use in a scenic area in Changsha, Hunan Province. The robot named Yoyo showed tourists around and gave a brief introduction for the scenic spot. It could sing and dance to amuse visitors. And thanks to voice recognition software, it could even answer questions from tourists.

Technology used in accommodation

The latest technology, including artificial intelligence and intelligent robots, has also been used in some hotels.

In August 2017, China's first artificial intelligence voice control hotel was opened in Hangzhou. It was developed by Fliggy, the travel brand of Chinese tech giant Alibaba. By speaking to an intelligent speaker in their hotel room, guests can control the lighting, curtains, and the television. They can also request information about things like the meal times, call room service, and book a taxi.

Intelligent robots have been employed in a high tech hotel in Chengdu in March, 2018. They are capable of keeping customers company, and entertaining them with singing and storytelling.

Technology used in transportation

High-tech transportation services give tourists in China a more pleasant and efficient travel experience. The high-speed railway network enables tourists to travel to faraway places for less money and time. China Southern Airlines has started online seat selection for all domestic flights and paperless e-boarding passes since 2018. And the facial recognition systems used at an increasing number of railway stations and airports help speed up security screening and ticket checks for travelers.

To sum up, technologies have great impact on China's tourism. The future of travel is technology-based, so tourism jobs will require both technical and advanced skills used to effectively manage smart operations. The greatest impact of digital transformation on tourism may be the effect on the sector's workforce, which directly and indirectly represents 1 in every 10 jobs worldwide.

(source:http://chinaplus.cri.cn/news/china/9/20180927/188985.html?from=singlemessage&isappinstalled=0)

New words and expressions

transform [træns'fɔ:m] *vt.* 变换，改变

theme [θi:m] *n.* 主题，题目

apply [ə'plaɪ] *vt.* 应用，申请

interactive [ˌɪntər'æktɪv] *adj.* 互动的，互相作用的

digital ['dɪdʒɪtl] *adj.* 数字的，数据的

helmet ['helmɪt] *n.* 头盔，钢盔

landmark ['lændmɑ:k] *n.* 里程碑，纪念碑

minister ['mɪnɪstə(r)] *n.* 部长，大臣

combine [kəmˈbaɪn] *v.* 使结合
gallery [ˈɡæləri] *n.* 画廊
amuse [əˈmjuːz] *vt.* 娱乐，逗乐，使人发笑
faraway [ˈfɑːrəweɪ] *adj.* 遥远的
workforce [ˈwɜːkfɔːs] *n.* (国家或行业等)劳动力
represent [ˌreprɪˈzent] *vt.* 象征，代表
virtual reality (VR) 虚拟现实
augmented reality(AR) 增强现实
artificial intelligence (AI) 人工智能
internet-plus 互联网+
historical relic 历史文物
technology-based 基于技术的

Notes

  1. World Tourism Day：世界旅游日。9月27日是世界旅游日。世界旅游日是由世界旅游组织确定的旅游工作者和旅游者的节日。1970年9月27日，国际官方旅游联盟在墨西哥城举行的特别代表大会上通过了世界旅游组织章程。为纪念这个日子，1979年9月世界旅游组织第三次代表大会正式把9月27日定为世界旅游日。世界旅游组织从1980年起每年都为世界旅游日确定一个主题，各国旅游组织根据主题和要求开展一系列庆祝活动。

  2. Tourism and the Digital Transformation：旅游与数字化转型。2018年，世界旅游日的主题是"旅游与数字化转型"，探索通过大数据、人工智能和数字平台等技术进步为旅游业提供的机会，帮助推动旅行体验走向更加无缝、无摩擦、高品质的轨道。

  3. virtual reality(VR)：虚拟现实技术，它是一种可以创建和体验虚拟世界的计算机仿真系统。它利用计算机生成一种模拟环境，是一种多源信息融合的、交互式的三维动态视景和实体行为的系统仿真，使用户沉浸到该环境中。

  4. augmented reality(AR)：增强现实，它是一种实时地计算摄影机影像的位置及角度并加上相应图像的技术，这种技术的目标是在屏幕上把虚拟世界套在现实世界并进行互动，这种技术最早于1990年提出。随着随身电子产品运算能力的提升，增强现实的用途越来越广。

  5. artificial intelligence(AI)：人工智能。它是计算机科学的一个分支，它企图了解智能的实质，并生产出一种新的能以人类智能相似的方式做出反应的智能机器。该领域的研究包括机器人、语言识别、图像识别、自然语言处理和专家系统等。

  6. Internet-plus："互联网+"代表着一种新的经济形态，它指的是依托互联网信息技术实现互联网与传统产业的联合，以优化生产要素、更新业务体系、重构商业模式等途径来完成经济转型和升级。"互联网+"计划的目的在于充分发挥互联网的优势，将互联网与传

统产业深入融合，以产业升级提升经济生产力，最后实现社会财富的增加。

7. The Palace Museum/the Forbidden City：故宫，其为中国明、清两代(公元1368～1911年)的皇宫。北京故宫博物院建立于1925年10月10日，位于北京故宫紫禁城内，是在明、清两代皇宫及其收藏的基础上建立起来的中国综合性博物馆，也是中国最大的古代文化艺术博物馆，其文物收藏主要来源于清代宫中旧藏。从2014年1月1日起，北京故宫博物院几乎每周一闭馆。2018年10月，故宫博物院发布首款主题功能游戏和首张古画主题音乐专辑，拉开"智慧故宫"序幕。

8. digital gallery：数字美术馆

9. Fliggy：飞猪，它是阿里巴巴全新品牌。2016年10月27日，阿里巴巴集团宣布，将旗下旅行品牌"阿里旅行"升级为全新品牌"飞猪"，英文名"Fliggy"。飞猪是阿里巴巴旗下的综合性旅游出行服务平台，它整合数千家机票代理商、航空公司、旅行社、旅行代理商资源，直签酒店、客栈卖家等为广大旅游者提供特价机票、酒店预订等产品和服务。

10. high-speed railway：高速铁路。中国高速铁路(China Railway High-Speed, 简称CRH)，它是指新建设计开行250公里/小时(含预留)及以上动车组列车，初期运营速度不小于200公里/小时的客运专线铁路。2018年底中国高铁运营里程超过2.9万公里，占全球高铁运营里程的三分之二以上，超过其他国家总和。2019年，计划确保投产高铁新线3200公里。

11. China Southern Airlines：中国南方航空集团有限公司(简称南航)，IATA国际代号CZ，总部设在广州，成立于1995年3月25日，以蓝色垂直尾翼镶红色木棉花为公司标志，是中国运输飞机最多、航线网络最发达、年客运量最大的航空公司。2018年10月，中国南方航空集团有限公司登上福布斯2018年全球最佳雇主榜单。11月15日，中国南方航空宣布2019年起退出天合联盟。

Exercises

1. Reading Comprehension: Choose the best answer for the following questions.

(1) _____ is World Tourism Day, which has been celebrated each year by the United Nations World Tourism Organization(UNWTO) since _____.

  A. June 5th；1980   B. September 28th；1982

  C. September 27th；1980   D. June 8th；1982

(2) _____ have gradually employed in the tourism industry of China.

  A. Virtual reality(VR)

  B. Augmented reality(AR)

  C. Artificial intelligence (AI) and Internet-plus

  D. All above

(3) A wide range of the newest technologies have been applied in almost every part of

Unit 3 Online Travel Service

China's tourism industry, including ____.

    A. at scenic spots   B. in accommodation

    C. in transportation   D. all above

(4) In April 2018, an intelligent robot tour guide was put to use in a scenic area in ____.

    A. Hangzhou   B. Chengdu

    C. Changsha   D. Guangzhou

(5) China's first artificial intelligence voice control hotel was opened in ____.

    A. Hangzhou   B. Chengdu

    C. Changsha   D. Guangzhou

(6) The workforce of tourism sector directly and indirectly represents ____ jobs worldwide.

    A. 1%   B. 10%

    C. 12%   D. 15%

2. Fill in the blanks with the appropriate form of the words or phrases given below in the box.

a wide range of	put on	employ	theme
be applied to	landmark	amuse	technology-based

(1) This government believes _____ innovation will be one of the key drivers for the growth of tourism industry.

(2) The play has been planned to _____ today but it was put off because of the bad weather.

(3) The new technology _____ farming.

(4) The police had to _____ force to enter the building.

(5) _____ colours and patterns are available.

(6) This is Xi'an's _____, the Dayan Pagoda.

(7) My funny drawings _____ the kids.

(8) The _____ of the conference is Tourism and Innovation.

3. Translate the following expressions into English or Chinese.

(1) United Nations World Tourism Organization(UNWTO) _____

(2) virtual reality(VR) _____

(3) artificial intelligence(AI) _____

(4) theme park _____

(5) historical relic _____

(6) voice control _____

(7) 高铁 _____

(8) 网上选位 _____

(9) 电子登机牌 _____

(10) 人脸识别系统 _____

(11) 检票 _____

(12) 安全检查 _____

4. Translate the following sentences into Chinese.

(1) Virtual reality(VR), augmented reality(AR), artificial intelligence(AI), Internet-plus—these terms have gradually become familiar to people traveling in China.

_____

(2) A growing number of China's tourist attractions, including theme parks, museums, and even zoos are applying those technologies to attract visitors.

_____

(3) The robot named Yoyo showed tourists around and gave a brief introduction for the scenic spot. It could sing and dance to amuse visitors. And thanks to voice recognition software, it could even answer questions from tourists.

_____

(4) Intelligent robots have been employed in a high tech hotel in Chengdu in March, 2018. They are capable of keeping customers company, and entertaining them with singing and storytelling.

_____

(5) China Southern Airlines has started online seat selection for all domestic flights and paperless e-boarding passes since 2018. And the facial recognition systems used at an increasing number of railway stations and airports help speed up security screening and ticket checks for travelers.

_____

5. Translate the following paragraph into English.

支付宝(Alipay)是中国最大的第三方在线支付平台，由阿里巴巴集团(Alibaba Group)于2004年创建。截至2012年底，支付宝拥有用户超过7亿。用户可利用这一平台支付各种费用，如网购、电话费、学费等。以网购为例，买家先将钱存到支付宝账户，收到商品后，再通过支付宝将钱转给卖家。支付宝为其用户提供了"简单、安全、快速"的在线支付方式，保护了买卖双方的利益。

6. Activity

Group work: If you are going to develop more online travel services for customers, what else online services will you offer? Why?

Writing: Visa Application and Invitation 签证的申请与邀请

1. Writing Skills

出境旅游经常要事先准备好签证，所以需要向相应目的地国家领馆提交签证申请表和各项旅客资料，有的国家还需要面签，比较常见的申请签证的资料表如下：护照、签证照片、户口簿、身份证、个人经济担保(银行流水)、签证申请表、家庭情况表、在职证明，申根签证还需要提供往返机票订单、行程安排、旅游保险等。

2. Useful Expressions and Sentences

Schengen visa　申根签证

applicant　申请人，申请者

nationality　国籍(注意：国籍填写要用该国家人，比如国籍是中国，要填写 Chinese)

minor　未成年的

legal guardian　监护人

marital status　婚姻状况

specify　注明

education establishment　教育机构

transit　过境

member state　成员国

sponsor　赞助者，资助者

EU (European Union)　欧盟

EEA (European Economic Area)　欧洲经济区

CH citizen　瑞士公民

spouse　配偶

ascendant　祖父母

decline　拒签

embassy　大使馆

consulate　领馆

旅游英语

3. Sample Writing

Sample1: Application for Schengen Visa

1. Surname (Family name)			
2. Surname at birth (Former family names)			
3. First name (Given name)			
4. Date of Birth (day-month-year)	5. Place of birth	7. Current nationality Nationality at birth, if different	
	6. Country of birth		
8. Sex Male Female	9. Marital status Single Married Separated Divorced Widow(er) other (please specify)		
10. In the case of minors: Surname, first name, address (if different from applicant's) and nationality of parental authority /legal guardian			
11. National identity number, where applicable			
12. Type of travel document Ordinary passport Diplomatic passport Service passport Official passport Special passport other travel document (please specify)			
13. Number of travel document	14. Date of issue	15. Valid until	16. Issued by
17. Applicant's home address and e-mail address		Telephone number(s)	
18. Residence in a country other than the country of current nationality No. Yes. Residence permit or equivalent No. _____ Valid until _____			
19. Current occupation			
20. Employer and employee's address and telephone number. For students, name and address of educational establishment.			
21. Main purpose(s) of the journey: Tourism Business Visiting family or friends Cultural Sports Official visit Medical reasons Study Transit Airport transit Other (please specify)			

22. Member State(s) of destination	23. Member State of first entry

24. Number of entries requested
    Single entry   Two entries
    Multiple entries
	25. Duration of the intended stay or transit indicate number of days

26. Schengen visas issued during the past three years
    No.
    Yes.   Date(s) of validity from _____ to _____

27. Fingerprints collected previously for the purpose of applying for a Schengen visa
    No.   Yes.
_____ date, if known

28. Entry permit for the final country of destination, where applicable
Issued by _____ Valid from _____ until _____

29. Intended date of arrival in the Schengen area	30. Intended date of departure from the Schengen area

31. Surname and first name of the inviting person(s) in the Member State(s). If not applicable, name of hotel(s) or temporary accommodation(s) in the Member State(s)	
Address and e-mail address of inviting person(s)/hotel(s)/temporary accommodation(s)	Telephone and telefax
32. Name and address of inviting company/organization	Telephone and telefax of company/organization
Surname, first name, address, telephone, telefax, and e-mail address of contact person in company/organization	

33. Cost of traveling and living during the applicant's stay is covered

旅游英语

续表

by the applicant himself/herself
 	
Means of support
  cash
  Traveler's cheques
  Credit card
  Pre-paid accommodation
  Pre-paid transport
  Other (please specify)
	by a sponsor (host, company, organization), please specify
	_____ referred to in field 31 or 32
	_____ other(please specify)
	Means of support
	  Cash
	  Accommodation provided
	  All expenses covered during the stay
	  Pre-paid transport
	  Other (please specify)

34. Personal data of the family member who is an EU, EEA or CH citizen

Surname		First name(s)
Date of birth	Nationality	Number of travel document or ID card

35. Family relationship with an EU, EEA or CH citizen
  spouse   child   grandchild   dependent ascendant

36. Place and date	37. Signature (for minors, signature of parental authority/legal guardian)

Sample 2：外国人签证、居留许可申请表

外国人签证、居留许可申请表

VISA AND RESIDENCE PERMIT APPLICATION FORM

1. 英文姓名 _____

Name in English (as it appears in your passport)

中文姓名 _____   国籍 _____

Name in Chinese (if applicable)   Nationality

性别 男 ☐ 女 ☐   职业 _____

Sex M   F   Occupation

照片 PHOTO

Unit 3 Online Travel Service

出生日期　　　年　　月　　日　　　　　出生地 _____
Date of birth　　Y　　M　　D　　　　　Place of birth

2. 护照或者证件种类　　　　外交 □　公务 □　普通 □　其他 _____
   Type of passport or certificate　Diplomatic　Service　Ordinary　Others

   护照或者证件号码 _____　有效期至　　　年　　月　　日
   Passport or certificate number　　　　Valid until　　Y　　M　　D

3. 现持签证或者居留许可号码 _____　　签发机关 _____
   Current visa or residence permit number　　　　　Issued by

   签证种类或者居留事由 _____　有效期至　　　年　　月　　日
   Type of visa or purpose of residence　　　Valid until　　Y　　M　　D

4. 在华邀请单位名称或者个人的姓名、地址和电话 _____
   Company or person to visit in China, name(s), address and telephone number
   _____

   申请人在华住址、电话 _____
   Address and telephone number of applicant in China
   _____

5. 使用同一护照的偕行人　Accompanying persons included in passport

姓名	性别	出生日期	与申请人关系
Name	Sex	Date of birth	Relationship to applicant
_____	_____	_____	_____
_____	_____	_____	_____

6. 申请签证的种类　Type of visa you are applying for

   F 商务 □　　　C 乘务 □　　　J-2 记者 □　　　G 过境 □
   Business　　　Crew　　　　　Correspondent　　Transit

   L 探亲 □　　　L 旅游 □　　　L 因其他私人事务 □
   Visiting relatives　Sight seeing　For other private purposes

7. 申请签证的有效次数和有效期 Number of entries and validity of visa you are applying for

零次 ☐	一次 ☐	二次 ☐	多次 ☐	有效期至 ____ 年 ____ 月 ____ 日
Zero	Once	Twice	Multiple	Valid until Y M D

8. 申请居留许可 Applying for residence permit

居留事由	学习 ☐	记者 ☐	记者家属 ☐
Purpose of residence	Study	Correspondent	Family member of correspondent
任职 ☐	家属 ☐	就业 ☐	家属 ☐
Taking up post	Family member	Employment	Family member

有效期至 ____ 年 ____ 月 ____ 日
Valid until   Y   M   D

9. 申请居留情况变更登记 _____
Register such changes _____

住址 ☐	就读院校 ☐	任职或者就业单位 ☐	其他 ☐
Address	Educational institute	Place of work	Others

10. 申请其他证件 Applying for other certificate

外国人出入境证 ☐	外国人旅行证 ☐	其他 ☐
Aliens' Exit-Entry Permit	Aliens' Travel Permit	Others

我谨声明我已如实和完整地填写了上述内容并对此负责
(如属代办，代办人签字)

I hereby declare that the information given above is true, correct and complete. I shall take full responsibility for the above information.

申请人签字 _____   代办人签字 _____   ____ 年 ____ 月 ____ 日
Applicant signature   Agent signature   Y   M   D

Sample 3：Visa invitation for CITIE

Visa Invitation

With greetings from GZL International Conference and Exhibition Service Ltd, the executive unit of CITIE 2017, China (Guangdong) International Tourism Industry Expo will be held in Canton Fair Complex, Guangzhou, China from 8th to 10th Sep.. I would hereby invited _____ (the delegation or the name of the company) led by you_____ (the name of the leader), to come over to Guangzhou, China for this Expo.

续表

During the Expo, you will stay here for _____ days, from _____ to _____. Visa application deadline is 1st Aug, 2017. Only exhibitors and hosted buyers are available for visa application.

IMPORTANT:

Visa can be applied in Chinese Embassy (Consulate General / Consulate/ Office) in or the Commissioner's Office of China's Foreign Ministry in _____ SAR:

We are looking forward to greeting you in China very soon!

Yours sincerely

Yang Yunxi

Senior Project Manager GZL International Conference and Exhibition Services Ltd.

No.1 Lejia Road, Jichang West Road, Guangzhou, 510403, PR China

Mobile: +86-13808819862

Email: yangyx@gzl.com.cn

Name list of the invited

Name	Gender	Passport No.	Date of birth	Position

4. Writing Practice

(1) Invited by John, the manager of SIC TURISMO SRL, one of the famous travel agencies in Europe, you will go to Italy, French and Germany for business trip from 2nd Aug. to 20th Sep. Your first entry is in Italy, and final entry is in Germany. Complete the application form for Schengen visa in Sample 1.

(2) Kate Smith is from Australia. Invited by Zheng Huan, the supervisor of China International Travel Service in Beijing, Kate Smith, the CEO of Hilton Hotel in New York, will come to China for business negotiation from 3rd Mar. to 15th Mar. It is her first time to come to China. Now she needs to apply for the visa of China. Her passport No. is AZ098. As her secretary, please fill in the visa application form in Sample 2.

旅游英语

Supplementary Reading

The Current Development of Ctrip

1. Baidu signs comprehensive deal with Ctrip

Chinese internet search giant Baidu Inc inked an in-depth partnership with China's largest online travel agency Ctrip, in its latest efforts to drive the development of intelligent tourism in China.

Under the agreement, Baidu will deploy its cloud services and artificial intelligence capabilities to provide Ctrip with solutions tailored to tourism scenarios and businesses. Baidu Cloud, the cloud unit of Baidu will help Ctrip improve operational efficiency and customer experience and reduce costs in marketing and sales, customer acquisition and online traffic conversion.

The two companies will also continue to explore a variety of smart services in more scenarios based on Baidu's AI capabilities, such as speech technology and autonomous driving.

The tourism industry is growing rapidly and Ctrip is the industry leader. Baidu looks forward to working with Ctrip to upgrade tourism services with "cloud plus AI", enhance customer experience, and explore a viable path to intelligent tourism for the entire industry. '

With the vigorous development of tourism, consumer needs are more and more diversified. To better serve our customers, Ctrip needs to be enabled by advanced cloud computing and AI technologies.

Ctrip hoped to collaborate with Baidu to create smarter customer service and more value for users.

This partnership is not limited to IT infrastructure. With Baidu Cloud's capabilities, big data analytics can be conducted on users' interests, habits and preferences. Different tourism products can be packaged by Baidu's AI and machine learning technologies to offer every user customized solutions.

(source: http://www.ecns.cn/news/2019-02-15/detail-ifzeratr8869559.shtml)

2. Ctrip ups Japan tourism market investment via Yokohama tie-up

China's biggest online travel agency Ctrip has inked a strategic cooperation agreement with Yokohama to boost the appeal of the Japanese city to global travelers, Chinese tourists in particular. The two sides will partner in tourism product development and destination branding among others.

The move is expected to facilitate two-way travel between China and Japan and jointly develop the cross-border cultural tourism industry. This year marks the 45th anniversary of the establishment of sister-city ties between Yokohama and Shanghai, where Ctrip is headquartered.

Japan is one of Chinese tourists' favorite travel destinations. China remains Japan's largest source of travelers for three consecutive years, according to Ctrip, citing Japanese official data. The company predicted Chinese visitors will make more than 8 million trips to Japan this year, a record high.

Ctrip has been investing heavily in exploring Japanese market in recent years. The company established a Japanese branch to better serve travelers to Japan in 2015. Earlier this year, it launched Trip.com, an independent brand primarily serving clients in Asia Pacific markets, in Tokyo to offer timely travel-related services. Construction of an around-the-clock Ctrip call center in Japan is currently underway.

The Nasdaq-listed firm looks to gain a bigger global tourism market share by accelerating international business expansion.

(source: http://www.xinhuanet.com/english/2018-11/21/c_137622512.htm)

Useful words and phrases

comprehensive [ˌkɒmprɪˈhensɪv] *adj.* 全面的，广泛的
deploy [dɪˈplɔɪ] *vt.* 开展，施展
acquisition [ˌækwɪˈzɪʃn] *n.* 获得
upgrade [ˌʌpˈɡreɪd] *vt.* 提升，提高
vigorous [ˈvɪɡərəs] *adj.* 有力的，大力的
tie-up [ˈtaɪ ʌp] *n.* 联合，协作
facilitate [fəˈsɪlɪteɪt] *vt.* 帮助，促进
consecutive [kənˈsekjətɪv] *adj.* 连续的，连贯的
tailored to 量身定做，定制的
Nasdaq-listed firm 纳斯达克上市公司

Read the passage and decide whether the following statements are true(T) or false(F).

1. _____ Baidu will deploy its cloud services and artificial intelligence capabilities to provide Ctrip with solutions tailored to tourism scenarios and businesses.

2. _____ The tourism industry is growing rapidly and Ctrip is the industry leader.

3. _____ This partnership between Ctrip and Baidu is limited to IT infrastructure.

4. _____ According to Ctrip, citing Japanese official data, the company predicted Chinese visitors will make more than 6 million trips to Japan this year.

5. _____ Construction of an around-the-clock Ctrip call center in Japan is currently underway.

Module Two

Hospitality

Unit 4　Hospitality Industry

Learning Objectives

After learning this unit, you should:
- Acquire the knowledge and information of the concept of hospitality industry.
- Grasp professional English words and expressions for hospitality industry.
- Get some practical knowledge about the range of hospitality industry.
- Be familiar with varies areas of hospitality industry.
- Get some cultural knowledge about Club Med.

Keywords

hospitality industry, service industry, Club Med

Information search

Please search some information about the topic of this unit by scanning the QR codes: (Travel Column of *China Daily*), (China Plus), (World Tourism Organization), (Travelogue of CCTV), (Ministry of Culture and Tourism of the People's Republic of China). After reading the information, please share with your classmates some information about the topic of this unit.

Warm-up

Task 1: Work in pairs, match the words with the pictures.

1. theme park _____
2. cruise line _____
3. event planning _____
4. lodging _____

(A)

(B)

旅游英语

(C)   (D)

Task 2: Discuss with your partner and find out more services in hospitality industry.

Passage A   The Hospitality Industry

The hospitality industry is a broad category of fields within the service industry that includes lodging, event planning, theme parks, transportation, cruise line, traveling and additional fields within the tourism industry.

The hospitality industry is a multibillion-dollar industry that depends on the availability of leisure time and disposable income. A hospitality unit such as a restaurant, hotel, or an amusement park consists of multiple groups such as facility maintenance and direct operations (servers, housekeepers, porters, kitchen workers, bartenders, management, marketing, and human resources etc.).

Before structuring as an industry, the historical roots of hospitality was in the western world in the form of social assistance mainly for christian pilgrims directed to Rome. For such a reason, the eldest public hospital in Europe was the Ospedale di Santo Spirito in Sassia founded in Rome in the eighth century A.D. on the model of the oriental world.

The hospitality industry is one that is primarily focused on customer satisfaction. For the most part, it is built on leisure or is luxury-based, as opposed to meeting basic needs. Hotels and resorts, cruise lines, airlines and other various forms of travel, tourism, special event planning, and restaurants all generally fall under the realm of the hospitality industry.

This service-based industry thrives on the leisure activities of patrons. Some of the business that the hospitality industry garners is transient and intermittent, but collectively, it accounts for a large source of its revenue. For example, a vacationing family may fly from one country to another, book a hotel room for the duration of their visit, dine at local restaurants, and tour theme parks or other area attractions. All of these activities involve the services provided by various areas of the hospitality industry.

Exceptional service is usually very important for all of these businesses. Customer satisfaction usually leads to consumer loyalty, which helps to ensure the success of a company in the hospitality industry. For example, if an individual chooses a particular airline and has a positive experience, he or she is likely to use it again in the future. Alternatively, if the flight is unpleasant, the airline attendants are rude, or the customer is otherwise displeased with the service, he or she is less likely to return to that airline the next time the opportunity arises.

Other services in the hospitality industry include special event planning for social and corporate functions. This may include the organization of a wedding that requires multiple vendors, such as florists, entertainers, cake bakers, and invitation designers. A wedding planner may also arrange for ground transportation and hotel accommodations for out-of-town guests. When all of these elements come together, a combination of local vendors within the hospitality industry collectively creates the overall experience for the wedding couple, their families, and the guests.

Similarly, corporate event planners commonly also arrange transportation for multiple individuals and secure hotel accommodations. Depending on the type of program the corporation is hosting, it is very likely that meeting space, audio visual equipment, food and beverage service, and other needs will also be arranged. Equipment rentals for trade shows — such as portable booths, pipe and drape, lighting, and signage — may also be required for the success of an event. Hospitality professionals that specialize in corporate events create an overall environment conducive for effective shows, meetings or conferences.

(source:https://www.wisegeek.com/what-is-the-hospitality-industry.htm)

New words and expressions

category ['kætɪg(ə)rɪ] *n.* 种类，分类
lodging ['lɒdʒɪŋ] *n.* 住宿
assistance [ə'sɪst(ə)ns] *n.* 援助，帮助
oriental [ɔːriˈentl] *adj.* 东方的
realm [relm] *n.* 领域，范围
garner ['gɑːnə] *vt.* 获得，得到
transient ['trænzɪənt] *adj.* 短暂的
intermittent [ˌɪntə'mɪt(ə)nt] *adj.* 间歇性的，不间断的
collectively [kə'lektɪvlɪ] *adv.* 共同地，全体地
alternatively [ɔːl'tɜːnətɪvlɪ] *adv.* 非此即彼，二者择一地

vendor ['vendɔː] n. 小贩，卖主

accommodation [əˌkɒməˈdeɪʃn] n. 住处，膳宿

booth [buːð] n. 展位，货摊

signage ['saɪnɪdʒ] n. 引导标志

event planning 活动策划

theme park 主题公园

cruise line 邮轮

a multibillion-dollar industry 数十亿的行业

disposable income 可支配收入

customer satisfaction 顾客满意度

thrive on 因……而成长，因……而发展

Notes

1. christian pilgrim: 基督教朝圣者，朝圣者都是朝着他们认为的天堂方向朝拜的，一般都是庙宇和高山等。朝圣者目的地一般为耶路撒冷、麦加或西藏(分属世界三大宗教基督教、伊斯兰教、佛教)。基督徒为了证明他们的虔诚，会到罗马、圣地亚哥的康普提拉甚至耶路撒冷朝圣。

2. the Ospedale di Santo Spirito in Sassia: 萨西亚的圣灵大教堂，始建于1633年，1642年完工，属巴洛克建筑风格。最初曾是天主教女修道院的主教堂。1860年，该教堂转为东正教教堂。1870年教堂开设圣灵修士修道院。20世纪50年代上半叶，对教堂内部进行过一次维修。70年代末到80年代初，对教堂进行最后一次修葺并保持至今。教堂中供奉着一些宗教珍品，如明斯克圣母圣像等。

3. all generally fall under the realm of the hospitality industry: 一般都归于酒店行业的范围。

4. This service-based industry thrives on the leisure activities of patrons. thrives on 繁荣兴旺；整句翻译：这个以服务为基础的行业是靠顾客的休闲活动发展起来的。

5. corporate function: 企业的职能

6. portable booth: 便携式展位

7. signage: 引导标志

8. Hospitality professionals that specialize in corporate events create an overall environment conducive for effective shows, meetings or conferences. 这是一个由that引导的定语从句，修饰 hospitality professionals(酒店业专业人士们)，conducive 有益于，有助于；整句意思：专门从事企业活动的酒店业专业人士为有效的展示、集会或会议创造了有利的整体环境。

Unit 4　Hospitality Industry

Exercises

1. Answer the following questions according to the passage.

(1) What areas does hospitality industry include?
_____

(2) What is the definition of hospitality industry?
_____

(3) According to the passage, what is the eldest hospital in Europe?
_____

(4) When was hospitality rooted in the western world?
_____

(5) What helps to ensure the success of a company in the hospitality industry?
_____

(6) What vendors do we need for a wedding?
_____

(7) What does an event planner need to do when organizing an event?
_____

(8) What is hospitality industry based on?
_____

2. Fill in the blanks with the appropriate form of the words given below in the box.

categories	booth	assistance	realm	transient
oriental	vendor	alternatively	garner	intermittent

(1) Cyberspace is a new _____, we have many, many years of hard-won understandings to guide us in this new space.

(2) The results can be divided into three main _____.

(3) She said that although her face was _____, she was, at heart, a westerner.

(4) How do we get legal _____?

(5) Being more attractive could help a candidate _____ more votes.

(6) Their happiness was _____, for the war broke out soon after they got married.

(7) Supplies of water and electricity are _____, also in health care facilities.

(8) If you do not like it, change it. _____, accept it.

(9) She looked at the _____ who cheated her the other day with distaste.

(10) The American walked to a telephone _____, "Hello. Is that the bank?"

3. Translate the following expressions into English or Chinese.

(1) the hospitality industry _____

(2) broad category _____

(3) Christian pilgrims _____

(4) customer satisfaction _____

(5) the leisure activities of patrons _____

(6) cruise lines _____

(7) fall under the realm of the hospitality industry

_____

(8) corporate events _____

(9) 服务业 _____

(10) 婚礼策划师 _____

(11) 展会 _____

(12) 主题公园 _____

(13) 小贩 _____

(14) 可支配收入 _____

(15) 东方的 _____

(16) 帮助 _____

4. Translate the following sentences into English with the words or phrases given in the brackets.

(1) 这些准则都是基于企业员工对于客户满意度的承诺。(customer satisfaction)

(2) 如果他的数字是准确的，就意味着中国消费者的可支配收入比官方估计的数字高出90%。(disposable income)

(3) 孩子能够在日常安排中茁壮成长。(thrive on)

(4) 东京迪士尼乐园是唯一一个在美国本土外赢利的主题公园。(theme park)

(5) 这条邮轮航线经过温哥华吗？(cruise line)

(6) 作为一名导游要安排和协调旅游活动，并为游客提供交通、膳宿、观光、购物和娱乐服务。(accommodation)

Passage B   Club Med

Club Med SAS, commonly known as Club Med and previously known as Club Méditerranée SA, is a private company headquartered in France, specializing in premium all-inclusive holidays. The company is primarily owned by Fosun Group and either wholly owns or operates over seventy premium all-inclusive resort villages in a number of exotic locations around the world.

Club Med

Foundation

The Club was started in 1950 by Belgian entrepreneur Gérard Blitz. Blitz had opened a low-priced summer colony of tents on the island of Majorca. Gilbert Trigano supplied the tents, and in 1953 Blitz wooed him into a partnership. The first official Club Med was built the next year in Palinuro, Salerno Italy. The original villages were simple: Members stayed in unlit straw huts on a beachfront, sharing communal washing facilities. Such villages have been replaced with modern blocks or huts with ensuite facilities.

Expansion

In 1961, the company was purchased by the 35-year-old Baron Edmond de Rothschild after he had visited a resort and enjoyed his stay. With Rothschild financing, the number of villages increased greatly under Trigano's leadership from 1963 to 1993. Winter villages, providing skiing and winter sports tuition, were introduced in 1956 at Leysin, Switzerland. In 1965, the first club outside the Mediterranean was opened in Tahiti. Club Med broadened its reach by opening villages in the Caribbean and Florida where English rather than French was the main language.

Originally attracting mainly singles and young couples, the Club later became primarily a destination for families, with the first Mini Club opening in 1967.

Club Med 2 is a 5-masted cruise ship owned by Club Med. The sails are automatically deployed by computer control. Club Med 2 was launched in 1992 in Le Havre, France. The ship, carrying up to 400 passengers with a crew of 200, cruises the Mediterranean, Caribbean and Atlantic.

The Club has also ceased to be a club in the legal sense, changing from a not-for-profit association to a for-profit public limited company (French SA) in 1995. However, each new customer is still charged a membership fee upon joining, and returning customers are charged an annual fee as well.

Services

Each resort provides a list of services and activities in one single package. This includes lodging, food, use of facilities, sports activities, games, and shows. Certain items such as premium alcoholic beverages previously required the use of beads or tickets as a form of payment; this is not required anymore.

Staff

Club Med staff are called "GOs", or Gentils Organisateurs (Gracious/Nice Organizers). Clients are "GMs", or Gentils Members (Gracious/Nice Guests/Members). The resort is known as a village. The resort manager is called the Chef de Village (Village Chief).

(source:https://en.wikipedia.org/wiki/Club_Med)

New words and expressions

headquarter [ˌhedˈkwɔːtə] vt. 在……设总部
primarily [ˈpraɪm(ə)rɪlɪ] adv. 首先，主要地
premium [ˈpriːmɪəm] adj. 优质的
exotic [ɪgˈzɒtɪk] adj. 异国的，外来的，异国情调的
tuition [tjuːˈɪʃ(ə)n] n. 讲授，指导
mediterranean [ˌmedɪtəˈreɪnɪən] n. 地中海 adj. 地中海的
resort [rɪˈzɔːt] n. 度假胜地
previously [ˈpriːvɪəslɪ] adv. 以前，预先
ensuite [ɒŋˈswiːt] adj. 带有浴室的套间的
charge [tʃɑːdʒ] v. 收(费)，(向……)要价
all-inclusive holidays 全包假期
cease to be 不再是
alcoholic beverage 酒精饮料

Notes

1. all-inclusive holiday: 一价全包假期

2. The Club was started in 1950 by Belgian entrepreneur Gérard Blitz. 该俱乐部于1950年由比利时企业家杰拉德·布利茨创办。

3. Blitz had opened a low-priced summer colony of tents on the island of Majorca. 布利茨在西班牙的马略卡岛(Majorca)开设了一处夏季廉价帐篷营地。

4. ...Blitz wooed him into a partnership: woo sb. into a partnership 恳求某人成为他的合作伙伴。

5. cease to be a club in the legal sense: cease to be，不再是；整句意思：不再是法律意义上的俱乐部。

6. Each resort provides a list of services and activities in one single package. 每个度假村在一个包里面提供一系列的服务和活动。这就是 all-inclusive holiday 一价全包假期。

7. Club Med staff are called GOs, or Gentils Organisateurs (Gracious/Nice Organizers). 地中海俱乐部的员工被称为GO，就是亲切的组织者的意思。

8. Clients are GMs or Gentils Members (Gracious/Nice Guests/Members). 俱乐部的顾客被称为GM或亲切的成员。

9. The resort is known as a village. 度假村被称为村子。

10. The resort manager is called the Chef de Village(Village Chief). 度假村经理被称为村长。

Exercises

1. Reading Comprehension: Choose the best answer for the following questions.

(1) The full name of Club Med is _____.
  A. Club Méditerranée SA   B. Club Médicine SA   C. Club Médical SA

(2) Club Med is a private company headquartered in _____.
  A. France   B. England   C. Swiss

(3) Club Med was started in 1950 by the Belgian entrepreneur _____.
  A. Gerfany Bezel   B. Mercedes Bens   C. Gérard Blitz

(4) Club Med broadened its reach by opening villages in the Caribbean and Florida where _____ was the main language.
  A. French   B. Italian   C. English

(5) In 1995, new customer is charged _____ upon joining.
  A. an annual fee   B. a membership fee   C. a renewing fee

(6) Club Med staff are called _____.
   A. GOs   B. CEO   C. GEO
(7) Each resort provides a list of services and activities in _____ package(s).
   A. two   B. one single   C. multiple
(8) The resort is known as a _____.
   A. village   B. town   C. county

2. **Fill in the blanks with the appropriate form of the words or phrases given below in the box.**

| Premium | Mediterranean | exotic | tuition |
| cease to be | resort | ensuite | charge |

(1) He declined to say what level of _____ would be acceptable.
(2) The Straits of Gibraltar are the strategic passage between the _____ and Atlantic.
(3) When it finally came, it _____ a dream and became my everyday reality.
(4) There is a larger room and a smaller room which has a larger _____.
(5) Find out which of these are native plants and which are _____.
(6) The _____ varies from 5 *yuan* to 10 *yuan*.
(7) I have no income and I have to pay my _____.
(8) We run the most expensive _____ in Sanya, on Yalong Bay.

3. **Translate the following words or expressions into English or Chinese.**

(1) headquarter _____
(2) supply _____
(3) all-inclusive holiday _____
(4) straw hut _____
(5) not-for-profit _____
(6) 地中海 _____
(7) 营利性的 _____
(8) 酒精饮料 _____
(9) 年费 _____
(10) 村长 _____

4. **Translate the following sentences into Chinese.**

(1) Club Med SAS, commonly known as Club Med and previously known as Club Méditerranée

SA, is a private company headquartered in France, specializing in premium all-inclusive holidays.
___

(2) The original villages were simple: Members stayed in unlit straw huts on a beachfront, sharing communal washing facilities.
___

(3) Originally attracting mainly singles and young couples, the Club later became primarily a destination for families, with the first Mini Club opening in 1967.
___

(4) This includes lodging, food, use of facilities, sports activities, games, and shows.
___

(5) Certain items such as premium alcoholic beverages previously required the use of beads or tickets as a form of payment; this is not required anymore.
___

5. Translate the following paragraph into English.

广州中国大酒店是一家五星级酒店，坐落于广州城市中心，毗邻广州火车站。广州中国大酒店拥有八百余间豪华客房(elegant accommodation)，客房空间大，有高速网络(high-speed Internet)，配有降噪窗户(noise-reduction windows)。酒店内有8间中西餐厅和酒吧，你可以尽情品味中外美食之旅。健康中心配备完善，桑拿浴室、按摩池、健身室、室外泳池(outdoor swimming pool)等设施应有尽有，为你带来舒适的享受。酒店内配置银行、港式茶餐厅、美式快餐等。中国大酒店是你的理想(ideal)选择。

6. Activity

Group work: Suppose you are the marketing manager of a hotel group in the world. In an expo, you are to introduce your hotel group to purchasers. Please introduce your hotel group with pictures or short videos. Each group makes a presentation for about 8 minutes.

Writing: Reservation Letter 预订信

1. Writing Skills

游客在出行前要预定各种票务、酒店、门票等，所以要进行电话或者网络预订。旅游服务机构为客户提供相应的预订服务。有些海外旅游、参展除了电话预订外，个人和团体还可以通过书信、电子邮件、网络及传真等方式完成预订。预订信属商务书信的一种，需要符合商务信函的撰写要求，包含信头、称呼、正文、结束语、签名等五个主要部分。

预定票务信函的内容应包括准确的预订人数、具体的日期、地点、航班号或者车次、座位等级要求等信息。如果预定酒店客房，内容应包括预定日期、房间类型、入住人数、餐饮要求等。

2. Useful Expressions and Sentences

(1) I would like to make a reservation of a double bed deluxe room in your hotel for the dates from November 28th to 30th.

(2) Settlement of payment shall be made in full upon our arrival.

(3) Please respond with a confirmation on my reservation. Please feel free to contact me as soon as possible for any clarification.

(4) Please reserve a single room under the name of Mr. Lin.

(5) I would like to book a flight to Paris on January 8 on Air France, First Class and round trip.

(6) We are pleased to confirm your reservation: one double room for four nights from November 5th to 9th at RMB860 per night.

(7) We would like to fly from Beijing to New York on the earliest flight.

(8) I have enclosed a check for $100 to serve as my deposit.

(9) Please charge my credit card for the initial deposit required.

(10) Thank you for your prompt attention and I look forward to receiving a reply confirming my reservation.

3. Sample Writing

A Letter of Reservation for Hotel Room

Feb. 20th, 2018
the Reservation Manager,
Grand View Hotel
112 Sun Street
Shanghai, 200010, Fax 012-7821868

Dear Sir/Madam,

I am writing to make a reservation for one suite from 4th March to 8th March, in which I am going to attend a trade fair in Shanghai. Please kindly reserve a suite for me for four nights, including breakfast. Please confirm the booking as soon as payment is made. Bank of China has been instructed to pay the fare and booking fees.

If there is no room available, please inform me other room options. Or I must look for another hotel.

I am looking forward to receiving your reply. Thank you.

Yours faithfully,

Joe Johnson

The following is the reservation confirmation form.

订房确认书

Reservation Confirmation Form

致： 由：
To: _____ From: _____

传真号码：
Fax No. : _____

亲爱的宾客：

感谢您预订×××酒店客房，我们对您的订房做出以下确认，如有任何疑问或需要做任何更改，请与我们联系。

Dear Guest,

Thank you for your reservation at ××× hotel. If you have any questions or changes about your reservation, please contact us as soon as possible.

客人姓名：   房间类型：
Guest name:_____   Room Type:_____

入住日期：   离店日期：
Arr. Date:_____   Dept. Date:_____

房价：
Room rate:

付款方式：   现金   转账   信用卡
Payment: Cash   Transfer accounts   Credit card

信用卡：   卡号：   有效期：
Credit card:_____   Card No._____   Valid:_____

备注：

续表

Remarks:_____

经办人：　　　　　　　　　　　日期：
Prepared by:_____　　Date:_____

Thank you for your reservation.

如果抵店时间未明确相告，所订的房间将保留至当天下午6:00。

Should arrival time is not stated, reserved room will be held until 6:00 p.m.

为了确保您的订房，请将您的信用卡号码及有效期限通知我们，或预付一晚房租的定金。

To guarantee your booking, please inform us your credit card number and date of valid or deposit in advance.

×××酒店预订部

Reservation Dept. ××× Hotel

地址(Address):　　　　　　　　　　邮政编码(Post Code):

电话(Tel):　　　　　传真(Fax):　　　　电子邮件(E-mail):

4. Writing Practice

Mr. Li Ming will fly to London on July 24th to attend a conference. Please write to China Eastern Airlines to reserve a first-class seat and the fare will be settled by Bank of China.

Supplementary Reading

China Aims to Make Hainan an International Tourism Island

For years China's Hainan province has been developing its tourism industry, with the key decision made by central authorities that aims to turn the island into an international tourist destination. Thirty years after Hainan island became a province and a special economic zone, Chinese President Xi Jinping called for an acceleration of its development into a center for international tourism and consumption.

Hainan's tourism industry has grown rapidly, but it's suffered from "growing pains". During the Spring Festival of 2018, thousands of holidaymakers returning home were stuck in a massive traffic jam on the island. When asked about it at this year's plenary session of the national legislature, delegate A Dong, also the mayor of Hainan's major tourist city of Sanya said there was a need for improvement. He said that the tourism industry in Hainan lacks high-end and competitive

Unit 4　Hospitality Industry

products. "The quality of relevant services cannot meet international standard yet", he added.

President Xi announced a series of favorable policies covering tourism, aiming to make Hainan an international resort. The efforts include carrying out major infrastructure projects like international routes and airlines while embracing intelligent and network infrastructure. In order to develop Hainan into an international hub of tourism and consumption, the government will open up the duty-free policy to boost sales. Xi also called for new tourism programs and better services.

Sanya set up China's first tourist police patrol in 2015 to standardize the tourism sector and offer better quality services to tourists. The captain of the division told CGTN that they are specialized in answering queries, resolving disputes and cracking down on crimes. In the future, they will equip themselves with more high-tech devices to quickly respond to emergencies, to monitor tourist sites and to translate. Police officers are also being trained in foreign languages to overcome the language barrier and better help overseas tourists.

The province is also seeking innovative ways to attract tourists by offering them diverse and exclusive experience. For instance, luxury hotel resorts are introducing cultural and educational programs to accommodation, which somewhat reflects Hainan's ambition to turn itself into the Dubai of China.

China also plans to further extend the offshore duty-free shopping policy in Hainan to cover all outbound tourists. Hainan has already had one of the world's largest duty-free shopping centers and it's now the fourth island in the world to pilot the policy.

The government wants Hainan to welcome more global investors, becoming a free trade zone by 2020 and a free trade port by 2025. In Sanya, the Phoenix Island International Cruise Port being upgraded is welcoming an increasing number of people internationally and the island can look forward to a brighter future.

(source:http://www.chinadaily.com.cn/a/201804/18/WS5ad695c0a3105cdcf6518e8b_1.html#_cofs_)

Useful words and phrases

ambition [æm'bɪʃ(ə)n] *n.* 雄心，志向
acceleration [əkˌselə'reɪʃn] *n.* 加速，促进
consumption [kən'sʌm(p)ʃ(ə)n] *n.* 消费，消耗
hub [hʌb] *n.* 中心
standardize ['stændədaɪz] *vt.* 使标准化
diverse [daɪ'vɜːs] *adj.* 不同的，多种多样的
central authorities 中央，最高领导机构
international tourist destination 国际旅游目的地
massive traffic jam 严重的交通堵塞

Read the passage and decide whether the following statements are true (T) or false(F).

1. _____Hainan has became a province and a special economic zone island for thirty-one years.

2. _____The tourism industry in Hainan lacks high-end and competitive products.

3. _____Hainan wants to become the Dubai of China.

4. _____Haikou set up China's first tourist police patrol in 2015 to standardize the tourism sector and offer better quality services to tourists.

5. _____Hainan has already had one of the world's largest duty-free shopping centers and it's now the third island in the world to pilot the policy.

Unit 5   Food and Beverage Services

Learning Objective

After learning this unit, you should:
- Be able to communicate with foreigners in English in a restaurant.
- Acquire the knowledge and information of Chinese Cuisine and Western Cuisine.
- Grasp professional English words and expressions for cuisine.
- Get some practical knowledge about Chinese table manners.
- Get some cultural knowledge about western catering.
- Master the basic words and expressions about the technique of cooking.
- Find ways to improve your writing skills about menu.

Keywords

Chinese cuisine, western cuisine, China's eight great cuisines, table manners

Information search

Please search some information about the topic of this unit by scanning the QR codes: (Travel Column of *China Daily*), (China Plus), (World Tourism Organization), (Travelogue of CCTV), (Ministry of Culture and Tourism of the People's Republic of China). After reading the information, please share with your classmates some information about the topic of this unit.

Warm-up

Task 1: Search on the Internet, and write down the names of the following dishes. Besides, try to list the famous cuisines of your hometown.

旅游英语

Task 2: A guest is making a complaint to the headwaiter in a restaurant. Please make a dialogue in groups and discuss.

What are they talking about?

Why is the guest making a complaint?

Example

Guest: Excuse me, are you the headwaiter? I'd like to have a word with you.

Head waitress: Yes, sir. What can I do for you?

Guest: I'm sorry to bother you, but my friend and I have been waiting half an hour for our last two dishes.

Head waitress: I'm sorry sir. Our staff are very busy this evening. Could you tell me what you've ordered?

Guest: Kun-pao chicken, beancurd with pepper and chili sauce.

Head waitress: Don't worry. Your meal will be ready soon.

Passage A Chinese Cuisine

Chinese cooking has a long history and is famous all over the world for its rich flavor and delightful colorings. It was the Chinese who invented the technique of making and using soy sauce, vinegar, wine, jams, and spices during the Yin-Zhou period, some 3000 years ago. Every Chinese local dish, special cuisine, and local snack has its own characteristics. Here are some of the most famous dishes, China's eight great cuisines.

1. Sichuan Cuisine

Sichuan cuisine is one of the four most famous dishes in China, and are enjoyed with great popularity all over the country, because of their distinct and various flavors. Some of the most famous flavors are derived from fish flavors, pepper powder boiled in oil, strange flavor and sticky-hot. The raw materials of a Sichuan dish are always wild edible herbs, and the meat of domestic animals and birds. The techniques used in cooking are sauting, stir-frying without stewing, dry braising, and Hui (frying and then braising with corn flour sauce). Famous Sichuan dishes include Sichuan Hotpot, Zhang Tea Duck, Mapo Beancurd, and Water Boiled Beef.

Sichuan Hotpot

Water Boiled Beef

2. Cantonese Cuisine

The Cantonese are widely recognized as gourmets as their food catalogue is very extensive and varied. Because of the location of Guangdong Province and its climate features, the Cantonese are fascinated by light, refreshing and aquatic food, in which the tender and original taste of the ingredients is kept intact. Famous Cantonese dishes are White Cut Chicken, Char Siu, Boiled Prawns.

3. Huaiyang Cuisine

Huaiyang cuisine mainly consists of Yangzhou and Zhenjiang. It originated in water villages south of the Yangtze River, and is characterized by the strictness in material selection. The emphasis of the fine workmanship is cutting, matching, cooking, and arranging. The flavor of lightness, freshness and mildness are the features of these dishes. Special attention is paid to retaining the natural juices and flavors. Famous dishes include Crystal Meat, Squirrel with Mandarin Fish, Liangxi Crisp Eel, and Duck Triplet.

4. Shandong Cuisine

Shandong cuisine with a long history has a great impact on other cuisines. With historical roots originating in sophisticated cuisine, the ingredients selected are more costly than others, usually are sea food due to the favorable location. Besides, its long duration of cold weather makes local chefs skilled in producing high-calorie and high-protein dishes. Major cooking techniques are quick-fry and deep-fry, which create distinctive crispy texture of the dishes. Famous dishes are Stewed Pork Hock, Four Joys Meatballs.

5. Hunan Cuisine

Hunan cuisine consists of local dishes from the Xiangjiang River area, Dongting Lake area and Western Hunan mountain area. Typical dishes are Dongan Fledgling Chicken, Hot-Spiced and Peppered Fledgling Chicken, Steamed Pickled Meat, Lotus Seed with Rock Candy and Mutton Soup with Tortoise.

6. Zhejiang Cuisine

Characterized by the mellow and non-greasy flavor, Zhejiang Cuisine serves as representative of the food from along the lower Yangtze River. Situated in the "land of fish and rice", Zhejiang has a substantial scope of local produce, nutrients and taste for its diners. The main methods of cooking are quick frying, stir-frying, braising and deep-frying.

7. Fujian Cuisine

Fujian cuisine sources from the native cooking style of Fujian Province shares a few common characteristics with nearby Taiwan and Guangdong. There's a wealth of seafood and woodland-based ingredients forming dazzling choices for diners.

8. Anhui Cuisine

The excellent geographical advantage of the Huangshan Mountains endows local people with a great deal of fresh flora and tasty fauna, composing the major ingredients of the dishes. Anhui cuisine chefs focus a lot of attention on preserving the original taste and nutrition of the materials, but they sometimes add ham or sugar candy to improve their dishes' taste.

(source:https://www.chinatravel.com)

New words and expressions

cuisine [kwɪˈzi:n] *n.* 菜肴，烹饪，烹调法
flavor [ˈfleɪvə] *n.* 味，香料 *vt.* 给……调味
vinegar [ˈvɪnɪgə] *n.* 醋
gourmet [ˈgʊəmeɪ] *n.* 美食家
location [ləʊˈkeɪʃn] *n.* 位置
freshness [ˈfreʃnəs] *n.* 新鲜度，(气味)清新
mildness [ˈmaɪldnəs] *n.* 淡，清淡
ingredient [ɪnˈgri:dɪənt] *n.* 配料，佐料，材料
steamed [sti:md] *adj.* 蒸熟的

style [staɪl] *n.* 风格，类型
geographical [ˌdʒi:ə'græfɪkl] *adj.* 地理的，地理学的
taste [teɪst] *n.* 滋味，风味 *vt.* 品尝
nutrition [njuˈtrɪʃn] *n.* 营养，营养学
ham [hæm] *n.* 火腿，(动物)后腿
raw material 原材料
have a great impact on 对……有很大的影响
land of fish and rice 鱼米之乡
common characteristics 共同特点
soy sauce 酱油

Notes

1. …is famous for its rich flavor: 以其浓郁的风味而闻名；be famous for sth.: 以……而闻名。Be famous for fine preparation, seasonableness, excellent colour, smell, taste and form. 以烹调精良，适应时令，色、香、味、形俱佳而著称。

2. "It is(was)+强调部分+who(that)…"强调句结构，如文中 It was the Chinese who invented the technique of making and using soy sauce, vinegar, wine…

(1) It was Tom and his friends who had a party in the club yesterday.

(2) It was because the book is so useful for my work that I bought it.

3. be widely recognized as: 被公认为

(1) The Cantonese are widely recognized as gourmets as their food catalogue is very extensive and varied.

(2) He strove to be recognized as a musician.

4. consist of: 由……组成。consist of , comprise, make up, constitute, be composed of, be comprised of, compose, 以上各词均表示由某些人或事物组成，或构成某事物。例句：Their diet consists largely of vegetables.

5. be characterized by: 其特点是……

(1) Huaiyang cuisine are characterized by the strictness in material selection.

(2) Mark Twain's works are characterized by humor and biting satire.

6. originated in: 起源于……

(1) The quarrel originated in a misunderstanding.

(2) Chinese culture originated in the Yellow River valley farming culture.

7. Soup with Tortoise: 甲鱼汤。中国家常菜谱的惯用表达方式：烹饪方式+主菜(+配菜/

配料)。例如：红烧鸡 braised chicken；栗子烧鸡 braised chicken with chestnuts；麻辣鸡丁 diced chicken with chili pepper.

8. quick-fry: 快炒。部分最常用烹饪术语：加调味佐料的 seasoned，炒 fry，炖 stew，焖 braise，加香料的 spiced，烤 bake，(roast, toast)，涮 instant-boil，烩 ass，盐腌的 salted，煨 simmer，熏 smoke，烧烤 barbecue.

9. focus a lot of attention on: 把注意力集中在…… With the final exam coming, they focus a lot of attention on the review of the textbook.

Exercises

1. Answer the following questions according to the passage.

(1) What have you learnt about Chinese cuisine from this passage?
_____

(2) What are the characteristics of Cantonese dishes?
_____

(3) What are the main condiments of Chinese cuisine?
_____

(4) What do you think are the four most famous dishes in China?
_____

(5) What are the ingredients selected in Shandong cuisine?
_____

(6) What special attention should be paid to in cooking Huaiyang dishes?
_____

(7) Why is the Sichuan cuisine famous in China?
_____

(8) What do you think Chinese cooking is famous for?
_____

2. Fill in the blanks with the appropriate form of the words or phrases given below in the box.

| originate | impact | taste | steamed | ingredient | nutrition |
| be recognized as | consist of | be characterized by | | common characteristics | |

(1) Tourism has a great _____ on in this city's economy.

(2) Where did the customs and traditions _____ ?

(3) What are their _____ and interest?

Unit 5 Food and Beverage Services

(4) The _____ buns are cold, and let's heat them up.

(5) Beijing Roast Duck _____ one of the most famous dishes in China.

(6) Sugar is a necessary _____ in any kind of cake.

(7) Assignments for this class _____ one individual assignment and one group discussion.

(8) He finished his aperitif and _____ the wine the waiter had produced .

(9) Vegetables are generally very low in calories, very high in fiber, and full of flavor and _____.

(10) The little girl _____ her long hair and big eyes.

3. Translate the following expressions into English or Chinese.

(1) Yin-Zhou period _____

(2) local snack _____

(3) China's eight great cuisines _____

(4) Sichuan Hotpot _____

(5) the raw materials _____

(6) boiled prawns _____

(7) squirrel with mandarin fish _____

(8) 主要成分 _____

(9) 水煮牛肉 _____

(10) 水晶肘子 _____

(11) 独特多样的口味 _____

(12) 野生食用草药 _____

(13) 广泛多样 _____

(14) 三套鸭 _____

(15) 酥脆质地的菜品 _____

4. Translate the following sentences into English with the words or phrases given in the brackets.

(1) 中国是一个有五千年历史的文明古国。(has a long history)

_____

(2) 地方餐饮风味独特。(local cuisine)

_____

(3) 因为兴趣不同，每个人出游所选旅游目的地也不同。(because of)

_____

(4) 这个谈判的重点是双方沟通合作良好。(the emphasis of)

_____

(5) 中国菜和西方菜的味道不同。(flavor)

_____

(6) 这道菜的优点是清爽可口。(the advantage of)

_____

Passage B　Western Cuisine

European cuisine, or alternatively western cuisine, is a general term collectively referring to the cuisines of Europe and other western countries, including that of Russia, as well as non-indigenous cuisines of the Americas, Oceania, and Southern Africa, which derive substantial influence from European settlers in those regions.

The cuisines of western countries are diverse. Compared with traditional cooking of Asian countries, for example, meat is more prominent and substantial in serving-size. Steak and cutlet in particular are common dishes across the West. Western cuisines also put substantial emphasis on grape wine and on sauces as condiments, seasonings, or accompaniments. Many dairy products are utilised in the cooking process, except in nouvelle cuisine. Cheeses are produced in hundreds of different varieties, and fermented milk products are also available in a wide selection. Wheat-flour bread has long been the most common source of starch in this cuisine, although the potato has become a major starch plant in the diet of Europeans and their diaspora since the European colonisation of the Americas, particularly in Northern Europe. Maize is much less common in most European diets than it is in the Americas, while corn meal is a major part of the cuisine of Italy and the Balkans. Although flatbread and rice are eaten in Europe, they do not constitute an ever-present staple. Salad is an integral part of European cuisine.

Formal European dinners are served in distinct courses. Usually, cold, hot and savory and sweet dishes are served strictly separately in this order, appetizer, soup, main course, and dessert. A service where the guests are free to take food by themselves is termed a buffet, and is usually restricted to parties or holidays.

French cuisine is one of the most famous cuisines in the world. Traditional French cooking is butter-based and centers on meat, poultry and fish. Today, however, the chefs of many Parisian restaurants are becoming more interested in regional food, home-style fare which relies on fresh, seasonal ingredients. French cooking tends not to be highly spiced, although fresh herbs like chives and parsley are essential ingredients in the sauces that accompany most savory dishes.

Unit 5 Food and Beverage Services

One of the most enjoyable aspects of Paris is diverse places to eat. Bistros are small, often moderately-priced restaurants with a limited selection of dishes. Brasseries are larger, bustling eateries with immense menus. Most serve food throughout the day and are open late. Cafes (and some wine bars) open early and usually close by 9:00 p.m. They serve drinks and food all day long from a short menu of salads, sandwiches and eggs. At lunch most offer a small choice of hot daily specials.

Restaurants in Paris

New words and expressions

alternatively [ɔ:l'tɜ:nətɪvli] adv. (引出第二种选择或可能的建议)要不，或者
non-indigenous [ɪn'dɪdʒənəs] adj. 非本土的
influence ['ɪnfluəns] n. 影响，有影响的人(或事物) vt. 影响，感染
traditional [trə'dɪʃənəl] adj. 传统的，惯例的
condiment ['kɒndɪmənt] n. 调味料，调味汁(或酱料等)
accompaniment [ə'kʌmpənimənt] n. 佐餐物
utilize ['ju:təlaɪz] v. 使用，利用
nouvelle [nu:'vel] n. 中篇小说
colonisation [ˌkɔlənai'zeiʃən] n. 殖民化
buffet ['bʊfeɪ] n. 自助餐
restricted [rɪ'strɪktɪd] adj. 受限制的，有限的，保密的
enjoyable [ɪn'dʒɔɪəbl] adj. 愉快的，快乐的
brasserie ['bræsəri] n. 餐馆
immense [ɪ'mens] adj. 巨大的，非常好的
compared with 与……比较

Notes

1. western cuisine: 东方人通常所说的西餐主要包括西欧国家的饮食菜肴，当然同时还包括东欧各国、地中海沿岸等国和一些拉丁美洲如墨西哥等国的菜肴。

2. Cheeses are produced in hundreds of different varieties, and fermented milk products are also available in a wide selection. 奶酪有数百种不同的品种，发酵乳制品也有多种选择。

3. grape wine: 葡萄酒。按酒的颜色可分为白葡萄酒、红葡萄酒、桃红葡萄酒；按含糖量可分为干葡萄酒、半干葡萄酒、半甜葡萄酒、甜葡萄酒。

4. in this order: 按此顺序。西餐上菜顺序一般为：头盘(也称开胃品)，汤，副菜，主菜，蔬菜类，甜品，咖啡或茶。

5. buffet: 自助餐，亦称顿饭，有时亦称冷餐会。它是目前国际上所通行的一种非正式的西式宴会，在大型的商务活动中尤为多见。

6. French cuisine is one of the most famous cuisines in the world. 法国菜是世界上最著名的菜肴之一。世界三大烹饪王国是中国、法国和土耳其。

7. While corn meal is a major part of the cuisine of Italy and the Balkans. 而玉米餐是意大利和巴尔干半岛菜肴的主要组成部分。a major part of: 主要组成部分。

8. Salad is an integral part of European cuisine. 沙拉是欧洲菜肴中不可或缺的一部分。沙拉主要有三类，分别为水果沙拉、蔬菜沙拉、其他沙拉。

Exercises

1. Reading Comprehension: Choose the best answer for the following questions.

(1) Which of the following is the main characteristic of French cuisine? ____
   A. Good use of spices.　　　　　　B. Noodles rich in varieties.
   C. Easy cooking, rich in characteristic.　　D. Nutrition.

(2) Which of the following is not made up of western cuisine? ____
   A. Appetizer.　　B. Liquor.　　C. Soup.　　D. Main course.

(3) Which of the following is not categorized as western cuisine ingredients? ____
   A. Meat.　　B. Aquatic.　　C. Wine.　　D. Egg and milk.

(4) What is the correct composition of western cuisine?
   A. Appetizer, soup, main course, dessert.　　B. Appetizer, soup, main course, dessert.
   C. Appetizer, main course, dessert.　　D. Appetizer, main course, dessert.

(5) Cold dishes are usually made from vegetables, fish, shrimp, chicken, ____, meat and other raw materials.
   A. crab　　B. duck　　C. fruit　　D. others

(6) The common cooking methods of western cuisine do not include ____.
   A. frying　　B. roasting　　C. grilling　　D. steaming

Unit 5　Food and Beverage Services

　　(7) The world's three major culinary kingdoms are China, ____ and Turkey.
　　　A. Britain　　　B. America　　　C. France　　　D. Japan
　　(8) ____ have become the main starch plant in the diet of Europeans and their immigrants.
　　　A. Tomatoes　　　B. Potatoes　　　C. Cucumbers　　　D. Cabbages

2. **Fill in the blanks with the appropriate form of the words or phrases given below in the box.**

| Enjoyable | non-indigenous | traditional | utilize |
| Immense | alternative | refer to | compared with |

　　(1) In Latin America, indigenous groups have far less schooling than _____ groups.
　　(2) _____, you can go to Beijing by high-speed train.
　　(3) The cook will _____ the leftover ham bone to make soup.
　　(4) It is always important to choose _____ and nutritious foods.
　　(5) Please _____ the right-hand column of page 200 of this tourism brochure.
　　(6) _____, the Chinese New Year's celebrations last for about two weeks.
　　(7) Overall tourism industrial production was up _____ last year.
　　(8) The _____ square was a sea of flowers.

3. **Translate the following expressions into English or Chinese.**

　　(1) 以及_____
　　(2) 非本土菜系_____
　　(3) 重大影响_____
　　(4) 传统烹饪_____
　　(5) 葡萄酒_____
　　(6) in a wide selection_____
　　(7) a major part of_____
　　(8) main course_____
　　(9) home-style fare_____
　　(10) moderately-priced restaurants_____

4. **Translate the following sentences into Chinese.**

　　(1) European cuisine, or alternatively western cuisine, is a general term collectively referring to the cuisines of Europe and other western countries.

_____

(2) The cuisines of western countries are diverse.

_____

(3) Maize is much less common in most European diets than it is in the Americas.

_____

(4) Formal European dinners are served in distinct courses.

_____

(5) French cuisine is one of the most famous cuisines in the world.

_____

5. Translate the following paragraph into English.

俗话说,"到北京,不到长城非好汉,不吃烤鸭(roast duck)真遗憾!"烤鸭是北京的地方风味,已有 1600 多年的历史。对于那些想更多地了解中国菜和中国文化习俗的人来说,北京烤鸭就是一个不错的选择。脆皮(crisp skin)和嫩肉是北京烤鸭的特点。北京最出名的老字号(centuries-old/time-honored brand)烤鸭店是"全聚德"。创建于 1864 年的全聚德备受各国元首、政府官员及国内外游客的喜爱。

6. Activity

Group work: Suppose you are the manager of one of the restaurants in Guangzhou, and you have to make dining arrangements for a tour from Australia. Please fill in the form below by listing the dishes that you arrange for the tour in a day, including breakfast, lunch and supper.

Breakfast	
Lunch	
Supper	

Unit 5 Food and Beverage Services

Writing: Menu 菜单

1. Writing Skills

菜单是宴会点餐时和供应菜肴的详细清单，它是餐厅餐食产品种类和价格的一览表，常见的菜单种类有零点菜单、套餐菜单、宴席菜单，或者按照餐别划分为早餐菜单、午餐菜单、晚餐菜单、夜宵菜单。

设计菜单要注意以下几点：(1)菜单的设计应明确餐厅的目标市场及消费定位，了解菜单设计是为谁设计，以及目标顾客的社会背景及生活习惯等；(2)现代餐饮菜单的设计，应注意每一个菜品的营养均衡，注意人体所需要的蛋白质、脂肪、碳水化合物、维生素和无机盐五大营养成分的平衡；(3)菜单要有吸引人的独特性，口味也应丰富多彩，富于变化。

2. Useful Expressions

a la carte	按菜单点菜
alcohol(liquor)	烈酒
entrée/main course	主菜
self-served	自助的
appetizer	开胃菜
take-out/take-away	外卖
cutlery	刀叉
specials	特价菜
dressing	酱料
dessert	甜点，甜品
side dish	配菜
seasoning	佐料，调味料
grill	烧烤
beverage	饮料
highchair	儿童专用餐椅
pickled	腌制的
deep fried	油炸的
coupon	优惠券

旅游英语

3. Sample Writing

Sample 1:

Smokey Joe's Bar & Grill Menu

SNACKS

Mozzarella Sticks	8.99	Fried Green Beans	8.99
Mozzarella deep fried and served with our marinara sauce		Green beans deep fried and served with wasabi sauce	
Calamari	11.99	Southwest Egg Rolls	7.99
Calamari and mild banana peppers lightly dusted in flour, fried and served with our marinara sauce		2 egg rolls served with house salsa	
Eggplant Fries	10.99		
Deep fried and sprinkled with parmesan cheese and our marinara sauce			

~~~ Flat Bread Pizza ~~~

Buffalo Chicken Pizza 11.99
4-cut flat bread pizza brushed with bleu cheese dressing, mozzarella and grilled chicken drizzled with hot sauce

Pulled Pork Pizza 11.99
4-cut flat bread pizza brushed with bbq sauce, mozzarella and topped with pulled pork

Cheese Pizza 9.99
4-cut flat bread pizza ladled with marinara sauce and topped with shredded mozzarella

Caprése Pizza 11.99
4-cut flat bread pizza topped with fresh tomatoes, olives, garlic, mozzarella, and drizzled with aged balsamic vinegar and extra virgin olive oil

~~~ Chicken Wings ~~~

Hot / Medium / Mild 12.99
Chicken wings served with bleu cheese and carrot sticks

Bourbon BBQ 12.99
Chicken wings served with house slaw

Garlic Parmesan 12.99
Chicken wings served with Caesar dressing

Barbeque 12.99
Chicken wings served with house slaw

GREENS

Smokey Joe's Salad 9.99
Fresh mixed greens, tomatoes, cucumbers, red onion, olives and banana peppers

Grilled Chicken Caesar Salad 12.99
Grilled juicy chicken with Romaine lettuce, parmesan cheese and croutons

Caesar Salad 9.99
Romaine lettuce, parmesan cheese and croutons

Grilled Chicken Salad 12.99
Grilled chicken with fresh mixed greens, tomatoes, cucumbers, red onion, olives and banana peppers

Buffalo Chicken Salad 12.99
Grilled spicy chicken with fresh mixed greens, tomatoes, cucumbers, red onion, olives and banana peppers

House Salad 6.99
Fresh mixed greens, tomatoes, cucumbers and red onion

Dressings: Italian, Balsamic Vinaigrette, Bleu Cheese, Ranch

SANDWICHES

~ ~ Sandwiches served on a toasted roll with chips ~ ~
(substitute french fries, sweet potato fries for 2.00)

Pulled Pork 9.99
Our famous slow roasted pork, shredded and glazed with our bbq sauce

Carolina Pulled Pork 11.99
Our famous slow roasted pork, shredded and glazed with our bbq sauce topped with house slaw

Grilled Chicken Breast 9.99
Grilled seasoned chicken breast with lettuce, tomato, mayonnaise (barbecue on request)

Philly Steak & Cheese Sandwich 12.99
Shaved steak, melted cheese, peppers and onions served on toasted garlic bread

Sausage, Peppers and Onions 10.99
Tender sausage sautéed with fresh peppers and onions served on a toasted roll

Buffalo Chicken 10.99
Grilled chicken breast with lettuce, bleu cheese dressing and hot sauce

Hot Italian Meatball Sandwich 11.99
Italian meatball sandwich served on a toasted garlic sub roll

Brant's Fish Sandwich 9.99
Batter dipped, deep fried golden brown and topped with lettuce

Sample 2：美国中餐馆的菜单

Appetizers

1. 韭菜猪肉锅贴　　　　Fried Pork with Chives Dumping

Unit 5 Food and Beverage Services

2. 素菜水饺　　　　　Vegetable Steamed Dumpling
3. 芝麻大饼　　　　　Sesame Pancake
4. 葱油饼　　　　　　Scallion Pancakes
5. 牛肉夹饼　　　　　Beef Pancake
6. 红豆莲子粥　　　　Rice & Bean Congee

Soups
1. 酸辣汤　　　　　　Hot & Sour Soup
2. 云吞汤　　　　　　Pork Wonton Soup
3. 扁肉　　　　　　　Wonton Soup in Fuzhou Style
4. 蛋花汤　　　　　　Egg Drop Soup
5. 鸡饭汤　　　　　　Chicken Rice Soup
6. 素菜豆腐汤　　　　Tofu and Vegetable Soup
7. 鱼丸汤　　　　　　Fish Ball in Soup
8. 元宵　　　　　　　Pork Sticky Rice in Soup
9. 汤圆　　　　　　　Sweet Peanuts in Sticky Rice in Soup
10. 榨菜肉丝汤　　　　Sliced Pork with Preserved Cabbage in Soup

Noodles
1. 羊肉面　　　　　　Rice Noodle in Lamb Soup
2. 牛腩面　　　　　　Stew Beef With Noodle Soup
3. 拌面　　　　　　　Flat Noodle with Peanut Sauce
4. 煮切面　　　　　　Wild Yellow Noodle in Soup
5. 煮米线　　　　　　Steamed Rice Noodle
6. 雪菜肉丝面　　　　Shredded Pork with Salted Cabbage Noodle
7. 牛腩炒面　　　　　Tenderloin with Stir-Fried Noodle
8. 炒米粉　　　　　　Pan Fried Thin Rice Noodle
9. 虾汤面　　　　　　Shrimp with Noodle Soup

Rice
1. 青椒牛肉饭　　　　Pepper Steak with Onion on Rice
2. 酸菜牛肉饭　　　　Beef with Pickled Cabbage on Rice
3. 牛腩饭　　　　　　Tenderloin on Rice
4. 牛肉炒饭　　　　　Beef Fried Rice
5. 芝麻鸡饭　　　　　Sesame Chicken on Rice
6. 芥兰鸡饭　　　　　Chicken with Broccoli on Rice
7. 鱼香饭　　　　　　Chicken with Garlic Sauce on Rice

8. 京都排骨饭	Pork Chop with Salt & Pepper on Rice
9. 叉烧肉炒饭	Roast Pork Fried Rice
10. 虾炒饭	Shrimp Fried Rice
11. 扬州炒饭	House Special Fried Rice
12. 什菜饭	Mixed Vegetable on Rice

4. Writing Practice

You are going to open a Chinese restaurant and a western restaurant in the center of Beijing. Work in groups and design a Chinese food menu or a western food menu, and try to build a vocabulary list for Chinese dishes in English.

Supplementary Reading

Chinese Table Manners

As a country that pays great attention to courtesy, the food culture is deep rooted in China's history. As a visitor or guest in either a Chinese home or restaurant, you will find that table manners are essential, the distinctive courtesies displayed will invariably add to the enjoyment of your meals, and keep you in high spirits! A multitude of etiquette considerations occur also when dining in China. There are some special differences from manners in western countries.

A round dining table is more popular than a rectangular or square one, as many people can be seated comfortably around it and conveniently face one another. The guest of honor is always seated to the right of the host; the next in line will sit on his left. Guests should be seated after the host's invitation, and it is discourteous to seat guests at the place where the dishes are served.

Chinese people stress filial piety all the time. The practice of presenting the best food first to the senior members of the family has been observed for countless generations. In ancient times the common people led a needy life, but they still tried their best to support the elder mother or father who took it for granted.

Although the hosts in China are all friendly and hospitable, you should also show them respect. Before starting to eat dinner, the host may offer some words of greeting. Guests should not start to eat until the host says "Please enjoy yourself" or something like that, otherwise it suggests disrespect and causes displeasure. When hosts place dishes on the table, they will arrange the main courses at the center with the supporting dishes evenly placed around them. When the main dishes are prepared in a decorative form either by cut or other means, they will be placed facing the major guests and elder people at the table. This also embodies virtue.

Apart from soup, all dishes should be eaten with chopsticks. The Chinese are particular about the use of chopsticks. There are many taboos such as twiddling with chopsticks, licking chopsticks, or using them to stir up the food, gesture with them or point them at others. Never stick chopsticks in the center of rice, as this is the way to sacrifice and is therefore considered to be inauspicious.

(source:https://www.travelchinaguide.com/intro/cuisine.htm)

Useful words and phrases

etiquette [ˈetɪket] *n.* 礼仪，礼节
discourteous [dɪsˈkɜːtiəs] *adj.* 粗鲁的
hospitable [hɒˈspɪtəbl] *adj.* 好客的，热情友好的
chopsticks [ˈtʃɒpstɪks] *n.* 筷子
taboo [təˈbuː] *n.* 禁忌，忌讳
twiddle [ˈtwɪdl] *vt.& vi.* (心不在焉地)捻弄
lick [lɪk] *v.* 舔
inauspicious [ˌɪnɔːˈspɪʃəs] *adj.* 不祥的，不吉的
a multitude of 大量的
the guest of honor 贵宾
stir up 挑起，挑动，搅动

Read the passage and decide whether the following statements are true (T) or false(F).

1. _____ A square dining table is more popular than a rectangular or round one.
2. _____ In ancient times the common people led a rich life.
3. _____ All dishes should be eaten with chopsticks.
4. _____ Before starting to eat dinner, the host may offer some words of greeting.
5. _____ You can use your own chopsticks to bring dishes to others.

Module Three

Tourist Attractions

Unit 6　Tourism Product

Learning Objectives

After learning this unit, you should:
- Understand how to give travel information in terms of tourist attractions.
- Master the key words and expressions for travel information.
- Get some cultural knowledge about types of tourism and travel information.
- Be familiar with the six elements in tourism industry.
- Find ways to improve your writing skills about advertisement and brochures.

Key words

types of tourism, personalized tour, tourism product

Information search

Please search some information about the topic of this unit by scanning the QR codes: (Travel Column of *China Daily*), (China Plus), (World Tourism Organization), (Travelogue of CCTV), (Ministry of Culture and Tourism of the People's Republic of China). After reading the information, please share with your classmates some information about the topic of this unit.

Warm-up

Task: Suppose you are going to have a trip with your friends to the USA. Discuss the following questions with your partners.

(1) How would you plan your trip? What are the factors that you should take into consideration? (time, budget, accommodation, transportation, destination, etc.)

(2) Will you use some travel apps while planning the trip? What are they?

Examples of Travel Apps

Passage A   Types of Tourism

Tourism is one of the most flourishing industries in the world, making a significant contribution to the world's GDP. Every year, millions of people from across the globe travel miles and miles away from their homes, in order to see the distant lands and experience their culture. No matter what your aim is, traveling to distant places always tends to fascinate. Tourism, as a concept, has come a long way today, and the activity has been classified into various types (and still counting). With the development of new tourist infrastructure, and owing to the extreme competition in the sector, several new ideas of promoting tourism are coming up. The tourism sector today aims to cater to the needs and preferences of all types of tourists, and thus, seems to take into consideration specific areas of their interest. Therefore, today we have a plethora of tourism types and innumerable options to choose from. The different categories of tourism are as follows.

Pyramid in Egypt

Tian'anmen Square in China

Cultural Tourism

Also known as culture tourism, it can be further divided into three categories — cultural and traditional tourism, historical tourism and rural tourism. This kind of tourism involves the culture of a particular country or region. The concept of cultural tourism includes things, such as history of a given region, the lifestyle of local people, architectures, religions, festivals and so on. Activities of cultural tourism in the urban areas may involve visiting museums, theaters, art galleries, etc.; those in the rural areas may involve visiting indigenous cultural communities and having an insight into their traditions, lifestyle, and values.

Natural Tourism

Also known as nature tourism, this kind of tourism is based on the natural attractions of an area. There are several subtypes as well, among which ecotourism is the most popular one in recent decades. Ecotourism is a form of tourism involving visiting fragile, pristine, and relatively undisturbed natural areas. It means responsible travel to natural areas, conserving the environment, and improving the well-being of the local people. Natural tourism also encompasses the concepts of geo-tourism, wildlife tourism and agritourism.

Business Tourism

Business tourism is leisure activities in conjunction with business travel, because business travelers typically have some free time when they are away from home. Common activities involved in business tourism include attending meetings, conferences, and seminars, visiting exhibitions and trade fairs, etc. Business tourists are less cost-sensitive than leisure tourists, spending on average twice as much per day. Their purchase decisions are influenced primarily by their ability to use time efficiently within business travel schedules.

Leisure Tourism

Leisure travel is travel in which the primary motivation is to take a vacation from everyday life. Leisure travel is often characterized by staying in nice hotels or resorts, relaxing on beaches or in a room. The early form of leisure tourism is considered to be beach tourism, in which many tourists spend their holidays on beaches. They relax, go bathing or just enjoy the salty sea breeze and the ocean. Spending holidays on beaches has had a long tradition in western countries for over one and a half centuries.

Paragliding

Rock climbing

Special Interest Tourism

Special interest tourism is the provision of customized tourism activities that caters to the specific interests of groups and individuals. Special interest tourism can be categorized based on the type of interest that motivates people to travel, for example, adventure tourism, in which tourists look for thrilling activities and extreme sports, including mountaineering, rafting, trekking, bungee jumping, scuba diving, paragliding, rock climbing; sports tourism, in which tourists can either travel to another place in order to participate in a sport, or just to watch it being played;

wellness tourism, which refers to traveling for the purpose of maintaining and enhancing one's body, mind, and soul with the use of massages, body treatments or meditation.

New words and expressions

flourishing [ˈflʌrɪʃɪŋ] *adj.* 繁荣的，盛行的
fascinate [ˈfæsɪneɪt] *vt.* 使着迷，深深吸引
innumerable [ɪˈnjuːm(ə)rəb(ə)l] *adj.* 无数的
rural [ˈrʊər(ə)l] *adj.* 乡村的，田园的
architecture [ˈɑːkɪtektʃə] *n.* 建筑艺术
religion [rɪˈlɪdʒ(ə)n] *n.* 宗教
urban [ˈɜːb(ə)n] *adj.* 城市的
indigenous [ɪnˈdɪdʒɪnəs] *adj.* 本土的，土著的
subtype [ˈsʌbtaɪp] *n.* 子类型
fragile [ˈfrædʒaɪl] *adj.* 脆弱的，易损坏的
pristine [ˈprɪstiːn] *adj.* 洁净的，未开发的
conserve [kənˈsɜːv] *vt.* 保护，保存
well-being [ˈwel biːɪŋ] *n.* 幸福，繁荣
encompass [ɪnˈkʌmpəs] *vt.* 包含
seminar [ˈsemɪnɑː] *n.* 研讨会
cost-sensitive [kɒst ˈsensətɪv] *adj.* 对价格敏感的
primarily [ˈpraɪm(ə)rɪlɪ] *adv.* 首先，主要地
motivation [məʊtɪˈveɪʃ(ə)n] *n.* 动机
resort [rɪˈzɔːt] *n.* 度假胜地
customized [ˈkʌstəˌmaɪzd] *adj.* 定制的
thrilling [ˈθrɪlɪŋ] *adj.* 刺激的，令人兴奋的
enhance [ɪnˈhɑːns] *vt.* 提高，改进，增强
massage [məˈsɑːʒ] *n.* 按摩，推拿
meditation [medɪˈteɪʃ(ə)n] *n.* 冥想，沉思
cater to 迎合，为……服务
a plethora of 大量的，过多的
art galleries 美术馆
have an insight into 对……有深刻认识，洞察
in conjunction with 连同
trade fair 商品交易会，展销会

purchase decision 购买决策
go bathing (到大海里进行)海水浴
body treatment 身体护理

Notes

1. GDP: 全称为 Gross Domestic Product, 指国内生产总值。

2. With the development of new tourist infrastructure, and owing to the extreme competition in the sector, several new ideas of promoting tourism are coming up. 随着旅游业基础设施建设的不断发展，以及旅游业竞争的日趋激烈，促进旅游业发展的新思路不断涌现。owe to sth. 表示原因，相当于 because of，意为"由于；归功于"。

3. …those in the rural areas may involve visiting indigenous cultural communities and having an insight into their traditions, lifestyle, and values. 在乡村地区，可以参观当地文化社群，深入了解他们的传统习俗、生活方式和价值观。

4. ecotourism: 生态旅游, 这一术语最早由世界自然保护联盟(IUCN)于 1983 年首先提出。1993 年国际生态旅游协会把其定义为："具有保护自然环境和维护当地人民生活双重责任的旅游活动。"生态旅游的内涵更强调的是对自然景观的保护，是可持续发展的旅游(sustainable tourism)。

5. cost-sensitive: 对价格敏感的。在经济学理论中，价格敏感度(price-sensitive)表示顾客需求弹性函数，即由于价格变动引起的产品需求量的变化。通常情况下，若消费者对价格敏感度高，则当某产品价格高时该消费者的需求就降低(即不购买或少购买)；价格低时需求就增加(即购买或多买)。价格敏感度低的消费者，其需求则不会因为产品价格的高低而发生大的变化。

6. leisure tourism: 休闲旅游，是为了获得健康愉悦的体验的旅游活动，休闲旅游的关键就是要轻松。与传统的观光旅游相比，休闲旅游更注重身心的调整修养，不注重景点观光游览。

7. wellness tourism: 健康旅游，也称为"康体旅游""保健旅游"，是指一切能够增进旅游者身心健康的旅游活动，包括健身、美容、营养、食疗、放松、陶冶性情及精神放松和调解等。

Exercises

1. Answer the following questions according to the passage.

(1) What kinds of tourism are there according to the passage?

(2) Which type of tourism do you like best? Why?
_____

(3) What does cultural tourism mean? Can you name some cultural destinations?
_____

(4) What is ecotourism? What are the benefits of ecotourism?
_____

(5) What does SIT mean according to the passage? How is SIT categorized?
_____

(6) Do you know some leisure destinations in the world? Name one or two and give a brief introduction.
_____

2. Fill in the blanks with the appropriate form of the words given below in the box.

| conduct   expand   permit   primary   attract   purchase   religion   motivate   flourish   tour |

(1) I was the first Western TV reporter _____ to film a special unit caring for Pandas rescued from starvation in the world.

(2) A study of travelers _____ by the website Tripadvisor names Hangzhou as one of the top 10 destinations in the world.

(3) Sichuan is a fascinating place. But for tourists like me, pandas are its top _____.

(4) Cambridge is always full of _____ in the summer.

(5) The advertisement is aimed _____ at children.

(6) We may never know what _____ him to kill his wife.

(7) This product should be consumed on the day of _____.

(8) Business _____ and within six months they were earning 18,000 dollars a day.

(9) The ski resorts are _____ to meet the growing number of skiers that come here.

(10) This is a part of our belief and our _____.

3. Translate the following expressions into English or Chinese.

(1) the most flourishing industry _____

(2) tourist infrastructure _____

(3) in recent decades _____

(4) the provision of customized tourism activities _____

(5) the specific interests of individuals _____

(6) enhance one's body _____

(7) take a vacation from everyday life _____

(8) making a significant contribution to _____

(9) 参加体育赛事 _____

(10) 改善当地民生 _____

(11) 负责任的旅游者 _____

(12) 极限运动 _____

(13) 探险旅游 _____

(14) 对这个问题有深刻见解 _____

(15) 脆弱的生态环境 _____

(16) 古代建筑 _____

4. Translate the following sentences into English with the words or phrases given in the brackets.

(1) 这些措施可以提高我们的生活质量。(enhance)
_____

(2) 离开教室前请务必关掉所有电灯以节约能源。(conserve)
_____

(3) 为了迎合不断增多的中国游客，巴黎的奢侈品商店现在雇佣了很多会讲普通话的营业员。(cater to)
_____

(4) 这是一本有趣的书，充满了对人际关系的迷人见解。(insight)
_____

(5) 这片丛林还处于原始状态，看起来好像从来没有人到过那里。(pristine)
_____

(6) 这幅地图显示了其余的西部区域，覆盖了 9 个州。(encompass)
_____

Passage B Customized Tour

In a fast and constantly changing world, the Internet—one of the main contributors to this change—brought us infinite possibilities. The information is everywhere, and consumers are more educated than ever. Consequently, consumers are now more and more demanding. They can simply search for the same offer in dozens, or even hundreds, of retail and reservations websites with simple mouse clicks in a matter of minutes. The time when they had to accept whatever the market had to offer them is over. This market change has been imposing itself over the past couple of years and it has affected almost every industry. Naturally, tourism isn't an exception.

Customized tours are those with a personalized itinerary. It is a tourism mode that originated in developed countries first with the target customers being middle-aged and elderly tourists with a reasonably high disposable income. In China, on the contrary, the target customers are young people, and the growth rate is very fast.

Procedures for customizing your trip

According to the first *"Customized Travels of Chinese Visitors in Europe"* report, jointly released by China's online tour provider Ctrip.com and the China Outbound Tourism Research Institute, the number of customized tours by Chinese tourists grew by 130 percent year-on-year in 2017, which indicates there is a big demand for customized tours in China.

A screenshot of Ctrip.com

According to the report, Shanghai, Beijing and Guangzhou were the top three departure cities for customized tours, which make up 50 percent of the overall customized tours. Second-tier cities such as Harbin, Wuhan, Fuzhou and Nanjing are fast-growing source cities for such tours. The top three European destinations for Chinese tourists' customized tours in 2017 were the United Kingdom, Italy and France, the report says.

This trend forces tourism companies to quickly adapt if they want to take advantage of this opportunity. It implies creating new systems, new synergies between partners, and preparing the staff to help customers, in the most effective way, in the choosing process of all the options available.

Below is an excerpt from the website of Rainbow Trade Fair Tours, an Indian travel agency.

Benefits of opting for a customized package

Do you worry about spending so much money on booking your airline tickets? Rainbow assures to take up your traveling charges. You don't have to spend money during your travel to the destination, nor while coming back. The travelers have the advantages of visiting the places they want to explore and enjoy the life's best travel experience.

When people decide to visit a place, accommodation within their budget is the most important thing that they keep in the mind. They are given full information about the best hotels where they can stay. They do not have to panic about searching for an accommodation. The hotels or lodges where they wish to stay give them comfortable place where they can stay till their holiday ends.

The travelers are given theme related packages based on the choice such as honeymoon package, adventure package, or even wildlife package. Arrangements will be made from picking the travelers from their accommodation to dropping them after a day trip. Their safety is also ensured so that their whole day trip passes off smoothly and efficiently. The travelers will be guaranteed best food services during their stay to satisfy their taste buds as well. They will get to taste the authentic food items of the destination.

New words and expressions

constantly ['kɒnst(ə)ntlɪ] *adv.* 不断地，时常地
infinite ['ɪnfɪnət] *adj.* 无限的，(数量或程度上)极大的
consumer [kən'sjuːmə] *n.* 消费者，用户，顾客
consequently ['kɒnsɪkw(ə)ntlɪ] *adv.* 因此，结果，所以
demanding [dɪ'mɑːndɪŋ] *adj.* 要求高的
itinerary [aɪ'tɪnərərɪ] *n.* 旅行计划，预定行程
originate [ə'rɪdʒɪneɪt] *vi.* 开始，起源
indicate ['ɪndɪkeɪt] *vt.* 表明，显示

adapt [ə'dæpt] *vt.&vi.* (使)适应
imply [ɪm'plaɪ] *vt.* 意味，暗示
synergy ['sɪnədʒɪ] *n.* 协同，协同作用
option ['ɒpʃ(ə)n] *n.* 选择，可选择的东西
available [ə'veɪləb(ə)l] *adj.* 可用的，可获得的
benefit ['benɪfɪt] *n.* 利益，好处 *vt.* 有益于
budget ['bʌdʒɪt] *n.* 预算
guarantee [gær(ə)n'tiː] *n.&vt.* 保证，担保
authentic [ɔː'θentɪk] *adj.* 真正的，真实的
in a matter of minutes 在几分钟内
on the contrary 相反
growth rate 增长率
second-tier cities 二线城市
take advantage of 利用
taste buds 味蕾

Notes

1. disposable income: 指可支配收入，即居民工资收入中扣除掉基本养老保险、基本医疗保险、失业保险、公积金、个人所得税等剩下的那部分。

2. Ctrip.com: 携程旅行网，简称携程或携程网，是一家总部设立在上海的中国大型旅游网站，1999年创办。

3. This market change has been imposing itself over the past couple of years and it has affected almost every industry. 过去几年里，这种市场变化一直在强制发生，几乎影响到了每一个行业。impose sth. on sth./sb. 意为"强制实行，把……强加于"。

4. developed countries: 发达国家。(A developed country, industrialized country, or "more economically developed country" (MEDC), is a country that has a highly developed economy and advanced technology relative to other less industrialized nations.)发达国家、工业化国家或者经济更加发达的国家，指的是与工业化低的国家相比，经济更加发达、技术更加先进的国家。

5. departure cities: 出发城市，此处指旅游者进行旅游活动时的出发地，通常也可理解为客源地。

6. The travelers have the advantages of visiting the places they want to explore and enjoy the life's best travel experience. 旅游者可以尽情游览他们想要探索的地方，享受生命中最棒的旅行体验。

Unit 6 Tourism Product

Exercises

1. Choose the best answer for the following questions.

(1) Which of the following statements is not the reason why consumers are now more and more demanding? _____

A. The Internet has brought us infinite possibilities.

B. The information is easily accessible.

C. Consumers are more educated than ever.

D. People are much pickier than before.

(2) "This market change has been <u>imposing</u> itself over the past couple of years…". Which of the following statements has the similar meaning to the underlined word "imposing"? _____

A. Impacting on   B. Carrying out   C. Forcing people to accept   D. Happening

(3) Which of the following statements is true according to the passage? _____

A. Customized tours originated in developing countries first.

B. In China, the target customers of personalized tours are young people.

C. In western countries, customized tours are especially tailored for old, rich people.

D. Customized tours are not popular among young people because it's too expensive.

(4) According to the report, what were the top three departure cities for customized tours in 2017? _____

A. Shanghai, Beijing and Hangzhou.   B. Shanghai, Beijing and Shenzhen.

C. Shanghai, Beijing and Guangzhou.   D. Beijing, Harbin and Wuhan.

(5) The top three European destinations for Chinese tourists' customized tours in 2017 were _____, Italy and France.

A. the United States   B. the United Nation

C. German   D. the United Kingdom

(6) This trend forces tourism companies to quickly adapt if they want to _____ of this opportunity.

A. utilize   B. take advantage

C. take chance   D. seize

(7) "Rainbow assures to take up your traveling charges." What does this sentence mean? _____

A. Rainbow will pay everything for you.

B. You have to pay extra charges for the service provided by Rainbow.

C. Rainbow will give you a low price for the traveling charges.

D. Rainbow provides an all-inclusive service in the customized tour.

(8) Which of the following statements is not the benefit of opting for a customized package? _____

    A. Food services cannot be guaranteed since each person has a unique flavor preference.

    B. Tourists don't have to spend extra money during their travel to the destination.

    C. Tourists do not have to worry about searching for an accommodation.

    D. Tourists can determine the theme of the tour according to their personal interests.

2. Fill in the blanks with the appropriate form of the words given below in the box.

constantly consequently demand available option benefit itinerary indicate

(1) Do you have any double rooms _____ this weekend?

(2) Instead of a soft drink, she _____ for water.

(3) One of the obvious facts about life is that it is _____ changing.

(4) I feel that I have _____ greatly from her wisdom.

(5) We planned our _____ several weeks before the trip.

(6) Everything you do in life, every choice you make, has a(an) _____.

(7) Our survey _____ that one in four children is bullied at school.

(8) My present job doesn't stretch me, so I'm looking for something more _____.

3. Translate the following expressions into English or Chinese.

(1) procedures for customizing a trip _____

(2) a fast and constantly changing world _____

(3) retail and reservations websites _____

(4) a big demand for customized tours _____

(5) make up 50 percent of the overall market _____

(6) 个性化的行程 _____

(7) 目标市场/客户 _____

(8) 快速增长的人口 _____

(9) 在预算之内的住宿 _____

(10) 正宗的当地小吃 _____

4. Translate the following sentences into Chinese.

(1) The highlight of our tour of Beijing was visiting the Forbidden City.

_____

(2) I love my friends; they praise me and give me infinite strength and inspiration.

_____

(3) The number of customized tours by Chinese tourists grew by 130 percent year-on-year in 2017, which indicates there is a big demand for customized tours in China.

_____

(4) This trend forces tourism companies to quickly adapt if they want to take advantage of this opportunity.

_____

(5) The time when consumers had to accept whatever the market had to offer them is over.

_____

5. Translate the following paragraph into English.

胡同(Hutong)是北京的一大特色，有着与北京城一样久远的历史。最早的胡同出现在元朝(the Yuan Dynasty)，如今大部分胡同是在明清时代(the Ming and Qing Dynasties)形成的。据专家考证，"胡同"一词源于蒙古语(Mongolian)的"井"。自古以来胡同都是北京城里普通市民生息的场所，可以说是北京平民文化的代表。但随着人口的增加，很多古老的胡同已经消失，取而代之的是现代化的却没有特色的高楼大厦。

6. Activity

Group work: If you are going to design a customized tour for yourself and your friends, how do you design your tour (e.g. your itinerary and how to get the traveling information you need)? Discuss with your group mates, and each group makes a presentation for about 8 minutes.

Writing: Tourism Advertisement and Brochure 旅游广告与宣传册

1. Writing Skills

广告的目的就是告知大众相应的产品信息，通过丰富语言的组织和精美图片的编辑等手段吸引目标客户群体达到能够消费的目的。旅游行业常见的是酒店广告、旅游线路广告等。广告经常使用简单明了、醒目的广告标语，使其更有吸引力。为了节省版面，广告也常常使用缩略语；为了使广告更加形象生动，以吸引目标客户群体，广告多使用比喻、排比等手段，从而使读者对产品和服务有更多的感性认识。在广告中经常使用第一和第二人称，给读者亲切的感觉，仿佛是热情的友人在发出诚恳的邀请。

就酒店广告而言，酒店广告主要包含以下内容：酒店名称、地点、交通情况、酒店类型和档次、服务特色、联系方式，最后通常配有朗朗上口的酒店广告语。好的酒店广告要根据消费者定位，写出最吸引目标人群的亮点，突出酒店与其他酒店不同之处。

旅游广告的内容则包括行程特色、价格、包含的服务项目，如航班、酒店、餐饮、主要景点、旅行社联络方式、网址、地址等。

2. Useful Expressions and Sentences

(1) It lies in...with beautiful views of/featuring beautiful views of…

(2) It is famous/prestigious for…

(3) The hotel is situated/located in/near/located on the north/east/west/south side of…

(4) set in…

(5) close to/surrounded by/overlooking/facing…

(6) It offers highest levels of comfort, convenience and personalized services including…

(7) It is ideal for meetings, seminars and social events.

(8) It enjoys a sunny climate throughout the year and have hence been named the XXX.

3. Sample Writing

Sample 1: Hotel Advertisement

Marco Polo Shenzhen

Fuhua 1st Road, Futian CBD, Shenzhen 518048, China

Tel: (86 755) 8298-9888   Fax: (86 755) 3322-7777

http://shenzhen.marcopolohotels.com/

Marco Polo Shenzhen is an international 5-star business hotel in Shenzhen, strategically located in the heart of Futian District—the city's new CBD. The hotel is close to the Shenzhen City Hall, Shenzhen International Convention & Exhibition Center and Metro Subway Station. Marco Polo Shenzhen is a 20-minutes' drive from Lowu Railway Station, 25 minutes from Shekou Ferry Terminal & Shenzhen Baoan International Airport, and 5 minutes to Huanggang border.

Marco Polo Shenzhen's 391 rooms and suites overlook the bustling city and offer elegant and comfortable interiors. The hotel's Continental Club offers business travelers the highest levels of comfort, convenience and personalized services including priority check-in, complimentary breakfast, all-day coffee & tea, and evening cocktails in the exclusive Continental Club Lounge.

The range of dining options in this Shenzhen hotel is superb and features Asian & International specialties in Café Marco, gourmet Japanese cuisine in Nishimura, and Chiu Chow cuisine in the popular Carrianna Restaurant. The hotel has a delightful Lobby Lounge, a Cigar and Wine club—Wall Street Club, a Cigar and Wine Club and California juice bar, a snack and juice bar overlooking the outdoor pool.

The hotel's "lifestyle floor" on the 4th level features a state-of-the-art Gym, an outdoor swimming pool and the internationally-renowned Mandara Spa. The Marco Polo Ballroom & 30 function rooms (includes an Auditorium), can accommodate up to 3000 guests, providing the ideal venue in Shenzhen for meetings, seminars and social events.

Sample 2: Travel Advertisement

Visit Japan!

Spring is the best time to visit Japan. Starting in March, the country is bedecked with cherry blossoms as tourists from far and wide flock to the various viewing spots to be harmony with nature. It is also the time in Japan for festivals, when some of the most colorful and traditional festivals associated with the season's flowers are celebrated. Japan is a land of varied charm. It has something for everyone. Particularly enchanting are the off-the-beaten-track places that are well worth visiting, an added bonus being that they are less frequented by tourists. By far the most popular among them in the vicinity of Tokyo is the Fuji National Park area. In this area are camping sites, lakes for boating, skating resorts, riding,
hiking, hunting, fishing and water-skiing facilities, as well as a cluster of hot water springs for health-conscious tourists.

4. Writing Practice

Work in groups and design an advertisement for the travel route based on the following information:

Golden route in China during Spring Festival, including Beijing, Shanghai, Xi'an and Guilin for about 15 days.

Travel agency: Pacific Delight Tours, Inc. 132 Madison Ave. New York NY 10016

Telephone: 212-684-221-7179

Supplementary Reading

Data Reveals Spring Festival Holiday Travel Trends

A big data report jointly released by Ctrip, a Shanghai-based online travel agency, and Skyscanner, a leading global travel search site, reveals three features and trends of the recently-concluded Spring Festival holiday: Beijing tops the hotlist of places of departure; Beijing, Shanghai and Guangzhou are still the most popular destinations for inbound travelers, and the Spring Festival travel rush shows a hint of reversed direction.

Outbound travel market still booming

Due to the growing middle-class, the outbound tourism market is still vibrant. Traveling abroad has become a top option for Chinese people in developed cities like Beijing, Shanghai, Guangzhou, Shenzhen and Chengdu, with Beijing ranking at the top spot as the place of departure. It suggests that Chinese people in affluent areas have broken from tradition to some extent and are prone to new ways of celebrating Spring Festival. Instead of the traditional going back home for family reunion, they choose to take their family on a vacation abroad.

In terms of destinations, places near the Chinese mainland are the most popular. Thailand remains the most popular overseas destination on the list during this period, followed by Japan. What highlights this year's niche travel market is the Philippines; its city, Cebu, enjoyed a 145% increase in the number of tourist arrivals, which ranks at first place on the dark horse destination list.

Big cities make hot destinations for inbound travelers

As more and more Chinese tourists opt for a foreign vacation during the holiday, another noteworthy trend is that a considerable number of foreign expats come to China to experience the Chinese Lunar New Year. Beijing, Shanghai and Guangzhou are still the top three destinations for foreign visitors, as big cities can offer a vibrant urban life experience and convenient transportation. But second-tier cities like Chengdu, Xiamen, Chongqing, Wuhan, Fuzhou, Changsha and Kunming also make the list due to their folk culture, unique cuisine and pleasant climate.

Reversed Spring Festival travel rush

For Chinese people, the most important Spring Festival tradition is going back to their hometown for family reunion. So usually the Spring Festival travel rush unleashes China's largest seasonal migration of people. But according to data, this year's travel rush shows a reversed direction, that is, a growing percentage of people chose to pick up the elderly and other family members to join them in cities to celebrate Spring Festival. Five popular destinations for this reversed travel route are Shanghai, Beijing, Guangzhou, Shenzhen and Hangzhou. The rationale behind this trend is that people can avoid the transportation peak by choosing a reversed direction.

(source:http://www.chinadaily.com.cn/a/201902/19/WS5c6bcccea3106c65c34ea292_2.html)

Unit 6 Tourism Product

Useful words and phrases

reveal [rɪ'vi:l] *vt.* 显示，揭露
vibrant ['vaɪbrənt] *adj.* 充满活力的
migration [maɪ'greɪʃ(ə)n] *n.* 迁移，移民
reversed [rɪ'vɜ:st] *adj.* 颠倒的，相反的
recently-concluded 不久前结束的
inbound travelers 入境旅游者
outbound travel market 出境旅游市场
middle-class 中产阶级
ranking at the top spot 排名第一
be prone to 有……的倾向
Chinese mainland 中国大陆
niche travel market 利基旅游市场
tourist arrivals 到达(某地)的游客人数

Read the passage and decide whether the following statements are true (T) or false(F).

1. _____ Beijing, Shanghai and Guangzhou are the most popular destinations for domestic travelers.

2. _____ It has become more and more popular for Chinese people in affluent areas to take their family on a vacation abroad during the Spring Festival vacation.

3. _____ Japan is second to Thailand as an outbound tourist destination for Chinese people.

4. _____ Cities like Chengdu, Xiamen, Chongqing are most popular destinations for foreign tourists since they can offer a vibrant urban life experience and convenient transportation.

5. _____ According to data, this year's travel rush shows a reversed direction because people think it's too troublesome to go back to their hometown for family reunion.

Unit 7 Tourist Attractions

Learning Objectives

After learning this unit, you should:
- Be able to give a full presentation about World Cultural and Natural Heritage.
- Acquire the knowledge and information of World Cultural and Natural Heritage.
- Grasp professional English words and expressions for tourist attractions.
- Find ways to improve your writing skills about tour commentary.

Keywords

World Cultural Heritage, World Natural Heritage, UNESCO

Information search

Please search some information about the topic of this unit by scanning the QR codes: (Travel Column of *China Daily*), (China Plus), (World Tourism Organization), (Travelogue of CCTV), (Ministry of Culture and Tourism of the People's Republic of China). After reading the information, please share with your classmates some information about the topic of this unit.

Warm-up

Task 1: What does UNESCO stand for? How many World Heritage Sites are there in China and in the world? Please search the information on the Internet.

Task 2: Please match the scenic spots with their names.

A. The Great Wall B. Suzhou Classical Garden C. Mount Taishan
D. Danxia Mountain E. The Potala Palace F. Terra-Cotta Warriors

_____ _____ _____

Unit 7 Tourist Attractions

Passage A World Heritage

A World Heritage Site is a landmark or an area which is selected by the United Nations Educational, Scientific and Cultural Organization (UNESCO) as having cultural, historical, scientific or other form of significance, and is legally protected by international treaties. Heritage is our legacy from the past, what we live with today, and what we pass onto future generations. World Heritage Sites belong to all the peoples of the world, irrespective of the territory on which they are located. Places as unique and diverse as the wilds of East Africa's Serengeti, the Pyramids of Egypt, the Great Barrier Reef in Australia and the Baroque cathedrals of Latin America make up our world's heritage.

The criteria for selection: to be included on the World Heritage List, sites must be of outstanding universal value and meet at least one out of ten selection criteria. Until the end of 2004, World Heritage Sites were selected on the basis of six cultural and four natural criteria.

(1) To represent a masterpiece of human creative genius.

(2) To exhibit an important interchange of human values, over a span of time or within a cultural area of the world, on developments in architecture or technology, monumental arts, town-planning or landscape design.

(3) To bear a unique or at least exceptional testimony to a cultural tradition or to a civilization which is living or which has disappeared.

(4) To be an outstanding example of a type of building, architectural or technological ensemble or landscape which illustrates (a) significant stage in human history.

(5) To be an outstanding example of a traditional human settlement, land-use, or sea-use which is representative of a culture (or cultures), or human interaction with the environment especially when it has become vulnerable under the impact of irreversible change.

(6) To be directly or tangibly associated with events or living traditions, with ideas, or with beliefs, with artistic and literary works of outstanding universal significance.

(7) To contain superlative natural phenomena or areas of exceptional natural beauty and aesthetic importance.

(8) To be outstanding examples representing major stages of earth's history, including the record of life, significant on-going geological processes in the development of landforms, or significant geomorphic or physiographic features.

(9) To be outstanding examples representing significant on-going ecological and biological processes in the evolution and development of terrestrial, fresh water, coastal and marine ecosystems and communities of plants and animals.

(10) To contain the most important and significant natural habitats for in-situ conservation of biological diversity, including those containing threatened species of outstanding universal value from the point of view of science of conservation.

The United Nations Educational, Scientific and Cultural Organization seeks to encourage the identification, protection and preservation of cultural and natural heritage around the world considered to be of outstanding value to humanity. This is embodied in an international treaty called the Convention concerning the Protection of the World Cultural and Natural Heritage, adopted by UNESCO in 1972.

UNESCO's missions are as follows.

(1) Encourage countries to sign the World Heritage Convention and to ensure the protection of their natural and cultural heritage.

(2) Encourage States Parties to the Convention to nominate sites within their national territory for inclusion on the World Heritage List.

(3) Encourage States Parties to establish management plans and set up reporting systems on the state of conservation of their World Heritage Sites.

(4) Help States Parties safeguard World Heritage properties by providing technical assistance and professional training.

(5) Provide emergency assistance for World Heritage Sites in immediate danger.

(6) Support States Parties' public awareness-building activities for World Heritage conservation.

(7) Encourage participation of the local population in the preservation of their cultural and natural heritage.

(8) Encourage international cooperation in the conservation of our world's cultural and natural heritage.

As of July 2018, there are 1,092 World Heritage Sites located in 167 states. Of these, 845 are cultural, 209 are natural and 38 are mixed properties.

New words and expressions

landmark [ˈlændmɑrk] *n.* 地标，里程碑，转折点

treaty ['triti] *n.* (国家间的)条约，协定
irrespective [ɪrɪ'spektɪv] *adj.* 不考虑……的，不顾……的
criteria [kraɪ'tɪərɪə] *n.* (评判或作决定的)标准，准则
masterpiece ['mæstərpis] *n.* 杰作，名著，典范
interchange ['ɪntərtʃeɪndʒ] *n./v.* 交换，交流
monumental [ˌmɑnju'mentl] *adj.* 丰碑式的，意义深远的
testimony ['testɪməni] *n.* 证明，证据
ensemble [ɑn'sɑmbl] *n.* 整体，总体，全体
illustrate ['ɪləstreɪt] *v.* 展示，表明
vulnerable ['vʌlnərəbl] *adj.* 易受伤害的，易受影响的
irreversible [ˌɪrɪ'vɜːsəbl] *adj.* 不可逆转的
tangibly ['tændʒəblɪ] *adv.* 清晰可见的，摸得着的
superlative [suː'pɜːlətɪv] *adj.* 极佳的，卓越的
aesthetic [iːs'θetɪk] *adj.* 美的，艺术的，美感的
geomorphic [ˌdʒiə'mɔfɪk] *adj.* 地貌的
geological [dʒɪə'lɑdʒɪkl] *adj.* 地质学的
terrestrial [tə'restrɪəl] *adj.* 地球的，地球上的
irrespective of 不论……，不顾……
make up 构成，组成
World Heritage List 世界遗产名录
meet the criteria 满足标准
on the basis of 根据……，在……基础上
associated with 与……有关，与……相联系
in the preservation/conservation of 保护……

Notes

1. United Nations Educational, Scientific and Cultural Organization (UNESCO): 联合国教科文组织，it is a specialized agency of the United Nations based in Paris. Its declared purpose is to contribute to peace and security by promoting international collaboration through educational, scientific, and cultural reforms in order to increase universal respect for justice, the rule of law and human rights along with fundamental freedom proclaimed in the United Nations Charter.

2. East Africa's Serengeti, the Pyramids of Egypt, the Great Barrier Reef in Australia and the Baroque cathedrals of Latin America: 东非的塞伦盖蒂，埃及的金字塔，澳大利亚的大堡礁和拉美的巴洛克式教堂。

3. To contain the most important and significant natural habitats for in-situ conservation of biological diversity, including those containing threatened species of outstanding universal value from the point of view of science of conservation. in-situ: 原位，现场，原位的。本句意思是：从自然环境保护的角度来看，包含对生物多样性的保护最重要的自然栖息地，也包括那些具有突出的普遍价值的受到威胁的物种。

4. The United Nations Educational, Scientific and Cultural Organization seeks to encourage the identification, protection and preservation of cultural and natural heritage around the world considered to be of outstanding value to humanity. This is embodied in an international treaty called the Convention concerning the Protection of the World Cultural and Natural Heritage, adopted by UNESCO in 1972. International Treaty: 国际条约，1972年联合国教科文组织巴黎会议上通过；Convention concerning the Protection of the World Cultural and Natural Heritage: 保护世界自然文化遗产公约。

5. The General Conference of the United Nations Educational, Scientific and Cultural Organization meeting in Paris from 17 October to 21 November 1972, at its seventeenth session. 联合国教育、科学及文化组织大会于1972年10月17日至11月21日在巴黎举行的第十七届会议。

6. State Party: 缔约国。

7. As of July 2018, there are 1,092 World Heritage Sites located in 167 states. Of these, 845 are cultural, 209 are natural and 38 are mixed properties. mixed property: 自然与文化双重遗产。There are four mixed World Heritage Sites in China, which are Mount Taishan, Mount Huangshan, Mount Emei Scenic Area, including Leshan Giant Buddha Scenic Area and Mount Wuyi.

8. A total of 1,092 World Heritage Sites exist across in 167 countries, Italy with 54 sites, has the most of any country, followed by China (53), Spain (47), France (44), Germany (44), India (37) and Mexico (35).

Exercises

1. Answer the following questions according to the passage.

(1) Why are World Heritage Sites selected around the world?
_____

(2) How many World Heritage Sites are mentioned in the passage and what are they?
_____

(3) What is the general criterial for selection of World Heritage List?
_____

(4) What is adopted by UNESCO in 1972?
_____

(5) Until 2018, how many World Heritage Sites are selected?
_____

2. Fill in the blanks with the words given below in the box.

| Masterpiece | landmark | vulnerable | safeguard |
| Aesthetic | conservation | criteria | irrespective |

(1) The _____ are regularly revised by the Committee to reflect the evolution of the World Heritage concept itself.

(2) To be selected, a World Heritage Site must be an already classified _____, unique in some respect as a geographically and historically place having special cultural or physical significance.

(3) The World Heritage Sites are intended for practical _____ for posterity, which otherwise would be subject to risk from human or animal trespassing, or threat from local administrative negligence.

(4) Car manufacturers are looking for new ways to _____ passengers.

(5) Natural heritage consist physical and biological formations or groups of such formations, which are of outstanding universal value from the ____ or scientific point of view.

(6) Many doctors and researchers believe that loneliness harms the immune system, making us more _____ to a range of miner and major illness.

(7) When we think of green buildings, we tend to think of new ones—the king of high-tech, solar-paneled _____ that make the covers of architecture magazines.

(8) This service should be available to everybody, _____ of whether they can afford it.

3. Translate the following sentences into English.

(1) 被提名的遗迹必须是具有全球价值的，而且至少满足这其中的一条标准。(meet the criteria)
_____
_____

(2) 截至 2018 年 7 月，全球共计 1,092 处世界遗产，遍布 167 个国家，其中 845 处文化遗产，209 处自然遗产，38 处双重遗产。(be located in, mixed property)
_____
_____

(3) 森林和草原占了这个国家 75%的面积。(make up)
_____
_____

(4) 不论是属于哪个国家的世界遗产，都受到这项国际公约的保护。(irrespective of, belong to)

_____

(5) 这个景区风景优美，与这里的气候有很大关系。(be associated with)

_____

4. Translate the following paragraph into Chinese.

A World Heritage Site is a landmark or an area which is selected by the United Nations Educational, Scientific and Cultural Organization (UNESCO) as having cultural, historical, scientific or other form of significance, and is legally protected by international treaties. Heritage is our legacy from the past, what we live with today, and what we pass onto future generations. World Heritage Sites belong to all the peoples of the world, irrespective of the territory on which they are located. Places as unique and diverse as the wilds of East Africa's Serengeti, the Pyramids of Egypt, the Great Barrier Reef in Australia and the Baroque cathedrals of Latin America make up our world's heritage.

Passage B Mount Huangshan

Mount Huangshan, located in the humid subtropical monsoon climate zone of China's Anhui Province and covering an area of 15,400 hectare with a buffer zone of 14,200 hectare, is famed for its stunning and peculiar natural sceneries composed of four wonders, namely unique Guest-Greeting Pines, Absurd Stones, Sea of Clouds and amazing Hot Springs, as well as high peaks, strange pines and glacial landforms. It is also of outstanding importance to its botanical richness and the conservation of a number of locally or nationally endemic plant species, some of which are threatened with extinction.

Mount Huangshan, often described as the "loveliest mountain of China", has played an important role in the history of art and literature in China since the Tang Dynasty around the 8th century, when a legend dated from the year 747 described the mountain as the place of discovery of the long-sought elixir of immortality. Mount Huangshan became a magnet for hermits, poets and landscape artists, fascinated by its dramatic mountainous landscape consisting of numerous granitic peaks, many over 1,000 meters high, emerging through a perpetual sea of clouds. During the Ming Dynasty from around the 16th century, this landscape and its numerous grotesquely-shaped rocks and ancient trees inspired the influential Shanshui (Mountain and Water) school of landscape painting, providing a fundamental representation of the oriental landscape in the world's imagination and art.

Highlights in Mount Huangshan: Four Wonders

The famed four wonders are four unique scenic spots belonging to Mount Huangshan, namely Strange Pines, Absurd Stones, Sea of Clouds and Hot Springs respectively.

There are hundreds of rare pine trees in Mount Huangshan. As one of the landmarks of Mount Huangshan, the most famous Guest-Greeting Pine stretches out for about 10 meters (33 feet) from the sheer cliffs, like an usher in a respectful greeting gesture.

The absurd stones can be seen almost on every peak of Huangshan Mountain. From different viewing angles, the stones look like human beings, animals or other objects. Accordingly, they are given different vivid names such as Monkey Stone and Flying over Stone.

Sea of Clouds is known for its beauty, scarcity, marvelousness, and flexibility. You would be lucky to see this rarely seen scenery as it only occurs around 50 days in a year. The whole mountain is as pretty as a huge ink-wash painting when enveloped in the misty clouds. Looking at the floating clouds pouring down from mountaintops will highlight your Mount Huangshan trip.

As one of the four wonders, the Hot Springs keep an average temperature of around 42.5℃ (108.5℉) all year round. Taking a bath in hot spring while appreciating the wonderful natural landscapes will not only refresh your body and mind, but also help get away from the fatigue after a tiring Mount Huangshan hiking.

In 1990, Mount Huangshan was listed as both the world cultural and natural heritage sites. The fairyland-like Mount Huangshan national park occupying an area of 160.6 square kilometers (39,700 acres) boasts not only attractive scenery but also abundant resources and a great variety of zoological species. In different seasons around a year, the mountain has various and unique beauty, such as the wild spring flowers, specular summer waterfalls, colorful autumn leaves and white winter rime.

Strange Pines

Absurd Stones

旅游英语

Sea of Clouds

Hot Springs

New words and expressions

subtropical [ˌsʌbˈtrɑpɪkl] *adj.* 亚热带的
monsoon [ˌmɑnˈsun] *n.* 季风，季风季节
absurd [əbˈsɜrd] *adj.* 荒诞的，杂乱无章的
glacial [ˈgleʃəl] *n.* 冰川
botanical [bəˈtænɪkəl] *adj.* 植物学的
endemic [enˈdemɪk] *adj.* 地方性的，流行的
extinction [ɪkˈstɪŋkʃən] *n.* 灭绝，消亡
immortality [ˌɪmɔrˈtæləti] *n.* 不朽，长生
elixir [ɪˈlɪksə(r)] *n.* 灵丹妙药，长生不老药
hermit [ˈhɜrmɪt] *n.* 隐士
granitic [græˈnɪtɪk] *adj.* 花岗石的
perpetual [pərˈpetʃuəl] *adj.* 永久的，不断的，持续的
scarcity [ˈskersəti] *n.* 不足，缺乏
fatigue [fəˈtig] *n.* 疲惫，疲劳
abundant [əˈbʌndənt] *adj.* 大量的，丰富的
rime [raɪm] *n.* 白霜
buffer zone 缓冲地带
art and literature 文学艺术
landscape painting 风景画，山水画
ink-wash painting 水墨画

Notes

1. Mount Huangshan, often described as the "loveliest mountain of China", has played an important role in the history of art and literature in China since the Tang Dynasty around the 8th century, when a legend dated from the year 747 described the mountain as the place of discovery of the long-sought elixir of immortality. 黄山被誉为"震旦国中第一奇山"。黄山在中国文学艺术史上占有重要的地位，传说中华民族的始祖轩辕黄帝曾在此修炼升仙。唐天宝六年(公元747年)六月十六日改现名，被唐玄宗钦定为黄山的生日。

本句中 long-sought 是复合形容词，由"副词+表示被动的过去分词"组成，此类复合形容词还有 well-known, widespread 等。

2. During the Ming Dynasty from around the 16th century, this landscape and its numerous grotesquely-shaped rocks and ancient trees inspired the influential Shanshui (Mountain and Water) school of landscape painting, providing a fundamental representation of the oriental landscape in the world's imagination and art. 自明代(公元16世纪)开始，黄山的风景和无数奇石、古树都成为当时有极大影响力的山水画派的创作内容，生动再现了东方景观的魅力，对世界艺术史都极具影响力。

3. The absurd stones can be seen almost on every peak of Huangshan Mountain. From different viewing angles, the stones look like human beings, animals or other objects. Accordingly, they are given different vivid names such as Monkey Stone and Flying over Stone. 黄山已被命名的怪石有120多处，其形态各异。黄山怪石从不同的位置，在不同的天气观看，可谓"横看成岭侧成峰，远近高低各不同"。黄山几乎每座山峰上都有怪石，其形成期约在100多万年前的第四纪冰川期。奇松怪石，如位于北海的梦笔生花以及"喜鹊登梅"(仙人指路)、老僧采药、苏武牧羊、飞来石、猴子望太平(猴子观海)。

4. As one of the four wonders, the Hot Springs keep an average temperature of around 42.5℃ (108.5℉) all year round. 黄山"四绝"之一的温泉，源出海拔850米的紫云峰下，水质以含重碳酸为主，可饮可浴。传说轩辕黄帝就是在此沐浴七七四十九日得以返老还童、羽化飞升的，故又被誉为"灵泉"。温泉每天的出水量约400吨左右，长年不息，水温常年在42度左右，属高山温泉。

5. The fairyland-like Huangshan national park occupying an area of 160.6 square kilometers (39,700 acres) boasts not only attractive scenery but also abundant resources and a great variety of zoological species. 仙境般的黄山国家公园占地160.6平方公里(397,000亩)，不仅风景秀丽，而且资源丰富，动物种类繁多。

Exercises

1. Answer the following questions according to the passage.

(1) What are Four Wonders in Mount Huangshan?
_____

(2) Why is Mount Huangshan important in Chinese art and literature?
_____

(3) Why are the stones called Absurd Stones in Mount Huangshan?
_____

(4) Is it rare to see the Sea of Clouds?
_____

(5) Why is Mount Huangshan popular with tourists?
_____

2. Find the right translation in Column B that matches the words and expressions in Column A.

Column A	Column B
(1) monsoon climate	A. 国家公园
(2) art and literature history	B. 世界自然与文化遗产
(3) Hot Spring	C. 季风气候
(4) landscape painting school	D. 山水画派
(5) World Natural and Cultural Heritage	E. 温泉
(6) national park	F. 文艺史

3. Translate the following sentences into English with the words or phrases given in the brackets.

(1) 黄山以其壮丽的景色而著称，每年都吸引着从四面八方来的游客、诗人、画家和摄影家。(be famed for)
_____
_____

(2) 这个旅游团由来自世界各地的40位游客组成。(be composed of)
_____
_____

(3) 这座教堂是 15 世纪建成的，五年前在一次地震中被毁了。(dated from)
_____
_____

(4) 从不同的角度看，这座山看起来像一个人、一个动物或者其他物体。(from different viewing angles)
_____
_____

(5) 虽然这家宾馆不大，但是它拥有两个游泳池和一个高尔夫球场。(boast)
_____
_____

4. Translate the following paragraph into Chinese.

In 1990, Mount Huangshan was listed as both the World Cultural and Natural Heritage Sites. The fairyland-like Mount Huangshan national park occupying an area of 160.6 square kilometers (39,700 acres) boasts not only attractive scenery but also abundant resources and a great variety of zoological species. In different seasons around a year the mountain has various and unique beauty, such as the wild spring flowers, specular summer waterfalls, colorful autumn leaves and white winter rime.

5. Translate the following paragraph into English.

西安是中国古代 13 个王朝(dynasty)的首都。毫无疑问，它是中国历史与文化的完美代表。西安居于"中国古都"之首，在中国历史上建都时间最长、影响力最大。它是丝绸之路(the Silk Road)的起点，是中华文明的发祥地。西安到处都是令人惊叹的历史奇观，因此吸引着众多的国内外游客。那里有着中国最古老、最壮观的博物馆和寺庙，其中最著名的是拥有 2000 年历史的兵马俑博物馆(the Terracotta Warriors Museum)。

6. Activity.

Students are divided into groups. Each group is required to collect some information about one World Heritage Site, and introduce the site to the class via pictures or short videos.

Writing: Tour Commentary 导游词

1. Writing Skills

导游词是导游讲解员引导游客游览观光的讲解词。其作用有三：一是引导游客观光游览，二是宣传旅游景点，二者相辅相承、密不可分，三是调动游客的兴趣，弘扬灿烂的中华文化。导游词的内容必须准确无误，令人信服。

导游词的基本要素通常包括一般性介绍(General introduction)，如景观的名称(What)、地理位置(Where)、规模(How large)、性质(How)、用途(What for, Who for)、历史、娱乐、特色等和景点的具体性介绍。同时要注重深层次的内容，如同类事物的鉴赏，包括欣赏有关诗词、对联的点缀以及名家的评论、历史价值、艺术价值、文化价值等。另外，导游词应该围绕如何调动游客的游兴及如何欣赏景点的主题而展开。

导游语言是一种具有丰富表达力、生动形象的口头语言，因此在导游创作中要注意多用口语词汇和浅显易懂的书面语词汇；多用短句，以便讲起来顺口，听起来轻松。导游词语言应是文明、友好和富有人情味的语言，应言之有情、言之有理，让游客赏心悦耳、倍感亲切温暖。讲解景点还可以适时穿插趣味盎然的传说和民间故事，以激起游客的兴趣和好奇心理。幽默风趣是导游词艺术性的重要体现，可使其锦上添花，气氛轻松。

2. Useful Expressions and Sentences

(1) Ladies and gentlemen, we are now approaching the XXX Park—our first stop of the sightseeing in downtown city. We'll be visiting the historic interest and historic relics on the …

(2) Here I'd like to give you some information before we get there.

(3) The park is located in the northwest of XXX City which is the largest park in downtown, covering an area of 860,000 square meters (212.5 acres).

(4) be selected as/be famous for/be known as/be noted for

(5) Located in XXX City in southern XXX Province, the scenic area of the XXX Mountain covers an area of 154 square kilometers and is famous for its four wonders. It also features a natural zoo and botanical garden.

(6) It is the largest and best preserved imperial palace outside the capital. Many of the scenic spots around the resort's lake are mimic famous landscaped gardens in southern China.

(7) The most southern city Sanya in Hainan Island has the most pleasant climate, the fresh air and the warm sunshine, the blue of the sea, the soft sand, the most delicious seafood.

(8) It is not only a beautiful scenery, but also rich cultural relics, beautiful and moving legends, natural, humanities history, art, are skillfully fused together.

3. Sample Writing

Xixi National Wetland Park

Good morning, ladies and gentlemen, my warmest welcome to you all. A Chinese saying has put it well, "separated as we are thousands of miles apart, we come together as if by predestination". It is truly my pleasure to be your tour guide today. Please call me Joy. I hope my service and interpretation can bring you a joyful trip in Hangzhou.

Westlake in Hangzhou may be a household name for a lot of travelers like you. But today I am going to take you to a place a bit off the beaten track, a perfect escape from the crowd of the town. If West Lake is likened to a stunningly beautiful woman, then this is more like a quiet young girl. It is Xixi National Wetland Park, well-known for its rich ecological resources, natural landscape and profound culture.

As the first national wetland park in China, Xixi is a rare urban park that perfectly integrates farming and culture. For centuries, many famous poets, writers and artists were enchanted by this fairyland. They visited, they stayed, and they applauded Xixi's beauty with poems, articles and paintings.

Covering an area of 11.5 square km, 70% of this park is streams, ponds, lakes, and swamps. Six main waterways crisscross the entire park, many with branching streams and fishponds that together form this unique wetland scenery.

That's why we usually say the soul of Xixi lies in water, and it's the culture that brings life to the water. Here at Shentankou, which means Deep Pool, this soul might refer to a dragon. According to historical records, people couldn't cross the pool without a ferry, for it is deep enough to accommodate a dragon. It is at this place that the annual dragon boat racing event is held during the Duanwu or Dragon Boat Festival. But why here?

According to historical records, the paddy fields here were often devastated by summer floods. To ward off these disasters, people began to pray to the Dragon King, for his blessing of fine weather and good harvest. Later in the Ming Dynasty around 500 years ago, Hong Zhong, Director of the Ministry of Justice, personally led locals in repairing the dikes and solving their water problems. The people of Xixi have since been racing dragon boats to commemorate the event, and competitions have grown in popularity.

Later, the Qing Dynasty Emperor Qianlong was so impressed by the lively and grand wetland celebration that he bestowed on it the noble title of Longzhou Shenghui, meaning Dragon Boat Pageant.

The dragon boat, made out of Chinese fir wood to increase the buoyancy, is generally rigged with decorative Chinese dragon heads and tails, which are usually carved out of camphor wood. It takes a skilled craftsman nearly a month to make a boat like this.

But, ladies and gentlemen, we can't race it yet. Having a boat made is just the first step, as the boat hasn't got a soul yet. We have to wait until the "Awakening of the Dragon". But how? Do we have to get a dragon rider to do this job? Usually a highly respected person in the local village has the honor. What he has to do is just dipping a brush in red paint and dotting the bulging eyes on a dragon head to reanimate the creature's bold spirit of hearty racing.

When the day comes, local people flock here to watch the race. With a band of the drum, hundreds of dragon boats come alive, springing out on the tranquil waters of the Xixi Wetland. With drums beating, water splashing, and people cheering, the spirit of dragon soars from water. Strong and experienced paddlers power the boats, demonstrating the skills like sweeping the dragon tails and suppressing the waves.

For Hangzhou citizens, the event is more a public spectacle or a carnival than a race. The spirit of dragon boat racing has been passed down for thousands of years and it will be carried on for many generations to come.

Ladies and gentlemen, now it's the time. If you'd like to try your hand at paddling a dragon boat, please follow me. But be prepared to get soaking wet.

Thank you.

4. Writing Practice

Work in group and write tour commentary for a scenic spot in your hometown or your school campus.

Supplementary Reading

Great Barrier Reef

The Great Barrier Reef is a site of remarkable variety and beauty on the north-east coast of Australia. It contains the world's largest collection of coral reefs, with 400 types of coral, 1,500 species of fish and 4,000 types of mollusk. It also holds great scientific interest as the habitat of species such as the dugong ("sea cow") and the large green turtle, which are threatened with extinction.

As the world's most extensive coral reef ecosystem, the Great Barrier Reef is a globally outstanding and significant entity. Practically the entire ecosystem was inscribed as World Heritage in 1981, covering an area of 348,000 square kilometers. The Great Barrier Reef (hereafter referred to as GBR) includes extensive cross-shelf diversity, stretching from the low water mark along the mainland coast up to 250 kilometers offshore. This wide depth range includes vast shallow inshore areas, mid-shelf and outer reefs, and beyond the continental shelf to oceanic waters over 2,000 meters deep.

Within the GBR there are some 2,500 individual reefs of varying sizes and shapes, and over 900 islands, ranging from small sandy cays and larger vegetated cays, to large rugged continental islands rising, in one instance, over 1,100 meters above sea level. Collectively these landscapes and seascapes provide some of the most spectacular maritime scenery in the world.

The latitudinal and cross-shelf diversity, combined with diversity through the depths of the water column, encompasses a globally unique array of ecological communities, habitats and species. This diversity of species and habitats, and their interconnectivity, make the GBR one of the richest and most complex natural ecosystems on earth. There are over 1,500 species of fish, about 400 species of coral, 4,000 species of mollusk, and some 240 species of birds, plus a great diversity of sponges, anemones, marine worms, crustaceans, and other species. No other World Heritage property contains such biodiversity.

Useful words and expressions

mollusk ['mɒləsk] *n.* 软体动物
ecosystem ['i:kəʊsɪstəm] *n.* 生态系统
entity ['entəti] *n.* 实体，独立存在
latitudinal [ˌlætə'tjudənəl] *adj.* 纬度的
rugged ['rʌgɪd] *adj.* 崎岖的，凹凸不平的
maritime ['mærɪˌtaɪm] *n.* 海的，海上的
ecological [ˌikə'lɑdʒɪkl] *adj.* 生态学的
sponge [spʌndʒ] *n.* 海绵，海绵体
anemone [ə'nemoni] *n.* 海葵
crustacean [krʌ'steʃən] *n.* 甲壳纲动物(如蟹、龙虾)
biodiversity [ˌbaɪəʊdaɪ'vɜːsəti] *n.* 生物多样性
cross-shelf 大陆架
vegetated cay 植物礁
water column 水柱

Unit 8 Cruising

Learning Objectives

After learning this unit, you should:
- Be able to give a full presentation about history and development of cruising.
- Acquire the knowledge and information of Carnival Corporation and cruising lines.
- Grasp professional English words and expressions for cruising.
- Find ways to improve your writing skills about tour itinerary.

Keywords

cruising, tourism industry, Carnival Corporation,

Information search

Please search some information about the topic of this unit by scanning the QR codes: (Travel Column of *China Daily*), (China Plus), (World Tourism Organization), (Travelogue of CCTV), (Ministry of Culture and Tourism of the People's Republic of China). After reading the information, please share with your classmates some information about the topic of this unit.

Warm-up

Task 1: Please recognize the cruise liners of the pictures below, write down the names, and give a brief introduction of each one.

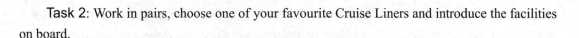

Task 2: Work in pairs, choose one of your favourite Cruise Liners and introduce the facilities on board.

Passage A   An Introduction of Cruising

A cruise ship (cruise liner) is a passenger ship used for pleasure voyages when the voyage itself, the ship's amenities, and sometimes the different destinations along the way (i.e., ports of call), form part of the passengers' experience. Cruise ship is not only the means of transportation to take the passengers from their usual places of residence (from their original port) to different destination (ports of call), but also a mix of accommodation and entertainment activities for travelers to get relaxation.

There are different types of cruising ships—ocean liners, small ships, river cruising, upmarket expensive cruises, budget-priced cruises to mention a few. Larger cruise ships have engaged in longer trips, such as transoceanic voyages which may not return to the same port for months. That is to say, ocean liners also usually have larger capacities for fuel, food, and other stores for consumption on long voyages. Some small cruise ships making two or three night round trips without any ports of call, for instance, Star Cruise in Hongkong. River cruise is a voyage along inland waterways, often stopping at multiple ports along the way, such as Yangtze River Cruise.

The leisure cruising began to appear in 1822, which started out as a shipping line with routes between England and the Iberian Peninsula, adopting the name *Peninsular Steam Navigation Company*. The company was incorporated by Royal Charter in the same year, becoming the *Peninsular and Oriental Steam Navigation Company*. The forerunner of modern cruise holidays, these voyages were the first of their kind, and P&O Cruises has been recognized as the world's oldest cruise lines. The practice of luxury cruising developed steadily for transatlantic crossings. In competition for passengers, more luxuries were added in the cruises. Titanic—being the most famous example — such as fine dining, luxury services and well-appointed staterooms.

Operators of cruise ships are known as cruise lines. Cruise lines have a dual character; they are partly in the transportation business, and partly in the leisure entertainment business. Historically, the cruise ship business has been volatile. The ships are large capital investments with high operating costs. Cruise lines have sold, renovated, or renamed their ships to keep up with travel trends. Larger holding companies appear and many cruise lines companies continue to operate as "brands" or subsidiaries of the holding company in the 1990s. Brands continue to be maintained partly because of the expectation of repeat customer loyalty, and also to offer different levels of quality and service. For instance, Carnival Corporation owns both Carnival Cruise Line, whose former image were vessels that had a reputation as "party ships" for younger travelers, and Holland America Line, whose ships cultivate an image of classic elegance.

Today a conventional cruise is a specially planned return voyage, with entertainment on board and organized shore excursions. Travelers normally return to their port of origin on the same vessel. The ship calls at many ports and islands, giving the passenger an opportunity to see a variety of new places of interest, and to venture beyond the confinement of the ship. Many cruises even offer a good choice for clients wishing to take fly-cruises mix—where the passenger first take a flight to destination city or country and then get aboard to begin the cruising holiday. Those package tour also comprises of hotel accommodation and shore sightseeing activities etc.

The majority of cruise ships are one-stop traveling experience, each passenger can enjoy the full fun of the ship. It offers different classes of accommodation, such as suites, ocean view cabins, balcony cabins, inside cabins as well as fine food in different dining rooms where passengers can enjoy a variety of cuisines, equal to a top-class hotel ashore. There are a variety of leisure activities you can choose from, such as deck games, swimming pools, keep-fit classes, navigational bridge visits, lectures, shows, bar etc. Many ships also provide families with good facilities for children and trained staff to care for them while the parents can enjoy their holidays carelessly. Actually, cruising is ideal for passengers traveling alone, even lone women feel safe.

Cruising has become a major part of the tourism industry, accounting for U.S.$29.4 billion, with over 19 million passengers carried worldwide in 2011. The main region for cruising was North America (70%), where the Caribbean islands were the most popular destinations. Next was Continental Europe (13%), the Mediterranean ports became the most visited ones. Rapid growth of the industries has seen nine or more newly-built ships catering to a North American clientele added every year since 2001, as well as others servicing European clientele. Smaller markets, such as the Asia-Pacific region, are generally serviced by older ships. These are displaced by new ships in the high-growth areas.

New words and expressions

amenities [əˈmenɪtiːz] *n.* (多用复数)便利设施，(环境的)舒适
upmarket [ˌʌpˈmɑrkɪt] *adj.* 高端的，高档的
capacity [kəˈpæsɪti] *n.* 容量，才能，性能
consumption [kənˈsʌmpʃən] *n.* 消耗，消费，耗尽
inland [ˈɪnlənd] *adj.* 内地的，内陆的
incorporate [ɪnˈkɔrpəreɪt] *v.* 包含，合并，混合

Unit 8 Cruising

forerunner [ˈfɔːrʌnə(r)] *n.* 先驱者，先锋
dual [ˈduəl] *adj.* 两部分的，二体的
volatile [ˈvɒlətaɪl] *adj.* 易变的，不稳定的
renovate [ˈrenəveɪt] *v.* 翻新，修复
subsidiary [səbˈsɪdiəri] *adj.* 附属的，次要的
vessel [ˈvesl] *n.* 船，飞船
cultivate [ˈkʌltɪveɪt] *v.* 培养，逐渐形成，教养
venture [ˈventʃə(r)] *v.* 冒险，尝试，勇于做
stateroom [ˈsteɪtˌruːm] *n.* 特等客舱
clientele [ˌklaɪənˈtel] *n.* 顾客，客户
Mediterranean [ˌmedɪtəˈreɪniən] *n./adj.* 地中海(的)
Caribbean [ˌkærɪˈbiːən] *n./adj.* 加勒比海地区(的)
Iberian Peninsula [aɪˈbɪəriən pəˈnɪnsjələ] 伊比利亚半岛
ports of call 沿途停靠的港
long voyage 远航
cater to 迎合，满足

Notes

1. A cruise ship (cruise liner) is a passenger ship used for pleasure voyages when the voyage itself, the ship's amenities, and sometimes the different destinations along the way (i.e. ports of call), form part of the passengers' experience. 游轮是一种用于游览航行的客船，航程本身、船上的设施、沿途停靠的不同目的地都是游客的旅行经历。

2. There are different types of cruising ships—ocean liners, small ships, river cruising, upmarket expensive cruises, budget-priced cruises to mention a few. 游轮的种类有很多种，比如远洋客轮、小型游船、江河游轮、高端奢华游轮、经济型游轮。to mention a few: 举几个例子。

3. Star Cruise in Hongkong: 香港丽晶游轮。

4. P&O: Peninsular and Oriental Steamship Company 半岛东方轮船公司

5. In competition for passengers, more luxuries were added in the cruises. Titanic—being the most famous example — such as fine dining, luxury services and well-appointed staterooms. 为了吸引客户，游轮上增添了更多奢华的成分，泰坦尼克作为世界闻名的游轮，增加了更豪华的餐厅，一流的服务和设施完善的特等客舱。well-appointed: 设施完善的。

6. Historically, the cruise ship business has been volatile. The ships are large capital investments with high operating costs. Cruise lines have sold, renovated, or renamed their ships to keep up with travel trends. 在历史上，游轮业就有不稳定的特征，游船是大资金的投资，需

要高的运营成本,所以当时很多公司出售、升级、改名他们的游轮就是为了追赶上旅游趋势。

7. customer loyalty/repeat customer: 客户的忠诚度

8. Carnival Corporation: 嘉年华集团

9. Many cruises even offer a good choice for clients wishing to take fly-cruises mix—where the passenger first take a flight to destination city or country and then get aboard to begin the cruising holiday. 许多游轮甚至提供给想要体验飞行和游轮一体的游客更好的选择,游客可以首先乘坐飞机到达目的地然后登船开始他们的游轮度假。

10. The majority of cruise ships are one-stop traveling experience, each passenger can enjoy the full fun of the ship. It offers different classes of accommodation, such as suites, ocean view cabins, balcony cabins, inside cabins. 大多数游轮提供的都是一站式旅游体验,每个游客可以充分享受整艘船上的休闲娱乐。游轮上提供不同等级的住宿,有套房、海景房、阳台房和内舱房。

Exercises

1. Answer the following questions according to the passage.

(1) What is a cruise ship?
_____

(2) How many types of cruise ships are mentioned in the passage?
_____

(3) Why did large cruise line companies appear?
_____

(4) What types of facilities are provided to the passengers aboard?
_____

(5) Which regions are popular with cruise ships?
_____

2. Fill in the blanks with the words given below in the box.

cruise	destination	brand	employment
consumption	schedule	headquarter	capacity

(1) Across our nine cruise line _____, we host over 12 million guests a year and visit over 700 ports of call around the world.

(2) Carnival Cruise Line Australia now has three ships, and offers _____ from Sydney and Melbourne to New Zealand, the Pacific Islands and Singapore.

(3) As we travel the world, it is important to us that our ships and crew are always warmly welcomed, that we bring goodwill and prosperity to the local residents and businesses at the _____ we visit.

(4) Carnival Corporation provides direct _____ onboard our ships to the crew members that may have limited opportunities due to socio-political situations in their home countries.

(5) Recycling the waste from our increased _____ is better than burning it.

(6) A total of 19 new ships are _____ to be delivered to Carnival Corporation between 2017 and 2022.

(7) The company established its Asia _____ in Singapore in 2013 and now operates a multitude of offices across Asia, including locations in China.

(8) Each stadium had a seating _____ of about 50,000.

3. **Translate the following sentences into English with the words or phrases given in the brackets.**

(1) 游轮就像一艘航行在海上的五星级度假酒店，包括餐厅、咖啡厅、酒吧、图书馆、电影院、商场、游泳池、健身房、网球场等设施。(amenity)

_____

(2) 客舱的大小尺寸不等，从一些小的单人间，到能够容纳 2~6 名游客的客舱，还有带单独客厅的客舱。(accommodate)

_____

(3) 北美作为游轮的主要客源市场，在过去的 12 年里游客每年增长 7%，在 2002 年达到七百万。(major)

_____

(4) 游轮可以停靠在各大洲的港口，游客和船员来自世界各个国家，游轮业可以使成千上万的国家和人民经济上受益。(ports of call)

_____

(5) 游轮业已经成为旅游业的重要组成部分，它不仅是运输业，还是一个休闲娱乐产业。(not only…but also…)

_____

旅游英语

4. Translate the following paragraph into Chinese.

Cruising has become a major part of the tourism industry, accounting for $29.4 billion, with over 19 million passengers carried worldwide as of 2011. The main region for cruising was North America (70%), where the Caribbean islands were the most popular destinations. Next was Continental Europe (13%), the Mediterranean ports became the most visited ones. The industries rapid growth has seen nine or more newly-built ships catering to a North American clientele added every year since 2001, as well as others servicing European clientele. Smaller markets, such as the Asia-Pacific region, are generally serviced by older ships. These are displaced by new ships in the high-growth areas.

Passage B   Carnival Cruise

If you're thinking of cruising, there's a very good chance you're considering a Carnival cruise. The launch of Carnival Cruise Lines is a classic tale of the American Dream. Started by the Ted Arison, the company began operation in 1972 with a boatload of vision, a single secondhand ship and just enough fuel to make a one-way trip from Miami to San Juan. Relying on little more than a contagious level of enthusiasm, Arison forged a partnership to build the young company into a full-fledged cruise line.

Carnival Cruise Line — "The World's Most Popular Cruise Line" — now carries millions of passengers every year. Carnival Cruise Line is proud to be part of a family of companies owned by Carnival Corporation, which includes sister lines Princess Cruises, Holland America Line and Cunard Line, In April 2003, agreements were finalized to combine Carnival Corporation with P&O Princess Cruises plc, creating the world's first global cruise operator encompassing 12 highly recognizable brands and making the new company one of the largest leisure travel companies in the world.

Carnival cruise ships can range in size from 2,700 people at full occupancy to 5,100, but because the line has invested heavily in regular updates, most ships feature the same standard—and popular—dining venues and bars.

Carnival ships are all about fun vacations at sea and ashore! There's so much variety that you can be as high-spirited or as low-key as you want. A Carnival cruise features day and night time entertainment like stage shows, musical performances, deck parties, casinos and more. When it comes to entertainment, all Carnival ships have a comedy club for family-friendly evening and adult-only night shows, as well as a main theater where you'll find about 40-minute high-energy song-and-dance shows.

Unit 8　Cruising

Considering the family holiday, Carnival ship is well-known for a family-friendly atmosphere, the Camp Ocean and Camp Carnival program for children offers age-appropriate, supervised activities for cruisers ages 2 to 11. For adults, Spa Carnival is an oasis of comfort and relaxation, providing body-care treatments and a complete fitness center. Aside from the main pool, which is the hub of much of the line's fun activities, almost every Carnival cruise ship also has at least one waterslide, with several having multi-slide water parks. Additionally, several have a top-deck Sport Square that features a colorful collection of outdoor amusements, including Ping-Pong, billiards, football, mini-golf, Twister and a SkyCourse ropes course.

Where the ships tend to differ is with specialty (extra-fee) restaurants. For instance, only 16 ships have a steakhouse, eight have a sushi place, five have an Italian trattoria and three have a pan-Asian restaurant.

Carnival's unprecedented rise to the world's largest cruise operator can be attributed to its ability to manage brand autonomy, with each major cruise line maintaining separate sales, marketing and reservation offices, as well as through the industry's most aggressive shipbuilding program. As of 2018, Carnival Cruise Line has a fleet of 26 cruise ships, with two more under construction and due for launch in 2019 and 2020, respectively. Another ship is scheduled to launch in 2022.

New words and expressions

contagious [kənˈtedʒəs] *adj.* 有感染力的，感染性的
forge [fɔrdʒ] *v.* 缔造，建立
full-fledged [ˌfʊl ˈfledʒd] *adj.* 成熟的，经过充分训练的，完备的
encompass [ɪnˈkʌmpəs] *v.* 包含，围绕
venue [ˈvenjuː] *n.* 地点，(体育比赛)场所
oasis [əʊˈeɪsɪs] *n.* 绿洲，乐土
hub [hʌb] *n.* 中心，核心，交通枢纽
waterslide [ˈwɔːtəslaɪd] *n.* 水上滑梯
billiard [ˈbɪlɪrd] *adj.* 台球的
deck [dek] *n.* 甲板，露天的舱面
trattoria [ˌtrætəˈriːə] *n.* 意大利餐馆
unprecedented [ʌnˈpresɪdentɪd] *adj.* 前所未有的，史无前例的
autonomy [ɔˈtɑnəmi] *n.* 自主，自主权
aggressive [əˈɡresɪv] *adj.* 积极进取的，竞争意识强的
range from…to… 范围从……到……

at full occupancy 满座

a fleet of 一队……

Notes

1. If you're thinking of cruising, there's a very good chance you're considering a Carnival cruise. The launch of Carnival Cruise Lines is a classic tale of the American Dream. 如果你想到游轮，极有可能你就会考虑嘉年华游轮，嘉年华游轮创业史是典型的美国梦代表。

2. P&O: Peninsular and Oriental Steamship Company 半岛东方轮船公司

3. San Juan：the capital and largest city of Puerto Rico 圣胡安，波多黎各的首都

4. Princess Cruises, Holland America Line and Cunard Line: 公主号游轮，荷美邮轮，冠达游轮

5. In April 2003, agreements were finalized to combine Carnival Corporation with P&O Princess Cruises plc. 2003 年 4 月，嘉年华公司与半岛东方公主号游轮公司合并最终实现。

6. Carnival ships are all about fun vacations at sea and ashore! There's so much variety that you can be as high-spirited or as low-key as you want. 嘉年华游轮提供船上岸上各种丰富的度假项目，有很多选择，如你所愿，可以尽情享受狂欢，也有安静的休闲。

7. As of 2018, Carnival Cruise Line has a fleet of 26 cruise ships, with two more under construction and due for launch in 2019 and 2020, respectively. Another ship is scheduled to launch in 2022。截止到 2018 年，嘉年华有 26 艘游轮船队，其中两艘正在建造中，预计分别在 2019 年和 2020 年将投放市场。另外一艘游轮预计将于 2022 年投放。

Exercises

1. Answer the following questions according to the passage.

(1) Who and in which year built the Carnival Cruise?
_____

(2) What types of fun activities passengers can enjoy aboard?
_____

(3) What kind of activities are provided for children on Carnival Cruise ship?
_____

(4) How many types of cuisine are provided on Carnival Cruise ship?
_____

(5) Why did Carnival Cruise become the largest cruise operator in the world?
_____

Unit 8 Cruising

2. Find the right translation in Column B that matches the words and expressions in Column A.

Column A	Column B
(1) cruise line	A. 归因于
(2) attribute to	B. 健身中心
(3) fitness center	C. 户外娱乐，户外休闲
(4) outdoor amusement	D. 预定处
(5) reservation office	E. 预期，按计划
(6) be scheduled to	F. 游轮航线

3. Translate the following sentences into Chinese.

(1) Prices range from $119 to $199, depending on different countries and areas.

_____
_____

(2) Considering he's only just started being a tour guide, he knows quite a lot about this job.

_____
_____

(3) The hotel has a fleet of limousines to take guests to the airport.

_____
_____

(4) I didn't accept the job because it was badly paid and aside from that, it wasn't very interesting.

_____
_____

(5) This restaurant features excellent cooking.

_____
_____

4. Translate the following paragraph into English.

京杭大运河(the Beijing-Hangzhou Grand Canal)是中国古代劳动人民创造的一项伟大工程。有着 2500 多年历史的大运河是世界上最古老、工程最大、里程最长的运河。春秋时期(the Spring and Autumn Period)，吴国(the State of Wu)开凿了从扬州到淮安的运河。后来历经几个朝代的翻修扩建，才形成现今的京杭大运河，运河北通北京南至杭州，全长约 1794 公里。它对中国南北地区经济、文化发展与交流起了巨大作用。

5. Activities

(1) For the current cruising industry, what are the advantages and problems? Work in groups and search the information from the Internet.

(2) Group work: Please introduce one of your favorite cruise lines. Each group makes a presentation for about 5 minutes.

Writing: Tour Itinerary 旅游线路

1. Writing Skills

旅游线路安排是旅行社提供给游客的一个旅游计划，让客人很清晰地了解旅游过程的吃、住、行、游览、观光、购物等重要内容。制定旅游线路应本着简洁明了的原则，多为表格形式，简易扼要，一目了然。当然，也可用开放式，如果各具体项目需要大篇幅描述时通常会用开放式。

旅游行程安排的主要内容包括七个要素。

(1) 时间：根据不同需要，可以是半天，一天 24 小时，也可以是具体的日期或一段时间。注意：交通工具的抵离时间要详尽到位。

(2) 事件：由于旅游观光活动基本是环绕吃、住、行、游、购、娱展开。因此，每一项内容均需彻底了解清楚、详细，安排具体、到位、得当。如果是一天的活动安排，通常会附上具体的时间和具体的安排；而如果是一段时间(如一周以上)的安排，则将时间按照"morning/afternoon/evening"来安排活动。

(3) 地点：具体地点(含景点、用餐、住宿、购物、文娱节目等)均须具体注明。

(4) 交通：短途运输、城市之间以及国家间的交通运输要具体明了(含飞机、车、船等)。

(5) 主要负责人：地接社、国内外组团社，地陪、全陪、领队情况以及联络方式等。

(6) 服务标准：吃、酒店、交通、娱乐等。

(7) 特别要求和注意事项。

2. Useful Expressions and Sentences

(1) who/who is in charge: local travel agency, both domestic and foreign tour organizer 国内外组团社 local guide/ national guide/ tour escort 地陪/全陪/领队

(2) pax: person/head's plural form 人头

(3) package tour, FIT (free and independent traveler) 包价游/自由行

(4) vegetarian 素食者

(5) twin room 双床房

(6) itinerary 行程安排，路线

(7) pick-up service/transfer service 接机/转机服务

(8) special request and points of attention 特殊要求和注意事项

(9) departure tax 离境税

3. Sample Writing

Sino-American Friendship Association Group Schedule

The following is the schedule for the 22-day tour to China from August 25th to September 10th, 2016. 30 pax: 14 males, 16 females, among whom there are 5 couples, 3 vegetarians, and 2 children under 10 (one is 8, the other is 9 years old). 15 twin rooms are needed and all booked by Beijing CITS. One coach of 40 seats is required for the whole trip. We hope you'll take good care of them.

Tour Organizer: Sino-American Friendship Association

Tour Code: Sino-America Friendship SAFA-160825

Destinations: Beijing—Kunming—Dali—Lijiang—Shangri-La—Guangzhou—Hong Kong—L.A.

Tour Escort: Philips Paul

Tour Dates	Transport	Destinations	Services Provided	Hotels	Meals	Received by
Day 1	Flight No.	Arrive in Beijing	Airport to Hotel Transfer (Beijing)	Great Wall	D	Beijing CITS
Day 2	Bus	Beijing	Temple of Heaven, The Forbidden City, The Tian'anmen Square	Great Wall	B/L/D	Beijing CITS
Day 3	Bus	Beijing	The Great Wall—Badaling Section, Sacred Way (Ming Tombs), Ming Tombs, Roast duck dinner	Great Wall	B/L/D	Beijing CITS
Day 4	Bus	Beijing	Summer Palace, Hutong Tours in Rickshaw	Great Wall	B/L/D	Beijing CITS
Day 5	Flight No.	Beijing to Kunming	Hotel to Airport Transfer (Beijing), Airport to Hotel Transfer (Kunming)	Green Lake	B/L/D	Kunming CITS
Day 6	Bus	Kunming	The Stone Forest and the Dragon Gate on Xishan/West Hill	Green Lake	B/L/D	Kunming CITS

续表

Tour Dates	Transport	Destinations	Services Provided	Hotels	Meals	Received by
Day 7	Flight No.	Kunming to Dali	Hotel to Airport Transfer (Kunming), Airport to Hotel Transfer (Dali), Zhoucheng elaborate batik crafts Houses of Bai People	Hillton Hotel	B/L/D	Kunming CITS
Day 8	Bus	Dali to Lijiang	Transfer to Lijiang by car (about 3~3.5 hours), The Black Dragon Pool, Lijiang Ancient City	Sheraton Hotel	B/L/D	Kunming CITS
Day 9	Bus	Lijiang	Jade Dragon Snow Moutain (incl. round trip cable car to Spruce Meadow), The Fresco in Baisha Village	Sheraton	B/L/D	Kunming CITS
Day 10	Bus	Lijiang to Zhongdian/ Shangri-La	Overlook for The First Bend of the Yangtze, Tiger Leaping Gorge, transfer to Zhongdian/Shangri-La	Sheraton Hotel	B/L/D	Kunming CITS
Day 11	Flight No.	Zhongdian/ Shangri-La to Kunming	Songzanlin Lamasery, Lake Bita & Lake Shudu, Airport Transfer (Zhongdian/Shangri-La) Airport to Hotel Transfer (Kunming)	Green Lake	B/L/D	Kunming CITS
Day 12	Flight No.	Kunming to Guangzhou	Hotel to Airport Transfer (Kunming), Airport to Hotel Transfer (Guangzhou)	White Swan	B/L/D	Shanghai CITS
Day 13	Bus	Guangzhou	the Yuexiu Park, (the Five Goats Stone Statues), the Western Han Dynasty Nanyue King Mausoleum Museum, the Sun Yat-sen Memorial Hall, Liurong (Six Banyan-Tree) Temple	White Swan	B/L/D	Guangzhou CITS

续表

Tour Dates	Transport	Destinations	Services Provided	Hotels	Meals	Received by
Day 14	Bus/Train	Guangzhou To Hong Kong	Chens' Ancestral Temple also known as the Academy of the Chen Clan, Baiyun Mountain (Yuntai Garden)	Sheraton Hotel	B/L	Guangzhou CITS
Day 15	Bus	Hong Kong	Cruising around the Hong Kong—Zhuhai—Macau Bridge	Sheraton Hotel	B/L/D	Hong Kong CITS
Day 16	Bus	Hong Kong	Disneyland Theme Park	Sheraton Hotel	B/L/D	Hong Kong CITS
Day 17	Flight No.	Hong Kong to L.A.	Avenue of Star		B/L	Hong Kong CITS

Date of Issue: /D. /M. /Y.   Issued by: Tour Guide Signature:

The fee includes:

1. All entrance fee in the itinerary;
2. All meals and shows in the itinerary;
3. Domestic flight service;
4. R/T transfer service;
5. Excellent English speaking tour guide service;
6. Hotel rate.

The fee excludes:

1. All the personal expenses;
2. Tips to drivers and guides;
3. Departure tax.

4. Writing Practice

Please complete the itinerary based on the following information:

The Tour, "Sino-America Friendship SAFA-080825 Tour", 30 pax, organized by an American travel agency—the Sino-America Friendship Travel Agency, will arrive in Beijing on flight CZ3111 from New York on September 14, 2016. It is a package tour who will visits the city for four days and stay in one of the famous deluxe five-star hotels—the Shangri-La Hotel and enjoy the world famous Chinese food in some good restaurants. Harry is their local guide who'll pick them up at the airport and escort them to tour around the city to see some well-known attractions in the city. After the visit to Beijing, the group leaves the city for Shanghai on flight CZ9275.

Local Tour Group Reception Schedule

Tour Code			Tour originating from (Country/District or city)		The United States of America	National Guide	
Name of Tour Organizer						Local Guide	
Total Pax		Male		Transport		Bus No.	
Children		Female				Driver	Ph. No.
Arr. Time					Dept. Time		
	Activity Program					Meals	Hotel
D1 D. M. H.						B. L. D.	
D2 D. M. H.						B. L. D.	
D3 D. M. H.						B. L. D.	
D4 D. M. H.						B. L. D.	
D5 D. M. H.						B. L. D.	
D6 D. M. H.						L. D. D.	
D7 D. M. H.						B. L. D.	

续表

Plan For Ticket Booking	Flight:
	Train:
	Ship:
Remark	

Supplementary Reading

Costa Cruises Offers Value and Exotic Destinations

Costa Cruises is the European arm of Carnival Cruise Lines, and sails to exotic ports, such as Dubai and Bombay. You can also explore breathtaking Norway, or colorful Thailand. When you arrive at a port of call, you'll have your choice of excursions. Did you know that Costa offers over 2,000 on-shore adventures? Visit nature reserves and coral reefs. You can even take custom excursions.

Entertainment and Attractions

On board all Costa ships you'll find a Casino with slot machines, roulettes and gambling tables. Entry is restricted to adult guests and the establishment is only open while the ship is sailing.

On the swimming pool deck of some Costa Cruises ships you'll find a giant eighteen square meter screen. You'll be able to enjoy the best music videos and great sporting events in maximum comfort and relaxation.

Whichever your favorite sport may be, on many Costa Cruise ships you'll find a multi-sport field to keep in shape playing five-a-side football, tennis, basketball and volleyball, an open-air jogging track, outdoor pools with sliding roofs suitable for all seasons and practical gyms fitted with the best Technogym equipment. And if you love group activities, join other guests for a free fitness course or book a Yoga or Pilates lesson.

Note: Fitness trainer and classes are an extra fee.

Dining Options

Costa Cruises offers Complimentary Dining options as well as Specialty Dining options (for an extra fee). Various options include: Preset dining, a la carte dining at the Club restaurant, Pizza place, snack bars, coffee bar, and afternoon tea.

Main Dining

All guests will have an option to choose time to dine at the Main Dining Restaurant. This option is not available for breakfast or lunch but only for dinner. You'll find the Table Booking Card in your cabin on arrival. You'll also be able to specify when and with how many people you wish to dine. Your request will be confirmed subject to availability in the restaurant.

Drinks

Drinks are not included in the price. In the buffet area you'll always find an ice dispenser and drinking water, including hot water to make yourself a cup of tea with the teabags provided. Cocktails, coffees and drinks can be purchased using your Costa Card from all the bars on the ship. For a moderate fee you can choose an option of "All Inclusive" which includes a selection of alcoholic and soft drinks by the glass and coffee, with the exception of premium brands and Mini Bar products.

Kids Activities

Babysitting Service is available only for kids of 3 or older! From morning to evening, Costa entertainment staff will make sure they have fun with lots of friends divided into four age groups from three to seventeen years old. If parents want to take part in any cruise events held in the evenings, they can also book a collective babysitting service one day in advance. This service is provided in the Mini-club between 11:30 p.m. and 1:30 a.m.

Useful words and expressions

exotic [ɪgˈzɑtɪk] *adj.* 外来的，具有异国情调的
reef [rif] *n.* 暗礁，礁石
roulette [ruːˈlet] *n.* 轮盘赌
establishment [ɪˈstæblɪʃmənt] *n.* 机构，企业，店
Pilates [pɪˈlɑːtiz] *n.* 普拉提，健身操
dispenser [dɪˈspensə(r)] *n.* 自动售货机
premium [ˈpriːmiəm] *adj.* 高端的
custom [ˈkʌstəm] *adj.* 订做的，量身设计的
nature reserve 野生生物保护区
subject to 受制于，以……为条件
a la carte 照菜单点
preset dining 事先备好餐食
slot machine 老虎机

Module Four

MICE

Unit 9 Introduction to MICE

Learning Objectives

After learning this unit, you should:
- Grasp professional English words and expressions for MICE.
- Get some practical knowledge about MICE.
- Be able to give a full presentation about MICE.
- Acquire the knowledge and information of incentive travel.
- Get some practical knowledge about incentive travel.

Keywords

meetings, incentives, conferences, exhibitions, incentive travel

Information search

Please search some information about the topic of this unit by scanning the QR codes: (Travel Column of *China Daily*), (China Plus), (World Tourism Organization), (Travelogue of CCTV), (Ministry of Culture and Tourism of the People's Republic of China). After reading the information, please share with your classmates some information about the topic of this unit.

Warm-up

MICE is an abbreviation; can you guess what they are standing for according to the pictures given below?

旅游英语

Passage A MICE

MICE stands for meetings, incentives, conferences and exhibitions, which is a type of tourism in which large groups, usually planned well in advance, are brought together.

IAPCO (the International Association of Professional Congress Organizers) publishes a book called "Meetings Industry Terminology" which functions as a dictionary for the meetings industry. The following are the definitions as put out by IAPCO.

Meeting—general term indicating the coming together of a number of people in one place, to confer or carry out a particular activity. Frequency: can be on an ad hoc basis or according to a set pattern, as for instance annual general meetings, committee meetings, etc.

Incentive—meeting event as part of a programme which is offered to its participants to reward a previous performance.

Conference—participatory meeting designed for discussion, fact-finding, problem solving and consultation. As compared with a congress, a conference is normally smaller in scale and more select in character—features which tend to facilitate the exchange of information. The term "conference" carries no special connotation as to frequency. Though not inherently limited in time, conferences are usually of limited duration with specific objectives.

Exhibition—Events at which products and services are displayed.

Recently, there has been an industry driven initiative to not use the "MICE Market" label and instead say "The Meetings Industry" which encompasses all the above.

ITE MICE—Visitors interested in outbound MICE

Of the 666 exhibitors of ITE 2018, which drew in its two trade days 2567 MICE/Corporate visitors and 6580 visitors from travel agents, 187 exhibitors present MICE travel products. Among MICE exhibitors, the three largest segments come mainly from Travel Agents/DMC, Hotel & Venue and NTO.

Moreover, majority of these visitors are interested in holding events overseas (Table 1); only half from small/medium size enterprises (Table 2); and likely they welcome holding together MICE and leisure travel for the affluent, as indicated in their interests (Table 3).

1 MICE/Corp visitors interested in/held before Overseas Events	
Products	%
Incentive Tour	51
Overseas Event/Exhibition	38
Overseas Meeting	36

2 Size of visitors' organizations by no. of staff	
No. of Staff	%
Below 50	50
50~250	19
Over 250	31

3 MICE/Corp visitors—Why Visit & Interest	
Kind of Information Seeking for	%
Destination	82
Travel Agents	95
Meeting/Event Venues	49
Transportation/Accommodation	74
Special Offer	35

  Admission in trade days requires registration. The second Trade Day of ITE is designated as MICE/Corporate Travel Day with a number of related seminars on, like Team Building Activities Abroad and Green Tourism; Industry Events like One Belt One Road Forum, Inauguration of Business Alliance in Bay Area (Pearl River Delta), Seminars by ILEA and on IT for Travel Trade etc.

  Exhibitors are holding theme travel seminars targeting MICE visitors. For example, Hong Kong Tourism Board held a trade seminar on "Holding meetings on Cruise", while others held a seminar of "Corporate Volunteer Programs" related to sustainable and green tourism, too.

  Many MICE exhibitors also target affluent FIT/private tours, who are present in tenths of thousand in ITE's public (FIT) days as 84% of its 90,000 visitors prefer FIT or private tour (See Section ITE—Public). Over the years, some 10 chambers of commerce and professional bodies help distribute ITE Guest Ticket (valid for both trade and public days) to members, with some requesting over 1,000 tickets.

For more details, please contact the Organizer—TKS Exhibition Services Ltd.
Email: travel@tkshk.com or fill in the Exhibiting Inquiry Form
Tel: (852) 31550600   Fax: (852) 35201500

TKS Exhibition Services Ltd., which was set up in August 2004 to acquire ITE Hong Kong, held ITE for the first time in June 2005. Despite the short time span for preparation, ITE 2005 grew to three halls from two largely through re-positioning and investments to upgrade services.

In 2006, TKS launched ITE MICE to be held concurrently, thus ITE Hong Kong used a total of 4 halls in 2006, then 5 halls but in two floors in 2007. Starting from its 2009 edition when HKCEC completed its expansion, ITE Hong Kong uses 5 halls in the same floor.

(source:https://www.itehk.com/ITEHK/index.php?menuid=main&module=content&topLevel=888&subLevel=802&lang=en)

New words and expressions

abbreviation [əbriːvɪ'eɪʃ(ə)n] n. 缩写，缩写词
incentive [ɪn'sentɪv] n. 动机，刺激
terminology [ˌtɜːmɪ'nɒlədʒi] n. 术语
fact-finding ['fækt faindiŋ] adj. 实情调查的
consultation [kɒnsəl'teɪʃ(ə)n] n. 咨询，磋商
encompass [ɪn'kʌmpəs] vt. 包含，包围
scale [skeɪl] n. 规模，比例
connotation [kɒnə'teɪʃ(ə)n] n. 内涵，含蓄
sustainable [sə'steɪnəb(ə)l] adj. 可以忍受的，可持续的
institution [ɪnstɪ'tjuːʃ(ə)n] n. 制度，公共机构
professional [prə'feʃ(ə)n(ə)l] adj. 专业的，职业的 n. 专业人员
academic [ækə'demɪk] adj. 学术的，理论的
seminar ['semɪnɑː] n. 讨论会，研讨班
exhibitor [ɪgˈzɪbɪtə] n. 参展商
segment ['segm(ə)nt] n. 段，部分
affluent ['æflʊənt] adj. 富裕的，丰富的
launch [lɔːntʃ] vt. 发射，发起，发动
expansion [ɪk'spænʃ(ə)n] n. 膨胀，扩张
green tourism 绿色旅游
team building activities abroad 海外团队建设活动

Unit 9　Introduction to MICE

Notes

1. hoc: House of Commons, (英国、加拿大的)众议院，下议院；ad hoc: 特别的，临时的；on an ad hoc basis: 权宜之计。

2. IAPCO (the International Association of Professional Congress Organizers)国际专业组织者协会；国际会议筹组人协会

3. ITE MICE: international travel expo，香港国际旅游展，会展部分

4. One Belt One Road Forum: 一带一路论坛，"一带一路"(The Belt and Road，缩写 B&R)是"丝绸之路经济带"和"21世纪海上丝绸之路"的简称，是 2013 年 9 月和 10 月由中国国家主席习近平分别提出的合作倡议。"一带一路"贯穿亚欧非大陆，一头是活跃的东亚经济圈，一头是发达的欧洲经济圈，中间广大腹地国家经济发展潜力巨大。丝绸之路经济带重点沟通中国经中亚、俄罗斯至欧洲(波罗的海)；中国经中亚、西亚至波斯湾、地中海；中国至东南亚、南亚、印度洋。

5. Inauguration of Business Alliance in Bay Area (Pearl River Delta): 珠三角地区大湾区商务联盟开幕式

6. holding meetings on Cruise: 邮轮上的会议

7. Team Building Activities Abroad 国外团队建设活动

8. Corporate Volunteer Programs 企业志愿者项目

9. IT for Travel Trade 旅游贸易的信息技术

10. chambers of commerce 商会

Exercises

1. Answer the following questions according to the passage.

(1) What does MICE stand for?

(2) What does IAPCO stand for?

(3) What is a conference?

(4) What do people do in exhibition?

(5) How many days does ITE 2018 HK last?

(6) What do the three largest segments mainly come from?

(7) What percentage of visitors are interested in overseas meetings?
_____

(8) What is the topic of the tourism seminar that Hong Kong Tourism Board held?
_____

2. Fill in the blanks with the words given below in the box.

| abbreviation | incentive | connotation | sustainable | scale |
| academic | segment | encompass | launch | seminar |

(1) As well as providing graduates with the "soft skills" employers want, "the arts and humanities _____ those things that make life worth living", he said.

(2) We will use this _____ in this article and throughout the series.

(3) Mission number one is satellite _____.

(4) To be _____ they have to think about the future and manage the waste and the sewage water.

(5) The _____ for most people when applying for a job is to survive.

(6) To actively develop energy cooperation and enrich _____ of bilateral relations.

(7) Welcome to the international _____ of chinese and its character system.

(8) In this _____, we will build our infrastructure.

(9) The _____ of the map is 1: 460000.

(10) _____ journals tend to be the primary source of news for science reporters because that is where researchers usually publish their findings.

3. Translate the following expressions into English or Chinese.

(1) limited duration with specific objectives _____

(2) medium size enterprise _____

(3) holding meetings on Cruise _____

(4) Corporate Volunteer Programs _____

(5) participants _____

(6) 企业旅游日 _____

(7) 私人旅游 _____

(8) 商会 _____

(9) 专业团体 _____

(10) 珠三角 _____

4. Translate the following sentences into English with the words or phrases given in the brackets.

(1) 这个段由系统上的所有进程共享。(segment)

_____

(2) 美国人出生时的平均预期寿命大约是 78 岁，这比大多数富裕国家的国民寿命要低。(affluent)

_____

(3) 首先，让我们来学习一些关于安全的概念和术语。(terminology)

_____

(4) 尽管如此，我仍然将宗教看作一种习俗来迷恋。(institution)

_____

(5) 这支足球队受过专业教练员的训练。(professional)

_____

(6) 一些展会需要额外的证件。(exhibitor)

_____

Passage B Incentive Travel

Most components of MICE are well understood, perhaps with the exception of incentives. Incentive tourism is usually undertaken as a type of employee reward by a company or institution for targets met or exceeded, or a job well done. Unlike the other types of MICE tourism, incentive tourism is usually conducted purely for entertainment, rather than professional or education purposes.

MICE events are usually centered on a theme or topic and are aimed at a professional, school, academic or trade organization or other special interest group. Examples: Medical Facilities, Theme Parks.

Travel incentives are a reward subset of an incentive program, recognition program or a loyalty program, which is a business tool designed to change consumer behavior to improve profit, cash flow, employee engagement and customer engagement. It has been described as business travel that is designed to motivate or trigger action, as a reward for these actions from employees or business partners. This fosters loyalty and encourages the best talent for an organization.

When an organization properly designs an incentive program, which includes looking at all departments which will be affected, rather than just the impact to the department that is sponsoring the incentive, the return on investment can be proven. Oxford Economics USA wrote in a 2009 study that incentive travel investments yielded a return of investment of more than $4:$1 and stated that in order to achieve the same effect of incentive travel, an employee's total base compensation would need to be increased by 8.5%.

The Incentive Research Foundation released a study in 2010 following the steps that an organization took to ensure that they received a return on their investment; they successfully merged acquired organizations into their company, and successfully merged their incentive programs.

Economic impact

Incentive trips, meetings and events account for 15% of all travel spending, which creates 2.4 million jobs, $240 billion in spending and $39 billion in tax revenue, according to the U.S. Travel Association. Incentive travel generates about $13 billion a year, according to the Incentive Research Foundation.

The economic impact and the AIG effect had negatively affected incentive travel programs in 2010, with spending on incentive travel being reduced.

Future of incentive travel

According to *Incentive Magazine*'s 2013 Travel IQ Survey—"The top benefits for 2013 range from recognizing performance (62.1%) and increasing sales (57.8%), to building morale (50%), improving employee loyalty (42.2%), and fostering teamwork (32.8%)".

(source: https://en.wikipedia.org/wiki/Travel_incentive)

New words and expressions

exception [ɪk'sepʃ(ə)n] *n.* 例外，异议
undertake [ʌndə'teɪk] *vt.* 承担，从事
target ['tɑːgɪt] *n.* 目标 *v.* 把……作为目标
exceed [ɪk'siːd] *vt.* 超过，胜过
motivate ['məʊtɪveɪt] *vt.* 刺激
trigger ['trɪgə] *vt.* 引发，触发
foster ['fɒstə] *vt.* 培养，养育
merge [mɜːdʒ] *vt.* 合并，使合并
generate ['dʒenəreɪt] *vt.* 使形成，发生
morale [mə'rɑːl] *n.* 士气，斗志
consumer behavior 消费者行为，消费者行为学
employee engagement 员工敬业度，员工参与

customer engagement 顾客参与

Notes

1. Most components of MICE are well understood, perhaps with the exception of incentives. "with the exception of"，也许……是一个例外。整句翻译：会展旅游大多数的构成都比较容易理解，也许奖励旅游是一个例外。

2. Travel incentives are a reward subset of an incentive program, recognition program or a loyalty program, which is a business tool designed to change consumer behavior to improve profit, cash flow, employee engagement and customer engagement. 这是个由 which 引导的非限定性定语从句，先行词是 incentive program, recognition program or a loyalty program，翻译为奖励项目、认可项目或忠诚度项目，从句的意思是，这是一种专门为改变顾客行为，提高利润、资金流、员工敬业度和员工忠诚度而设计的商业手段。

3. Oxford Economics USA: 美国牛津经济研究院

4. motivate or trigger action: 激励或触发行为

5. base compensation: 基本薪酬

6. U.S. Travel Association: 美国旅游协会

7. The Incentive Research Foundation: 奖励研究基金会

8. *Incentive Magazine*'s 2013 Travel IQ Survey: 奖励杂志 2013 年旅游智商调查

Exercises

1. Reading Comprehension: Choose the best answer for the following questions.

(1) Incentive tourism is usually conducted purely for _____ purposes.

   A. entertainment   B. professional   C. education

(2) _____ fosters loyalty and encourages the best talent for an organization.

   A. Travel incentive   B. MICE tourism   C. Event

(3) According to the passage, if a company invests one dollar in incentive, they will get more than _____ dollars.

   A. 2   B. 3   C. 4

(4) Incentive travel generates about _____ billion a year, according to the Incentive Research Foundation.

   A. $12   B. $13   C. $14

(5) Incentive trips, meetings and events account for 15% of all travel spending, which creates _____ million jobs.

   A. 3.4   B. 4.2   C. 2.4

(6) According to *Incentive Magazine*'s 2013 Travel IQ Survey—The top ONE benefits for 2013 was _____.

   A. recognizing performance

   B. increasing sales

   C. building morale

(7) According to *Incentive Magazine*'s 2013 Travel IQ Survey—The fifth top benefits for 2013 was _____.

   A. employee loyalty

   B. fostering teamwork

   C. building morale

(8) Travel incentive is a business tool designed to change _____ to improve profit, cash flow, employee engagement and customer engagement.

   A. employee behavior

   B. employer behavior

   C. consumer behavior

2. **Fill in the blanks with the words given below in the box.**

| exception | undertake | target | exceed |
| motivate | trigger | foster | merge |

(1) _____ an enterprise culture of safety and security.

(2) Everyone should keep discipline and you are no _____.

(3) They _____ you and teach you safe workouts you can do at home.

(4) When you click the _____, it pops up an alert.

(5) My _____ is to get into double figures so hopefully I can do that this season.

(6) _____ not what you cannot perform, but be careful to keep your promise.

(7) This allows you to combine and _____ XML and relational data.

(8) I _____ the excellent student who has excessive excellence.

3. **Translate the following expressions into English or Chinese.**

   (1) employee reward_____

   (2) professional purpose_____

   (3) reward subset_____

   (4) interest group_____

   (5) loyalty program_____

(6) 员工敬业度_____
(7) 顾客忠诚度_____
(8) 税收_____
(9) 激励研究基金会_____
(10) 经济影响_____

4. Translate the following sentences into Chinese.

(1) Most components of MICE are well understood, perhaps with the exception of incentives.
_____

(2) Travel incentives are a reward subset of an incentive program, recognition program or a loyalty program, which is a business tool designed to change consumer behavior to improve profit, cash flow, employee engagement and customer engagement.
_____
_____

(3) Oxford Economics USA wrote in a 2009 study that incentive travel investments yielded a return of investment of more than $4:$1.
_____

(4) Incentive trips, meetings and events account for 15% of all travel spending, which creates 2.4 million jobs, $240 billion in spending and $39 billion in tax revenue, according to the U.S.
_____

(5) According to *Incentive Magazine*'s 2013 Travel IQ Survey—"The top benefits for 2013 range from recognizing performance (62.1%) and increasing sales (57.8%), to building morale (50%), improving employee loyalty (42.2%), and fostering teamwork (32.8%)".
_____
_____

5. Translate the following paragraph into English.

在第7届中国——东盟首脑会议(China—ASEAN Summit)上，温家宝倡议，从2004年起每年在中国广西南宁举办中国——东盟博览会(China—ASEAN Expo)。他的提议受到东盟各国领导人的欢迎。设立博览会的目的是争取中国和东盟各国的互惠互利、共同繁荣。十年来，博览会极大推动了区域经济和贸易合作，为世界各地的商界带来了巨大机遇。今年，2,300多家来自中国和东南亚国家的公司参加了展会。

6. Activity

Group work: In the world, there are many conferences or exhibitions related to tourism.

Please introduce one of the conferences or exhibitions on tourism in or outside China. Each group makes a presentation for about 5 minutes.

Writing: Other forms in Tourism 旅游其他相关表格

1. Writing Skills

　　旅游行业是一个综合性行业，涉及很多不同行业和部门，因此相应地要填写一些必要的表格，如作为导游或者旅行社的计调人员应该很清楚国际机场的出境手续办理的各个流程及其所需的各种旅行文件，出入境部门所需检查的各种文件表格，如入境登记卡、出境登记卡、海关行李申报单、旅客健康申明卡以及客人的姓名、性别、年龄、国籍、地址、要申报或说明的内容、要前往的目的地、住宿、交通，如航班、车次等内容。所有表格应符合国内国际标准。

　　注：国际航班出境手续流程如下。

　　办理乘机手续→托运行李→检验检疫→海关→边防检查→安全检查→候机与登机 (出境)

2. Useful Expressions and Sentences

　　nationality 国籍
　　occupation 职业
　　issue 发证
　　accompany 伴随
　　guarantee 保证
　　currency 通货，货币；流通，通用，流行
　　ornament 装饰物
　　necessity 必需物品
　　procedure 手续，程序，步骤
　　antique 文物；古时制造的，古董的
　　symptom 症状
　　accommodation 住宿
　　delete 省略
　　registration 注册，登记
　　settlement 处理，解决
　　license 执照，牌照
　　snivel 流鼻涕

avian influenza 禽流感
diarrhea 腹泻
psychosis 精神病
venereal diseases 性病
active pulmonary tuberculosis 开放性肺结核
entry card/arrival card 入境登记卡
exit card/departure card 出境登记卡
visa application form 签证申请表
baggage declaration form 海关行李申报单
passenger's health declaration 旅客健康申明卡

3. Sample Writing

(1) Entry/Exit Card

Family Name	
Given Name	
Male　　　　Female　　　　Nationality	
Date of Birth	
Occupation	
Passport Type and No.	
Visa Type and No.	
Issued By	
Accompanied By	
Port and Date of Entry/Exit	
Signature	

(2) China Customs
Baggage Declaration Form For Outgoing Passengers

1. Surname			
Given Name			
2. Date of Birth	Year	Month	Day
3. Sex	Male	Female	
4. No. of Traveler's Document			
5. Nationality (Region)			

续表

| 6. Purpose of the trip | Official | Business | Leisure | Study |
| | Immigration | Visiting friends or relatives | Return | Others |

7. Flight No./Vehicle No./Vessel Name

8. Number of persons under the age of 16 traveling with you

I am (We are) taking out of China's Customs territory

9. Trip Necessities (Camera, video, laptop, etc) valued each at over RMB 5,000 which will be brought back at the end of the trip.　　　　Yes　No

10. Chinese currency in cash exceeding RMB 20,000 or foreign currencies in cash exceeding USD 5,000 if converted into US dollar.　　　Yes　No

11. Gold, silver and other precious metals.　　　　Yes　No

12. Cultural relics, endangered animals or plants and products thereof.　Yes　No

13. Radio transmitters, radio receivers, communication security equipment. Yes　No

14. Other articles which are prohibited or restricted form being taken out of the territory in accordance with the law of the People's Republic of China.　　Yes　No

15. Goods of commercial value, samples, advertisements.　　Yes　No

I Have Read the Instructions on the Reverse Side of This Form and Declare That the Information Given on This Form Is True

Passengers who are taking any articles included in items 9-14 shall fill out this form in detail

Description	Quantity	Value	Type/Model	Customs Remarks

Passenger's Signature　　　　　　　Year　　Month　　Date

(3) Health Declaration Form on Entry/Exit

Entry-Exit Inspection Quarantine of the P. R. China

Notice: For your and others' health, please fill in the form truly and completely. False information of intent will be followed with legal consequences.

Unit 9 Introduction to MICE

Name _____	Sex ____ Male ____ Female
Date of Birth _____	Nationality/Region _____
Passport No. _____	Flight No. _____

The contact address and telephone number _____

_____

1. Have you had close contact with poultry or bird in the past 7 days? Yes   No

2. Have you had close contact with patients or suspects suffering from avian influenza in the past 7 days? Yes   No

3. Please mark the symptoms and diseases you have got in the corresponding

 Fever   Snivel   Cough   Sore throat

 Headache   Diarrhea   Vomiting   Breath Difficulty

 Venereal Disease   AIDS/HIV   Psychosis

 Active pulmonary tuberculosis

I declare all the information given in this form are true and correct.

Signature _____   Date _____

Temperature (for quarantine official only) _____ ℃

4. Writing Practice

Please fill in the forms in sample 1, sample 2 and sample 3 according to your own situation.

Supplementary Reading

Adventures Outside the Box

About Us

 With so many companies offering business travel solutions, you may wonder what sets Adventures Outside the Box apart: our greatest advantage over competitors is that our division is one of several brands and companies owned and operated by Adventures Abroad Worldwide Travel, a high-end tour operator established in 1987.

 Not only do we have access to the resources, expertise and buying power of Adventures Abroad Worldwide Travel, but also to its travel agency, Roseway Travel, and its luxury yacht charter company, Magic Yacht Charters. Here is a breakdown pinpointing the specialties of each division and how their expertise comes to bear on Adventures Outside the Box operations.

Adventures Abroad Worldwide Travel

Specializes in small-group cultural tours to 120 countries, with in-house product development, flights and operations departments. Along with scheduled group tour departures, Adventures Abroad creates and operates custom itineraries to virtually every country on the globe. With a broad network of local and international contacts established over 25 years, a solid reputation within the industry and a high volume of travelers sent abroad annually, Adventures Abroad has the buying power and leverage to ensure Adventures Outside the Box corporate clients enjoy the best rates available without sacrificing quality.

Roseway Travel

A full-service travel agency in West Vancouver that boasts 31 years of servicing leisure and corporate clients, arranging hotels, flights, ocean and river cruises, and tours. Roseway Travel's wealth of local and national contacts means Adventures Outside the Box has a strong advantage in the realm of corporate travel in general and Destination Management in specific.

Magic Yacht Charters

The largest yacht charter company in the Lower Mainland, Magic Yacht Charters owns and operates four luxury vessels in downtown Vancouver that can accommodate events for between 80 and 400 people—the ideal venue in which Adventures Outside the Box can arrange and host corporate conferences and group or individual incentive initiatives.

Adventures Outside the Box's highly experienced staff has access to all the resources and expertise necessary to manage all your corporate travel logistics.

Our Services

Group & Individual Incentive Programs

Drawing on the expertise gained from 25 years of arranging leisure and corporate group travel to popular and obscure destinations worldwide, we know what it takes to create and operate custom travel solutions abroad and how to ensure their success.

Destination Management

Our extensive local knowledge, developed by way of running group-tour programs throughout North America, and our ever-growing database of travel industry contacts in B.C. stand us in good stead when it comes to delivering high-quality and cost-effective custom travel solutions in Vancouver and beyond.

Corporate Travel

Along with a wealth of international suppliers and agents, we have in-house flights and operations departments to arrange all air, accommodations and itinerary particulars at the best rates.

Conference & Meeting Management

The logistics of arranging travel to conferences, conventions and meetings locally can prove challenging enough, but doing so abroad is infinitely more difficult. At home or abroad, Adventures Outside the Box has the expertise, contacts and resources you need to guarantee a successful, hassle-free experience.

(source:http://www.adventuresoutsidethebox.com/about-us)

Useful words and phrases

competitor [kəm'petɪtə] *n.* 竞争对手
expertise [ˌekspɜːˈtiːz] *n.* 专门知识，专长
pinpoint ['pɪnpɔɪnt] *vt.* 查明，找准
in-house [ˌɪn ˈhaʊs] *adj.* 内部的
leverage ['liːv(ə)rɪdʒ] *n.* 手段，影响力，杠杆作用 *v.* 利用
vessel ['ves(ə)l] *n.* 船，舰
database ['deɪtəbeɪs] *n.* 数据库，资料库
set …apart 使……显得突出
yacht charter 游艇租赁
hassle-free 轻而易举的，毫无麻烦的

Read the passage and decide whether the following statements are true (T) or false(F).

1. _____ Adventures Abroad Worldwide Travel, a high-end tour operator, was established in 1987.

2. _____ Specializes in small-group cultural tours to 130 countries.

3. _____ Roseway Travel is a full-service travel agency in West Vancouver.

4. _____ Magic Yacht Charters owns and operates five luxury vessels in downtown Vancouver.

5. _____ Adventures Outside the Box has the expertise, contacts and resources you need to guarantee a successful, hassle-free experience, both at home or abroad.

Unit 10 Canton Fair

Learning Objectives

After learning this unit, you should:
- Acquire the knowledge and information of Canton Fair.
- Grasp professional English words and expressions for Canton Fair.
- Get some practical knowledge about Canton Fair.
- Get some cultural knowledge about Canton Fair.
- Understand how to give information about travel services for MICE.
- Find ways to understand tour contract and features of language for tour contract.

Keywords

Canton Fair, Travel Services for MICE

Information search

Please search some information about the topic of this unit by scanning the QR codes: ▣ (Travel Column of *China Daily*), ▣ (China Plus), ▣ (World Tourism Organization), ▣ (Travelogue of CCTV), ▣ (Ministry of Culture and Tourism of the People's Republic of China). After reading the information, please share with your classmates some information about the topic of this unit.

Warm-up

Task: Read the invitation below, ask and answer questions with your partners about the following information.
- Where was it located?
- Who can I contact?
- What is the booth number?
- Where can I go if I want more information about this company?

Unit 10 Canton Fair

Passage A Canton Fair

The Canton Fair is a trade fair held in the spring and autumn each year since the spring of 1957 in Canton (Guangzhou), China. It is the oldest, largest, and the most representative trade fair in China.

Its full name since 2007 has been China Import and Export Fair, renamed from Chinese Export Commodities Fair. The fair is co-hosted by the Ministry of Commerce of China and the government of Guangdong Province, and organized by China Foreign Trade Centre.

The National Pavilion (export section) of Canton Fair is sorted into 16 categories of products, which will be exhibited in 51 sections. Over 24,000 of China's best foreign trade corporations (enterprises) take part in the fair. These include private enterprises, factories, scientific research institutions, wholly foreign-owned enterprises, and foreign trade companies.

The fair leans to export trade, though import business is also done here. Apart from the above-mentioned, various types of business activities such as economic and technical cooperation and exchange, commodity inspection, insurance, transportation, advertising, and trade consultation are other activities that are also commonly carried out at the fair.

Basic information about Canton Fair

First held: April 1957.

Interval: Three phases per session; two sessions per year.

Spring session: April 15-19 (Phase 1); April 23-27 (Phase 2); May 1-5 (Phase 3).

Autumn session: October 15-19 (Phase 1); October 23-27 (Phase 2); October 31-November 4 (Phase 3).

Industries:

Phase 1: Electronics & Household Electrical Appliances, Lighting Equipment, Vehicles &

Spare Parts, Machinery, Hardware & Tools, Energy & Resources, Chemical Products, Building Materials, International Pavilion

Phase 2: Consumer Goods, Gifts, Home Decorations

Phase 3: Office Supplies, Cases & Bags, Recreation Products, Medical Devices and Health Products, Food, Shoes, Textiles & Garments, International Pavilion

Venue:

China Import and Export Fair (Pazhou) Complex, 380 Yuejiangzhong Road, Haizhu District, Guangzhou 510335

Gross exhibition space: 1,185,000 m^2.

Number of booths: Over 60,400 standard stands (122nd Session).

Varieties: Over 160,000.

Business turnover: 30,160 million USD (122nd Session).

Number of trading countries and regions: 213 (122nd Session).

Number of visitors: 191,950 (122nd Session).

Exhibitors: Over 25,000 (with 24,429 Chinese exhibitors, 620 international exhibitors, 122nd Session).

Five steps to attend Canton Fair

Five Steps to Attend Canton Fair

Step 1: Get invitation (E-invitation) to China for Canton Fair 2019

You will need the Canton Fair invitation to apply the visa to China and get registered for the Canton Fair Entry Badge (IC Card). *CantonTradeFair.com* provides free E-invitations for buyers who have booked Guangzhou hotels from us. Just save your time to apply E-invitation here.

Step 2: Apply visa to China

You can use Canton Fair E-invitation to apply visa to China at your country or regular residence place before arriving in China. For more information please check China Visa Application.

Step 3: Plan your trip to the Canton Fair host city—Guangzhou, China

There is a great surge in hotel demand for the Canton Fair every year, so it's highly recommended to plan your trip before hand. You can trust on us to book a hotel for you, or plan a Guangzhou Local Tour or China Tour for a more fantastic trip.

Step 4: Register and get entry badge to the Canton Fair

If you are a new comer to the Canton Fair, you need to get registered first with your Invitation & valid documents (check details) at the Canton Fair Pazhou Overseas Buyers' Registration Center or at the Appointed Hotels.

Regular buyers since the 104th Canton Fair can go to the Fair directly with the Entry Badge.

Step 5: Enter the Canton Fair and meet with exhibitors

You can get free booklets incl. layout, exhibits, exhibitors for the Fair at the Service Counter. It's highly recommended to take your own interpreter who will stand by your side and help for better communication.

(source: http://www.cantontradefair.com/cantonfair/index.aspx)

New words and expressions

category ['kætɪg(ə)rɪ] *n.* 种类，分类
co-hosted [kəʊ ˈhəʊstɪd] *adj.* 联合主办的
representative [reprɪ'zentətɪv] *adj.* 有代表性的 *n.* 代表
institution [ɪnstɪ'tjuːʃ(ə)n] *n.* 制度，建立
enterprise ['entəpraɪz] *n.* 企业
gross [grəʊs] *adj.* 总共的 *n.* 总额
insurance [ɪn'ʃʊər(ə)ns] *n.* 保险，保险业
advertising ['ædvətaɪzɪŋ] *n.* 广告，登广告
phase [feɪz] *n.* 时期
resource [rɪ'sɔːs] *n.* 资源
recommend [rekə'mend] *vt.* 推荐，介绍
interpreter [ɪn'tɜːprɪtə] *n.* 解释者，口译者
badge [bædʒ] *n.* 证章，标记
register ['redʒɪstə] *vt.* 登记，注册
Ministry of Commerce 商业部
lean to 倾向
commodity inspection 商检进出口，商品检验
trade consultation 贸易磋商，贸易商量

Notes

1. China Import and Export Fair: 中国进出口商品交易会

2. Chinese Export Commodities Fair: 中国出口商品交易会

3. The fair is co-hosted by the Ministry of Commerce of China and the government of Guangdong Province, and organized by China Foreign Trade Centre. " co-hosted": 联合协办。整句意思：交易会由中国商业部、广东省政府联合协办，由中国对外贸易中心组织。

4. The National Pavilion (export section) of Canton Fair is sorted into 16 categories of products, which will be exhibited in 51 sections. "be sorted into"：分成……类。整句意思：广交会的国内展馆(出口区)分成16类商品，将在51个区域展出。

5. wholly foreign-owned enterprises: 外资企业

6. The fair leans to export trade, though import business is also done here. "lean to"：偏向于。整句意思：交易会偏向于出口贸易，虽然也有进口贸易。

7. gross exhibition space: 展馆总面积

8. There is a great surge in hotel demand for the Canton Fair every year. "surge"：激增。整句意思：每年广交会期间酒店的需求量激增。

9. You can get free booklets incl. layout, exhibits, exhibitors for the Fair at the Service Counter. "incl."=including: 包括。整句意思：你可以在服务中心领取免费的宣传手册，包括展会布局、展品、参展商等信息。

10. It's highly recommended… 我们大力推荐……

Exercises

1. Answer the following questions according to the passage.

(1) What has been the full name of Canton Fair since 2007?

(2) Which season is Canton Fair held in?

(3) How many phases is Canton Fair held every season now?

(4) When was the first Canton Fair held?

(5) How to apply for a visa according to the passage?

(6) What business does Canton Fair lean to?
_____

(7) How can we get access to Canton Fair?
_____

(8) If you can not communicate freely in Canton Fair, what can you do?
_____

2. Fill in the blanks with the words or phrases given below in the box.

| category | gross | lean to | insurance | interpreter |
| badge | register | recommend | resource | advertising |

(1) On the outside, they are one of the leaders of search and _____ on the Internet.
(2) I should wholeheartedly _____ him.
(3) Most users fall into this _____.
(4) The young politician is beginning to _____ the opinions of the workers.
(5) That is quite low relative to the _____ flows in and out of unemployment.
(6) He works in an _____ company.
(7) Please queue up to _____.
(8) In short, the old _____ with the same While Alfa Romeo sports car has been known as one of today's well-known trademarks.
(9) It depends on how you utilise your _____.
(10) Have a gift for languages, he wants to become an _____.

3. Translate the following expressions into English or Chinese.
(1) Ministry of Commerce of China _____
(2) China Foreign Trade Centre _____
(3) categories _____
(4) scientific research institutions _____
(5) International Pavilion _____
(6) Electronics & Household Electrical _____
(7) Appliances _____
(8) Vehicles & Spare Parts _____
(9) E-invitation _____
(10) 医疗设备和健康产品 _____
(11) 纺织品服装 _____

旅游英语

(12) 入场券 _____

(13) 中国进出口商品交易会 _____

(14) 机器 _____

(15) 硬件和工具 _____

(16) 能源资源 _____

(17) 建筑材料 _____

4. Translate the following sentences into English with the words or phrases given in the brackets.

(1) 尽管如此，我仍然将宗教看作一种习俗来迷恋。(institution)
   _____

(2) 这次亚运会将由广州和三个临近城市东莞、佛山以及汕尾共同举办。(co-hosted)
   _____

(3) 他们选举汤姆作为他们的代表。(representative)
   _____

(4) 这家企业的愿景极其美好。(enterprise)
   _____

(5) 近几年，他们更倾向于出口高度专业化的产品。(lean to)
   _____

(6) 咱们有最好的公证行，即中国进出口商品检验局。(commodity inspection)
   _____

Passage B　Travel Services for MICE

It is with great pleasure that we invite you to a magical land called India with the most historic sights, beaches, backwaters, mountains, deserts and state of the art conferencing facilities. With such a vast array of options, India is fast developing into one of the most sought after conference destinations in the world.

And to this further, Cox & Kings is constantly introducing innovative events and suggestions to make every conference and event a memorable one.

Cox & Kings was the first to develop a world-class cell for international conferences and conventions in India. Backed by over a decade of award winning performance and a team of industry experts who can efficiently fuse modern amenities with local, this division is powered by a high-end platform of Information Technology that offers super-fast error free processing.

Cox & Kings caters for all aspects of conference organizing, business meetings, event management, seminars, exhibitions, product launches and incentives. Every event is fashioned to suit the specific requirements of our clients and every detail is handled with care, right from the pre-event preparations, during the event itself and through to post event settlements. Extensive planning and considerable research ensure the most comprehensive & memorable conference for all our clients.

Cox & Kings unveils a refreshingly different travel experience, not only across India but also across Nepal and Sri Lanka. India is fast emerging as one of the favoured destinations for meetings and conferences. It has a selection of world-class hotels and palace resorts with the latest state-of-art facilities. Efficiently connected to the globe via air and road, high speed broadband Internet and support facilities like video conferencing, hi-tech projectors, language interpretation capacities, India makes for a very comfortable meeting space. To add to the efficiency are professional destination management services, strong infrastructure to conduct training, spacious venues offering a range of seating arrangements and a gamut of leisure activities.

Cox & Kings has also introduced the concept which is exclusive. These are small touches, which go a long way in giving a taste of the essence of India. These include theme dinners, theme nights and royal dinners.

India and Cox & Kings look forward to taking you through one of the most incredible conferencing experiences available!

(source: https://www.coxandkings.com/mice/mice.shtml)

New words and expressions

backwater ['bækwɔ:tə] *n.* 死水，停滞不前的状态或地方
array [əˈreɪ] *n.* 排列，一系列
innovative ['ɪnəvətɪv] *adj.* 创新的，有创新精神的
memorable ['mem(ə)rəb(ə)l] *adj.* 难忘的，值得纪念的
fuse [fju:z] *vi.* 融合 *vt.* 使融合
efficiency [ɪˈfɪʃ(ə)nsɪ] *n.* 效率，功效
spacious ['speɪʃəs] *adj.* 宽敞的，广阔的
gamut ['gæmət] *n.* 全音域，整个范围
exclusive [ɪkˈsklu:sɪv] *adj.* 专有的，独有的
incredible [ɪnˈkredɪb(ə)l] *adj.* 难以置信的，惊人的
state of the art 最先进的
most sought after 最炙手可热的
error free 无差错，无误差

cater for 迎合，为……提供所需
suit the specific requirement 符合具体要求
make for 有助于，走向

Notes

1. It is with great pleasure that: 非常高兴……

2. And to this further: 更进一步地说，而且……

3. make every conference and event a memorable one: 把每一个会议和活动变成难忘的回忆。"one"是代词，指代前面的"conference and event"。

4. Cox & Kings was the first to develop a world-class cell for international conferences and conventions in India. "cell"是细胞、单元的意思，所以这句话应该译为：Cox & Kings 公司是印度第一家发展世界级国际会议业务的公司。

5. product launch: 产品发布会

6. a gamut of leisure activities: 全方位的休闲活动

7. is fashioned to suit the specific requirements of our client: "be fashioned to…"被塑成……

8. one of the most incredible conferencing experiences available: 现存的最难以置信的、美好的会议体验之一。

Exercises

1. Reading Comprehension: Choose the best answer for each of the following questions.

(1) This passage introduced _____ as one of the most sought after conference destinations in the world.

 A. China   B. India   C. Cuba

(2) Cox & Kings is good at efficiently fusing modern _____ with local ones.

 A. amenities   B. facilities   C. equipment

(3) Extensive _____ and considerable research ensure the most comprehensive and memorable conference for all our clients.

 A. surveying   B. marketing   C. planning

(4) Cox & Kings does not only provide travel services across India, but also across Nepal and _____.

 A. Maldives   B. Cambodia   C. Sri Lanka

(5) You can enjoy _____ services with Cox & Kings.

 A. conference   B. driving   C. wedding

Unit 10　Canton Fair

(6) Cox & Kings can provide you _____ hotels and palace resorts with the latest state-of-art facilities.

　　A. first-class　　　　　B. world-class　　　　C. super-class

(7) Cox & Kings can help you to efficiently get connected to the globe via air and road, high speed _____ Internet and support facilities.

　　A. broadband　　　　　B. projectors　　　　　C. highways

(8) This passage is a(an) _____ of Cox & Kings.

　　A. argumentation　　　B. introduction　　　　C. prose

2. Fill in the blanks with the words or phrases given below in the box.

| most sought after | spacious | destination | array |
| memorable | gamut | incredible | innovative |

(1) Happiness is the _____ human emotion.

(2) Start with an _____ to hold the character information.

(3) This includes decisions about where to go, where to stay and what to do while at a _____.

(4) Daniel is reading in the _____ and bright classroom.

(5) Car manufacturers have no choice but to get _____.

(6) One of the most _____ tragedies in history, the sinking of the Titanic in 1912 shocked the world.

(7) I hope you'll take the challenge and find _____ joy in the process.

(8) In short, our relationships in Asia certainly run the full _____ of global challenges.

3. Translate the following expressions into English or Chinese.

(1) historic sights _____

(2) international conferences and convention _____

(3) high-end platform _____

(4) theme nights _____

(5) pre-event preparations _____

(6) 最炙手可热的 _____

(7) 最佳的会议体验 _____

(8) 电视会议 _____

(9) 广阔的场地 _____

(10) 整个范围 _____

173

4. Translate the following sentences into Chinese.

(1) With such a vast array of options, India is fast developing into one of the most sought after conference destinations in the world.

_____

(2) Backed by over a decade of award winning performance and a team of industry experts who can efficiently fuse modern amenities with local, this division is powered by a high-end platform of Information Technology that offers super-fast error free processing.

_____

(3) Cox & Kings unveils a refreshingly different travel experience, not only across India but also across Nepal and Sri Lanka.

_____

(4) To add to the efficiency are professional destination management services, strong infrastructure to conduct trainings, spacious venues offering a range of seating arrangements and a gamut of leisure activities.

_____

(5) These are small touches, which go a long way in giving a taste of the essence of India. These include theme dinners, theme nights and royal dinners.

_____

5. Translate the following paragraph into English.

2010年世界博览会(World Expo 2010)于5月1日至10月31日在中国上海举行。世博会吸引了190个国家和56个国际组织参展。超过7,300万中外游客参观了世博园，参观人数是历届世博会中最多的一次。这届世博会的主题是"城市，让生活更美好"(Better City, Better Life)，体现了人类对更适宜居住环境、更美好生活的愿望。在世博园里所有的展馆(pavilion)中，中国展馆是最受欢迎的场馆之一。

6. Activity

Group work: If you are going to organize a conference on tourism recently, please discuss with your group mates and fill in the form below briefly. Then each group makes a presentation about the conference for about 5 minutes.

Theme	
Time	
Place(country, city and venue)	
Speakers(names and titles)	
Participants	
How to prepare for the conference	1.
	2.
	3.
	4.
	5.
	…

Writing: Tour Contract 旅游合同

1. Writing Skills

  旅游合同是保护旅游者与旅游经营者合法权益的法律文书，也是旅游质量监督管理部门受理旅游投诉、处理旅游纠纷、划分赔偿责任的重要依据。《旅行社管理条例》规定，旅行社组织旅游者旅游应当在出游之前与旅游者签订书面合同。内容要求：关于吃、住、行、游、购、娱；增加、减少、取消等合作方面的内容要面面俱到、周详；权益条款方面，要本着"共赢"的出发点，既要站在己方的利益立场，也要顾及对方的利益。

  旅游合同要求格式正确，用词准确、严谨，使用正规词、法律用语、行业术语等。旅游合同内容要素，即主要条款如下：

  (1) 标的：即合同当事人权利和义务共同指向的对象——旅游服务；互相交换旅游团或

互派代表团。

(2) 数量和质量。

(3) 价款或者报酬。

(4) 合同的期限、履行时间、地点和方式。

(5) 合同的双方权益条款。

(6) 违约责任。

(7) 解决争议的方法。

(8) 其他。

除合同主要条款以外，双方当事人应根据实际情况约定其他有关双方权利和义务的条款。在签订旅游合同时要注意以下事项。

(1) 明确服务质量标准。

现有的国内旅游组团合同通常包括旅游行程、旅游价格、双方义务和违约责任等基本内容。但旅行社提供的交通、餐饮、住宿服务，因标准不同而各有差异。因此，旅游者在选择适合自己的旅游行程时，应在合同中对所要求的服务项目及标准给予明确约定以保证质价相符。

(2) 重视旅游行程表。

旅游行程表是旅游合同的重要构件，具有同等法律效应，因此游客在签约后务必将合同与行程表一并保管好。旅游行程表应包括往返的具体时间、乘坐的交通工具、每日的具体行程、游览景点、住宿标准、用餐次数及标准、娱乐安排、购物安排、是否提供全程导游服务等项目。旅游者确认行程无误之后，应要求旅行社在行程表上盖章确认。

(3) 解除合同关系须慎重。

合同一旦签订，就具有法律效应，双方当事人既享有权利也要承担义务，如果没有有效合理的原因和对方书面同意，不可随意解除合同关系。在国内旅游组团合同中的违约责任条款明确规定，游客在旅游合同签订后，如单方面解除合同，必将承担违约造成的损失，同时，还将赔偿相应额度的违约金。

2. Useful Expressions and Sentences

(1) hereby: by means of ; by reason of this 特此，因此，兹

This contract is hereby made and concluded by and between XXXCo. (hereinafter referred to as Party A) and XXXCo. (hereinafter referred to as Party B) on XXX (date), in XXX (Place), China, on the principle of equality and mutual benefit and through amicable consultation.

本合同双方，XXX 公司 (以下称甲方) 与 XXX 公司(以下称乙方) 于 XXX (日期)在中国 XXX (地点)，本着平等互利和友好协商的原则特签订本合同。

(2) This contract will be effective, once signed by both parties, and valid until _____. After expiration, the validity of the contract can be extended under a written agreement confirmed by

both parties.

一经双方签署，此合同立即生效。其有效期至_____。期满后，合同的契约效力在经双方书面确认同意下可继续(延期)生效。

(3) This contract is written in Chinese and English versions. Both versions have the same authenticity. Whenever difference in explanation arises between the two versions, the Chinese version will be deemed to be the criterion of judgement.

本合同分为中文版本和英文版本。两个版本均具同样真实性。任何时候两个版本间出现不同解释，将以中文版本为判决的准则。

(4) Both parties should try to resolve their disputes, if any, in the execution of the contract through friendly consultation. If no solution could be found through consultation, both parties agree to submit their disputes to the Ministry of Culture and Tourism of the People's Republic of China for coordinated settlement in accordance with the Law of China.

如果在执行合同过程中出现争端，双方应当本着友好协商的方式进行解决。如果通过协商无法进行解决，双方应当根据中国法律，向中国文化和旅游部递交争端内容，寻求协调解决。

(5) The conclusion, alteration and abrogation of this contract or retrieval of breach of contract should be in line with the regulations specified in the "People's Republic of China Law Concerning Economic Contract with Foreign Countries". Without mutual consent, either party cannot transfer to a third party its right and commitments, as described in this contract.

本合同的订立、变更和废除或违约的追究应符合"中华人民共和国对外经济合同法"中的规定。根据本合同，未经双方同意，任何一方均不得把权利和承诺转让给第三方。

3. Sample Writing

The following is the sample "Contract and Appendix" for reference.

Sample Contract on Tours Arranged by Chinese and Foreign Travel Services (or Tourist Corporation)

中外旅行社(旅游公司)组团业务合同范本

This contract is hereby made and concluded by and between _____ China International Travel Service (hereinafter referred to as Party A) and _____ Co. (hereinafter referred to as Party B) on ×××(date), in ×××(Place), China, on the principle of equality and mutual benefit and through amicable consultation.

The contract and the appendix to the contract constitute an inseparable integrity. Both the transcript of the contract and the articles in the appendix to the contract hold the same authenticity.

Article 1

Party B plans _____ to organize _____ tours (or delegations) with tourists to visit China from _____ to _____.

Article 2

Party B is required to confirm to Party A the final booking on a tour (or a delegation), when accepted by Party A, 30 days prior to the scheduled arrival of the said tour (or delegation) at the port of entry in China.

Party A should acknowledge confirmation to Party B within three working days after receipt of confirmation from Party B.

Party B is required to send Party A, at least 20 days prior to the scheduled arrival of each tour (or delegation) at the point of entry in China, a detailed list with each participant's full name, sex, date of birth, occupation, nationality, passport number, arrival/departure flight or train number, points and dates of entry and exit, number of rooms required and requests on visits.

Article 3

Party B is free to propose at any time to Party A additional tours (or delegations) other than those planned. Upon receipt of a mail/fax/e-mail proposal from Party B, Party A is required to reply within three working days. Upon receipt of a reply from Party A, Party B is required to acknowledge confirmation to Party A also within three working days, with necessary information as required by Article 2.

Article 4

Party B agrees to make telegraphic remittance of total expenses for each tour (or delegation) to Party A bank account at least 15 days prior to the scheduled arrival in China of each tour (or delegation). If more than one remittance is made simultaneously, it is necessary for Party B to specify the exact amount for each tour (or delegation) on the remittance memo. Tour expenses are not to be settled in Chinese currency Renminbi.

Article 5

If Party B fails to make the remittance before the deadline as stipulated by Article 4, Party A has the right to take any of the three following options to deal with the overdue payment.

(1) Party A will not host the tour (or delegation) any longer, no matter whether the tour (or delegation) has entered into China or not. Party B will bear all responsibilities arising there from.

(2) Party A will report the case to the travel administration of the Chinese government and propose to all other travel services in China declining hospitality to the unpaid tour (or delegation) sent by Party B.

(3) Party A will charge Party B an overdue fine for any unpaid amount. After the conclusion of each tour (or delegation) in China, Party B is required to clear off any outstanding amount

within one month, otherwise an overdue fine is to be charged additionally in the following month, at a rate of 0.2% of the outstanding amount per day.

Article 6

Party A is committed to offer services according to the itineraries and package services confirmed by this contract and the appendix to the contract.

Party A has the obligation *to* instruct all its liaison or sales personnel, tour guides, drivers and other staff to render standard-oriented services to tourists. They are strictly forbidden to extort tipping from tourists.

Article 7

Except in situations beyond human control, Party A should provide compensatory service for tourists or refund to Party B the difference in payment for service rendered below standard.

Except in situations beyond human control, Party A will be held responsible for additional expenses resulting from the change, caused by Party A in itinerary, transportation vehicles, accommodation and meals.

However, Party A will not be held responsible for compensation resulting from change of itinerary under the following situations.

(1) The scheduled date of entry of a tour (or delegation) is changed off hand by Party B. Consequently Party B will be liable for compensation and complaints lodged by clients, resulting from change of accommodation, transportation and sightseeing programme. Party B is also liable for economic loss, if any, incurred to Party A.

(2) The itinerary is changed at the request of tour (or delegation) participants after arrival in China. Subsequent economic loss, if any, will be borne by tour (or delegation) participants rather than Party A.

(3) The tour schedule is changed by air/railway or steamship departments due to mechanical failure or bad weather.

(4)The tour schedule, itinerary and length of stay in China are changed due to unforeseen situation beyond human control. Any difference or balance in payment will be collected or reimbursed accordingly.

(5) Party A will not be held responsible for any harm sustained by tourists during their visit in China by airplane or train or steamship or during their stay in hotel, restaurant or tourist area. However, Party A is obligated to help Party B to retrieve the harm in humanitarian spirit.

Article 8

Party B reserves the right to lodge complaint to the travel administration of the Chinese government and moreover to request compensation for material loss, as a result of violation by

Party A of provisions for quality service.

Article 9

Party A should notify Party B, three months in advance of the scheduled arrival of a tour (or a delegation) in China, the adjustment, if needed under unusual circumstance, in the package rates after confirmed by both parties. Party A will charge the tour (or the delegation) based on original quotation within three months after the date of notification.

Article 10

It is necessary for Party A to make Party B acquainted with the policy and regulations of the Chinese government concerning tourist activities in China.

Party B is required to ask tourists to abide by policy and regulations. Tourists offend the Chinese policy and regulations, which will be dealt with by law in China, will not hold Party A responsible for any violation.

Article 11

Party A will quote a package rate for a tour (or a delegation) scheduled to China in accordance with Chinese pricing policy and regulation. After Party B confirms the quotation, both parties will sign an appendix to the contract. There is (are) _____ appendix (appendices) attached to this contract.

Article 12

Party A is committed to making overall arrangements at various cities in China for tours (delegations) sponsored by Party B, Party A cannot entrust any other party to become involved in separate arrangements for tours (delegations) at any city in China.

Party A can entrust, if necessary, a certified land operator in China to take care of travel arrangements. As an immediate agent for Party B, Party A will bear direct responsibility for tourist activities in China.

Article 13

To guarantee security for traveling in China, Party A will arrange for tourists' travel-accident-insurance, which will be covered in tour package rates, either party is liable for violation, if any, against regulations stipulated by the Chinese government concerning insurance coverage for overseas tourists during travel in China.

Article 14

The conclusion, alteration and abrogation of this contract or retrieval of breach of contract should be in line with the regulations specified in the "People's Republic of China Law Concerning Economic Contract with Foreign Countries". Without mutual consent, either party cannot transfer to a third party its right and commitments, as described in this contract.

Article15

Both parties should try to resolve their disputes, if any, in the execution of the contract through friendly consultation. If no solution could be found through consultation, both parties agree to submit their disputes to China National Tourism Administration for coordinated settlement in accordance with the Law of China.

Article16

This contract will be effective, once signed by both parties, and valid until _____. After expiration, the validity of the contract can be extended under a written agreement confirmed by both parties.

Article17

This contract is written in Chinese and English versions. Both versions have the same authenticity. Whenever difference in explanation arises between the two versions, the Chinese version will be deemed the criterion of judgement.

Article18

After both parties have signed this contract, Party A should submit a duplicate copy of the contract to its superior tourism authorities for record.

Name/Signature   Name/ Signature
Of Party A's Representative   Of Party B's Representative
Date/Place of Signing   Date/Place of Signing

Note: In terms of content, the above-mentioned model contract advances with the times.

4. Exercises: Translate the following sentences into Chinese.

(1) All disputes arising from the execution of or in connection with the contract shall be settled through friendly consultation between both parties. In case no settlement can be reached, the dispute shall be submitted for arbitration.

_____

_____

(2) Should any other clause in this contract be in conflict with the following supplementary conditions, the supplementary conditions should be taken as final and binding.

_____

(3) China International Travel Service (hereinafter referred to as A) and the Ocean Hotel (hereinafter referred to as B) desirous to strengthen the friendly relations between the two parties on the basis of equality and for their mutual benefit, have agreed to conclude this agreement as follows.

_____

_____

(4) We are entitled to cancel the contract which became overdue owing to buyer's no-performance.

___

(5) The present contract is made out in Chinese and English both versions being equally valid.

___

Supplementary Reading

History of Cox & Kings
Founded in 1758
250th Year Countdown Celebration

Cox & Kings holds pride of place as the world's longest established travel company. Our journey began when Cox & Kings was appointed as general agents to the regiment of Foot Guards in India. Today, more than 249 years later, Cox & Kings is the "Destination Management Company" of choice in India, a one-stop travel solutions provider. Cox & Kings offers a comprehensive range of conference arrangements in the subcontinent, pertaining to every aspect of travel, anywhere around the globe and to suit every budget.

At Your Service

Cox & Kings are truly the subcontinent experts, organizing travel to India since 1758. Our two hundred and forty-nine years of grand history gives us an unrivalled experience at organizing travels throughout the subcontinent.

One-stop Shop

Cox & Kings presents the answer to all your needs under one roof, right from Business and Corporate Travel to Destination Management for groups and individuals and Incentive holidays, from Charters and Cruises handling to Outbound and Domestic Tourism. We also have our in-house foreign exchange division and a specialised cell for Conferences, Conventions and Exhibitions & Trade Fairs.

Cox & Kings promises an enriching journey, familiarizing the traveller with a wide diversity of exotic leisure options. Meticulous planning, emphasis on safety, efficient staff and state-of-the-art equipment form the foundation of each of our programmes.

Network

Cox & Kings has a network of 14 offices and 44 associate offices offering round the clock quality service. We have a strong web of international and domestic marketing arms for effective and successful worldwide congress promotion.

Cox & Kings, India has over 25 associated offices connecting the length and breadth of India.

Cox & Kings International Offices and Representatives

Cox & Kings has international offices and representatives in UK, USA, Japan, Germany, Spain, South Africa, Russia, Italy, Sweden and Australia. Cox & Kings worldwide business associate is Radius, with a network of over 4,640 branches around the world.

Worldwide Business Associates

RADIUS, with a network of over 4,640 branches around the world. A global service that has set benchmarking standards in the corporate travel community.

Memberships that guarantee excellence

Cox & Kings is amongst the members of some of the highest standards of excellence like TAAI, IATA, PATA, ASTA, IATO, ICCA and ICPB Charter, which guarantee the quality of services Cox & Kings offers.

Hall of Fame

Cox & Kings is undoubtedly the best destination manager in the country. It has won seven National Awards for being the "Best Conference Agent", of the country of which seven were in a consecutive row. This prestigious award has been constituted by the Government of India, Department of Tourism to honour the best company in the field of conferences and incentives. Enjoy the Best of India & Beyond!

(source:https://www.coxandkings.com/mice/history.shtml)

Useful words and phrases

countdown ['kaʊntdaʊn] *n.* 倒数
subcontinent [ˌsʌbˈkɒntɪnənt] *n.* 次大陆
unrivalled [ʌnˈraɪv(ə)ld] *adj.* 无与伦比的，无敌的
cell [sel] *n.* 细胞，电池
benchmarking [ˈbentʃˌmɑːkɪŋ] *n.* 标杆管理，标记
guarantee [gær(ə)nˈtiː] *n.* 保证 *vt.* 保证，担保
prestigious [preˈstɪdʒəs] *adj.* 有名望的，享有声望的
one-stop travel solutions provider　一站式旅游解决方案提供商
round the clock　昼夜不停，不知疲倦地
standards of excellence　卓越的标准

Read the passage and decide whether the following statements are true (T) or false(F).

1. _____ Cox & Kings was held in 1758.

2. _____ Cox & Kings does not provide foreign exchange services in the company.

3. _____ Cox & Kings, India has over 25 associated offices connecting the length and breadth of India.

4. _____ Cox & Kings is not a member of some of PATA.

5. _____ Cox & Kings has international offices and representatives in China.

Module Five
Traditional Chinese Culture

Unit 11　Traditional Chinese Culture and Festivals

Learning Objectives

After learning this unit, you should:
- Understand how to introduce traditional Chinese culture and festivals.
- Master the key words and expressions for traditional Chinese culture and festivals.
- Get some cultural knowledge about Chinese values and belief.
- Find ways to improve your writing skills about farewell speech.

Key words

traditional Chinese culture, festivals, material and spiritual culture

Information search

Please search some information about the topic of this unit by scanning the QR codes: ▦ (Travel Column of *China Daily*), ▦ (China Plus), ▦ (World Tourism Organization), ▦ (Travelogue of CCTV), ▦ (Ministry of Culture and Tourism of the People's Republic of China). After reading the information, please share with your classmates some information about the topic of this unit.

Warm-up

Task 1: Watch a short video about China, and discuss the following questions in groups.
1. Can you say something about Chinese culture?
2. What do you think are the elements that consist of traditional Chinese culture?

Task 2: Watch the video again, and match the words and phrases in column A with those in column B.

Column A	Column B
1. silk road	A. 莫高窟
2. pottery and ceramic	B. 刺绣
3. Mogao Grottoes	C. 奇迹
4. wonder	D. 陶瓷
5. Terra Cotta Warriors	E. 兵马俑
6. embroidery	F. 丝绸之路

Passage A   A Glimpse of Traditional Chinese Culture

China is an extremely large country—first in population and third in area. There are 56 ethnic groups in China, among which the Han ethnic group is the largest one, constituting approximately 92% of the population of China. Each group is unique with their own customs and dialects of Chinese. China is also an ancient civilization aged more than 5,000 years old. The Chinese culture features an abundance of the material and spiritual values, unchanged over millennia. Chinese culture includes customs and traditions, language, music, dances, painting, arts and crafts, literature, cuisine, clothing, architecture and so on.

The 56 ethnic groups of China getting together

Values & Philosophy

The traditional cultural values that influence the Chinese people are mostly derived from Confucianism and Taoism. Confucianism, the most influential school of thought in China's history, was founded by Confucius (551–479 BC), a great philosopher and educator of the Spring and Autumn period. The core value of Confucianism is Ren (仁，benevolence) and Li (礼，ritual and etiquette).

Benevolence extends from the importance of familial ties and blood connections and is held in high esteem by the Chinese. "A peaceful family will prosper (家和万事兴)." is a famous and widely accepted saying. This benevolence, although based in familial ties, extends to friendships and social relationships, producing a full set of values that include justice, courtesy, wisdom, honesty, loyalty, self-discipline, and commitment.

Chinese people cherish etiquette. They believe that showing respect to heaven, the earth and people is important. In social life, etiquette means that people get along with each other harmoniously and respect the elderly.

Another significant value is harmony. The philosophic concept of harmony is expressed in both the Confucianism and the Taoism. The Taijitu, or Yin-Yang symbol, offers a visual representation of this concept. It depicts two opposing forces, each of which includes elements of the other and may transform into its opposite under certain conditions. The balanced interaction of these opposing forces creates a unified and harmonious whole. Confucius said, "The gentleman aims at harmony, and not at uniformity." Thus, a gentleman may hold different views, but he does not blindly follow others. Instead, he seeks to coexist harmoniously with them. According to the concept of harmony, the universe unites diversity. Modern Chinese society tries to maintain harmony between humankind and nature, people and society, mind and body and among members of different communities.

The portrait of Confucius   The symbol of Taiji in Taosim

Traditional Chinese Medicine

In the 2016 Rio Olympics, some reddish-purple, round bruises are displayed on the bodies of some athletes. The western people couldn't help wondering what those bruises are. In fact, they are caused by the traditional Chinese medicine therapy of cupping(拔罐). Traditional Chinese Medicine had long been mysterious to people from western countries. But nowadays, it has been accepted and become more and more popular with many western countries.

旅游英语

Olympic gold medalist Michael Phelps practices cupping, an ancient Chinese therapy

Traditional Chinese Medicine (TCM) is an ancient system of health and wellness that has been used in China for thousands of years. The practice of TCM includes various forms of herbal medicine, acupuncture and moxibustion, massage (Tuina), cupping, Qi exercise (Qigong), and dietary therapy. Different from western medicine, which focuses on treating disease, TCM looks at your entire well-being. Western medicine tends to view the body a lot like a car. It has different systems that need the right inputs and outputs. It's very concrete and logical. TCM, on the other hand, is based on balance, harmony, and energy. There are two central ideas that form the basis for TCM.

- Qi: In Chinese it means "vital force or life energy". It is invisible, running throughout the human body in the meridians, but is reflected in the functions of body organs or tissues. Any break in the flow is an indication of imbalance of the body functions, which may lead to diseases. Then TCM treatments often focus on ways to promote and maintain the flow of qi.
- Yin-yang: The Taoist philosophy Yin-yang describes the idea that everything in nature consists of two opposite phases or energies, for example, day and night, sun and moon, male and female, movement and tranquility, etc. Yin and yang are constantly changing. If one becomes unbalanced in the body, illness occurs. For example, since yin is cold, an excess of yin can cause illnesses such as insomnia and dry-mouth. Conversely, a yang deficiency can cause cold limbs. Good health then, is maintained by balancing yin and yang.

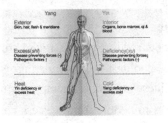

How yin and yang are manifested within the body

Unit 11 Traditional Chinese Culture and Festivals

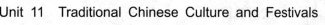

The traditional Chinese culture, both extensive and profound, starts far back and runs a long, long course. It is too difficult to put it in a short article. Still, you can learn it and experience it while touring the vast land of China.

New words and expressions

constitute ['kɒnstɪtjuːt] *vt.* 组成，构成
approximately [ə'prɒksɪmətlɪ] *adv.* 大约，近似地
dialect ['daɪəlekt] *n.* 方言
philosophy [fɪ'lɒsəfɪ] *n.* 哲学，哲理
influential [ˌɪnfluˈenʃl] *adj.* 有影响力的
benevolence [bɪ'nevələns] *n.* 仁慈，善行
ritual ['rɪtʃʊəl] *n.* 宗教仪式，典礼 *adj.* 仪式性的，传统的
etiquette ['etɪket] *n.* 礼节，礼仪
prosper ['prɒspə] *vi.* 繁荣，昌盛
courtesy ['kɜːtɪsɪ] *n.* 有礼的举止，礼貌
commitment [kə'mɪtm(ə)nt] *n.* 承诺
cherish ['tʃerɪʃ] *vt.* 重视，珍视
harmony ['hɑːmənɪ] *n.* 协调，和睦，融洽
visual ['vɪʒjʊəl] *adj.* 视觉的，视力的
depict [dɪ'pɪkt] *vt.* 描述，描绘
diversity [daɪ'vɜːsɪtɪ] *n.* (人或事物的)多样性，多元化
therapy ['θerəpɪ] *n.* 治疗，疗法
mysterious [mɪ'stɪərɪəs] *adj.* 神秘的，不可思议的
concrete ['kɒnkriːt] *adj.* 实在的，具体的
logical ['lɒdʒɪk(ə)l] *adj.* 合乎逻辑的，合理的
invisible [ɪn'vɪzɪb(ə)l] *adj.* 无形的，看不见的
meridian [mə'rɪdɪən] *n.* 经线(此处指中医里的人体"经络")
phase [feɪz] *n.* 阶段，时期
excess [ɪk'ses] *n.* 过多，过量 (an excess of)
deficiency [dɪ'fɪʃ(ə)nsɪ] *n.* 不足，缺乏
ethnic groups 民族
ancient civilization 古老的文明
an abundance of 大量的，丰富的
material and spiritual values 物质和精神财富

over millennia 数千年来
arts and crafts 艺术和手工艺
derive from 来自，从……中得到，衍生于
extend from… 从……延伸/扩展而来
self-discipline 自我约束，自律
seek to 追求，争取
coexist with 共存，共处
reddish-purple, round bruises 紫红色、圆形的瘀伤(指拔罐后留下的印迹)
couldn't help wondering 不免(会觉得)奇怪
herbal medicine 草药
dietary therapy 食疗
consist of 由……构成，包括

Notes

1. Confucianism: 儒家思想，又称儒学、孔孟思想，是先秦诸子百家学说之一，由孔子创立，经孟子等人的发展逐渐形成完整的儒家思想体系，成为中国传统文化的主流，影响深远。孔子思想以"仁"为核心，孔子认为"仁"即"爱人"，提出"己所不欲，勿施于人""己欲立而立人，己欲达而达人"等论点，并认为推行"仁政"应该以"礼"为规范，即"克己复礼为仁"。

2. Taoism: 既可以指春秋战国时期以老子、庄子为代表的道家学说，也可以指中国本土宗教——道教。道家学说以"道"为最高哲学范畴，认为"道"是宇宙万物的本源，提倡"道法自然""无为而治"，与自然和谐相处。而道教是在中国古代鬼神崇拜观念上，以道家思想为理论根据，承袭战国以来的神仙方术衍化形成的一种民间宗教，主要宗旨是追求长生不死、得道成仙。

3. Spring and Autumn period: 春秋战国时期，即公元前 770 年至公元前 221 年，是中国历史上的一段大分裂时期，也是百家争鸣、人才辈出、思想活跃的时代。

4. Taijitu and Yin-Yang: 阴阳，为源于古代中国哲学思想的一种二元论观念。古代中国把事物中对立又联合的现象，如天地、日月、昼夜、寒暑、牝牡、上下、左右、动静、刚柔、刑德等，用"阴阳"的概念来加以表述，其彰显出"相互对立又依存"的抽象关系。大约在北宋年间，出现了道教的太极图。太极图以一条曲线将圆形分为两半，形成一半白一半黑，白者像阳，黑者像阴，白中又有一个黑点，黑中又有一个白点，表示阳中有阴，阴中有阳。分开的两半，酷似两条鱼，所以俗称阴阳鱼。(摘自维基百科：https://zh.wikipedia.org/wiki/阴阳#太極圖)

5. It depicts two opposing forces, each of which includes elements of the other and may

Unit 11 Traditional Chinese Culture and Festivals

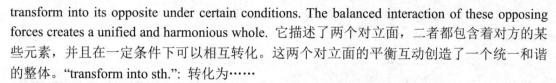

transform into its opposite under certain conditions. The balanced interaction of these opposing forces creates a unified and harmonious whole. 它描述了两个对立面，二者都包含着对方的某些元素，并且在一定条件下可以相互转化。这两个对立面的平衡互动创造了一个统一和谐的整体。"transform into sth.": 转化为……

6. Traditional Chinese Medicine (TCM): 中医，一般指以中国汉族劳动人民创造的传统医学为主的医学，所以也称汉医。中医学以阴阳五行作为理论基础，将人体看成是气、形、神的统一体，通过"望闻问切"四诊合参的方法，探求病因、病性、病位，分析病机及人体内五脏六腑、经络关节、气血津液的变化、判断邪正消长，进而得出病名，归纳出证型，使用中药、针灸、推拿、按摩、拔罐、气功、食疗等多种治疗手段，使人体达到阴阳调和而康复。(摘自百度百科：https://baike.baidu.com/item/中医)

7. Qi: 气，中医认为，气是构成人体和维护人体生命活动的最基本物质，在生理上具有推动、温煦、防御、固摄、气化等功能。气聚合在一起便形成了有机体，气散则形体灭亡。

8. For example, since yin is cold, an excess of yin can cause illnesses such as insomnia and dry-mouth. Conversely, a yang deficiency can cause cold limbs. 例如，阴为寒，阴盛就会导致失眠、口干等病症。反之，阳虚则会导致手足不温。

Exercises

1. Answer the following questions according to the passage.

(1) Why is it that people always say "Chinese culture is rich and profound"?

_____

(2) Who is Confucius? Please give a brief introduction.

_____

(3) What are the core values of Confucianism?

_____

(4) What should people do in pursuit of the philosophic concept of He (harmony)?

_____

(5) Could you please explain the Taoist philosophy of Yin-yang?

_____

(6) What is the difference between Traditional Chinese Medicine and western medicine?

_____

(7) What kinds of therapies are there in TCM?

_____

(8) Have you ever tried any of the therapies in TCM? Share your experience with your classmates.

_____

2. Fill in the blanks with the appropriate form of the words or phrases given below in the box.

| commitment | constitute | derive | mysterious | influence |
| cherish | harmony | depict | coexist | diversity |

(1) He is regarded as one of the most _____ film directors of his generation.

(2) I _____ the memories of the time we spent together.

(3) Your suggestions are not in _____ with the aims of this project.

(4) Many people support the idea that traditional Christian beliefs can _____ with science and evolution.

(5) China is a large country, boasting great geographical _____.

(6) China's ethnic minorities _____ less than 7 percent of its total population.

(7) Marriage is no longer always seen as a lifetime _____.

(8) The god is _____ as a bird with a human head.

(9) Medically, we will _____ great benefit from this technique.

(10) The police are investigating the _____ deaths of old people at the hospital.

3. Translate the following expressions into English or Chinese.

(1) the most influential school of thought in China's history _____

(2) get along with each other harmoniously _____

(3) blindly follow others _____

(4) a dialogue about concrete issues _____

(5) a new drug that is in the experimental phase _____

(6) a deficiency of safety facilities _____

(7) to maintain health by balancing yin and yang _____

(8) imbalance of the body functions _____

(9) 伟大的思想家和教育家 _____

(10) 家和万事兴 _____

(11) 春秋战国时期 _____

(12) 人与自然和谐相处 _____

(13) 传统中医疗法 _____

(14) 合理的结论＿＿＿＿＿＿＿＿＿＿＿＿＿＿＿＿＿＿＿＿＿＿＿＿＿

(15) 视觉表现形式＿＿＿＿＿＿＿＿＿＿＿＿＿＿＿＿＿＿＿＿＿＿＿

4. Translate the following sentences into English with the words or phrases given in the brackets.

(1) "仁"源于家庭关系和血缘关系的重要性，受到中国人的高度重视。(extend)
＿＿＿＿＿＿＿＿＿＿＿＿＿＿＿＿＿＿＿＿＿＿＿＿＿＿＿＿＿＿＿＿＿

(2) 按摩对放松和平衡身体各器官的机能来说很有帮助。(balance)
＿＿＿＿＿＿＿＿＿＿＿＿＿＿＿＿＿＿＿＿＿＿＿＿＿＿＿＿＿＿＿＿＿

(3) 简单来说，经络就是人体的气流经的通道。(flow)
＿＿＿＿＿＿＿＿＿＿＿＿＿＿＿＿＿＿＿＿＿＿＿＿＿＿＿＿＿＿＿＿＿

(4) 练太极有助于增强记忆力，改善平衡性，提高灵活性。(promote)
＿＿＿＿＿＿＿＿＿＿＿＿＿＿＿＿＿＿＿＿＿＿＿＿＿＿＿＿＿＿＿＿＿

(5) 孔子的社会和政治哲学的中心思想是"仁爱"。(philosophy)
＿＿＿＿＿＿＿＿＿＿＿＿＿＿＿＿＿＿＿＿＿＿＿＿＿＿＿＿＿＿＿＿＿

(6) "仁爱"的观念虽然建立在家庭关系的基础上，但也延伸到了友谊和社会关系中。(extend)
＿＿＿＿＿＿＿＿＿＿＿＿＿＿＿＿＿＿＿＿＿＿＿＿＿＿＿＿＿＿＿＿＿

Passage B　A Brief Introduction to Traditional Chinese Festivals

　　China's many ethnic groups place great emphasis on festival celebrations. The traditional festivals of the Han people include the Spring Festival (Lunar New Year), the Lantern Festival, the Festival of Clear Brightness (Qingming Festival), the Dragon Boat Festival, Praying for Wisdom Festival(the Double Seventh Festival), the Mid-autumn Festival and the Double Ninth Festival. Ethnic minority festivals include the Dai people's Water Sprinkling Festival, the Mongolian Festival of Nadam, the Tibetan Shoton Festival and the Festival of Fast-Breaking of the Hui People, etc. These festivals offer a vivid expression of traditional folk customs.

　　The Spring Festival is the most important of the traditional Han festivals. Families across the land make special New Year's purchases, wrap dumplings, paste New Year's couplets on their doors, display lanterns, hold Lion Dances, set off fireworks and drink toasts to the New Year. These customs have been passed down without a break since the Han Dynasty, thousands of years ago. The Spring Festival marks the start of the lunar year, and is a celebration of the renewal of nature and the rebirth of all living things. This holiday continues to be celebrated today just as it was thousands of years ago, with the same traditional activities and festive atmosphere. The only difference is that now, CCTV (China Central Television) broadcasts a Spring Festival special gala every year, consisting of first-class performers and a wide variety of colorful acts—a holiday "feast for the spirit" for all of China.

The Lantern Festival falls on the fifteenth day of the first lunar month. This festival might be considered as a holiday for lovers in the ancient times. The celebration reaches its peak in the evening, when every household has been decorated with colored lanterns. Families stroll through the streets, young and old together, admiring the lanterns and engaging in riddle guessing games. In classical times, even young unmarried women, generally confined to the home, were allowed outside to enjoy the lanterns on this holiday. Most traditional love stories about young scholars secretly meeting beautiful women are set on the Lantern Festival night.

The Dragon Boat Festival commemorates the poet Qu Yuan, a patriot who drowned himself to save his country 2000 years ago. On this day, it is traditional to eat the unique and delicious pastry known as Zongzi, and participate in dragon boat races.

The Mid-autumn Festival falls on the 15th day of the 8th lunar month. The festival has a long history. In ancient China, emperors followed the rite of offering sacrifices to the sun in spring and to the moon in autumn. People selected this day to celebrate because it is a season when crops and fruits are all ripe and weather pleasant. On the Mid-autumn Festival, all family members or friends get together and meet outdoor, putting moon cakes and melons on tables and admiring the moon while talking about life. How splendid a moment it is! The beautiful folk story of *Houyi shooting the sun* and *Chang E flying to the moon,* which are quite familiar to Chinese people, are closely related with the Mid-autumn Festival.

Poems about the moon

Viewing the Moon, Thinking of You

—Zhang Jiuling

As the bright moon shines over the sea,
From far away you share this moment with me.

Unit 11 Traditional Chinese Culture and Festivals

For parted lovers lonely nights are the worst to be.
All night long I think of no one but thee.
To enjoy the moon I blow out the candle stick.
Please put on your nightgown for the dew is thick.
I try to offer you the moonlight so hard to pick,
Hoping a reunion in my dream will come quick.
　　　　—Translated by Ying Sun

　　The Double Ninth Festival, held on the ninth day of the ninth lunar month, is a traditional festival of the Han people that dates back to ancient times. On this day, people go on excursions to the mountains, where they admire the fall chrysanthemums and adorn themselves with the fruit of the prickly ash, as described in the famous poem written by Wangwei, "All alone in a foreign land, I am twice as homesick on this day. When brothers carry dogwood up the mountain, each of them a branch—and my branch missing."

The fruit of the prickly ash

New words and expressions

lunar ['luːnə] *adj.* 月亮的，阴历的
wrap [ræp] *v.* (用纸或布等)包，裹
toast [təʊst] *n.* 祝酒，敬酒，干杯
renewal [rɪ'njuːəl] *n.* 更新，恢复，复兴
atmosphere ['ætməsfɪə] *n.* 气氛，氛围
gala ['gɑːlə] *n.* 庆典，演出盛会
first-class *adj.* 优秀的，第一流的
household ['haʊshəʊld] *n.* 全家人，家庭(指一户人家)
commemorate [kə'meməreɪt] *vt.* 纪念
patriot ['peɪtrɪət] *n.* 爱国者
splendid ['splendɪd] *adj.* 灿烂的，极好的
excursion [ɪk'skɜːʃ(ə)n] *n.* 远足，短程旅行

fall chrysanthemum 秋天的菊花
adorn with 佩戴
place emphasis on 重视，强调
paste New Year's couplets 贴对联
Lion Dances 舞狮
set off fireworks 放烟花
a wide variety of 多种多样的
feast for the spirit 精神的盛宴
reach its peak 到达顶峰
decorate…with… 用……装饰/布置
stroll through the streets 在街上漫步
engage in 参加，参与(活动)
admire the lanterns 赏花灯
riddle guessing games 猜灯谜
drown oneself 投水自尽
date back to 追溯到，从……开始有

Notes

1. Chinese lunar calendar: 阴历，中国传统历法之一，也被称为农历、旧历等。阴历在天文学中主要指按月亮的月相周期来安排的历法，以月球绕行地球一周为一月，即以朔望月作为确定历月的基础，一年为十二个历月的一种历法。

2. the Mongolian Festival of Nadam: "那达慕"大会是蒙古族历史悠久的传统节日。"那达慕"是蒙语的译音，意为"娱乐、游戏"。每年七、八月牲畜肥壮的季节举行的"那达慕"大会，是人们为了庆祝丰收而举行的文体娱乐大会。

3. the Tibetan Shoton Festival: 雪顿节是西藏、青海、甘肃、四川、云南等省、区藏族人民的传统宗教节日，大都在藏历二月初、四月中旬或六月中旬举行，具体日期各地不尽相同。雪顿节按藏语解释就是吃酸奶的节日，因此又叫"酸奶节"。因为雪顿节期间有隆重热烈的藏戏演出和规模盛大的晒佛仪式，所以有人也称之为"藏戏节""晒佛节"。

4. the Festival of Fast-Breaking of the Hui People: 回族的开斋节，亦称"肉孜节"，与"宰牲节"同为伊斯兰教两大节日。时间在伊斯兰教历 10 月 1 日。穆斯林在莱麦丹(第 9 月)全月斋戒，斋月最后一日寻看新月，见新月则次日开斋，即为开斋节；如未见新月，则继续封斋，节期顺延，一般不超过 3 天。

5. The Spring Festival marks the start of the lunar year, and is a celebration of the renewal of nature and the rebirth of all living things. 春节标志着农历新年的开始，也是庆祝自然复苏、

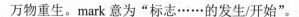

Unit 11　Traditional Chinese Culture and Festivals

万物重生。mark 意为"标志……的发生/开始"。

6. In classical times, even young unmarried women, generally confined to the home, were allowed outside to enjoy the lanterns on this holiday. 古时候，年轻的未婚女子通常是禁止外出的，但在这一天也可以外出赏灯。confine sb. to the home：将某人关在家里。

7. In ancient China, emperors followed the rite of offering sacrifices to the sun in spring and to the moon in autumn. 在中国古时候，帝王们遵循春天祭日，秋天祭月的仪式。rite 指祭祀的仪式、典礼；offer sacrifices to："把祭品献给……"，意指祭祀。

8. The fruit of the prickly ash: 此处指的是古人重阳登高时佩戴的茱萸。古人认为重阳节这一天插茱萸可以消灾避难，还能避免瘟疫。

9. Viewing the Moon, Thinking of You: 为唐代诗人张九龄《望月怀远》诗文的英译版。

10. the famous poem written by Wangwei: 此处指唐代诗人王维的名篇《九月九日忆山东兄弟》，全诗为"独在异乡为异客，每逢佳节倍思亲。遥知兄弟登高处，遍插茱萸少一人"。

Exercises

1. Choose the best answer for the following questions.

(1) Which of the following statements is not the major traditional festivals celebrated by Han people? _____

　　A. The Double Ninth Festival.　　B. The Dragon Boat Festival.
　　C. The Shoton Festival.　　D. The Lantern Festival.

(2) Which of the following statements is NOT a way that people celebrate the Spring Festival? _____

　　A. People will buy many new things for the festival, such as new clothes, candies and snacks, couplets, etc.
　　B. Lion Dances are held to celebrate the Spring Festival.
　　C. Families will get together, wrapping dumplings and setting off fireworks.
　　D. Women in the family will pray for health and wisdom.

(3) Which of the following statements about the Lantern Festival is true according to the passage? _____

　　A. Admiring the lanterns and engaging in riddle guessing games are traditional activities for this holiday.
　　B. The Lantern Festival falls on the fifteenth day of the eighth lunar month.
　　C. Women were not allowed to go out to the streets on the Lantern Festival in the ancient

times.

D. This festival is still considered a holiday for lovers today.

(4) "The Dragon Boat Festival commemorates the poet Qu Yuan…" What does the underlined word mean in this sentence? _____

    A. Remember.   B. Remind.   C. In memory of.   D. Honor.

(5) Which of the following folk stories is related with the Mid-autumn Festival? _____

    A. Kuafu Chasing the Sun.   B. Chang E Flying to the Moon.

    C. Jingwei Filling up the Sea.   D. Yugong Removing the Mountains.

(6) Which of the following statements about the Double Ninth Festival is NOT true? _____

    A. The Double Ninth Festival is held on the ninth day of the ninth lunar month.

    B. People usually put snacks and melons on tables and admire the moon in the open air.

    C. On this day, people go on excursions to the mountains.

    D. People will also put on the fruit of the prickly ash as a decoration.

2. Fill in the blanks with the appropriate form of the words or phrases given below in the box.

wrap   minority   decorate   admire   date back   celebrate   set   customary

(1) We stood for a few moments in front of the lake, _____ the picturesque view.

(2) Let's buy some champagne in _____ of her safe arrival.

(3) Every time when celebrating the New Year, the village still maintain its _____.

(4) The present was beautifully _____ in gold paper.

(5) All of the fossils _____ to 183 million years ago during the Jurassic period.

(6) We _____ our house with something red in the Spring Festival.

(7) Parents should _____ a good example to their children.

(8) This section of the bookstore caters for _____ interests.

3. Translate the following expressions into English or Chinese.

(1) a vivid expression of traditional folk customs _____

(2) dispel bad luck and bring good fortune _____

(3) family reunion dinner _____

(4) a nation with various ethnic groups _____

(5) seeing off the old year and greeting the new _____

(6) 中国农历 _____

(7) 流传千年的习俗 _____

Unit 11 Traditional Chinese Culture and Festivals

(8) 舞龙舞狮 _____

(9) 赏花灯，猜灯谜 _____

(10) 文化多样性 _____

4. Translate the following sentences into Chinese.

(1) On the first day of the Spring Festival, people pay New Year's calls, giving best wishes to one another.

_____

_____

(2) In 2005, the traditional couplet was added into the National Intangible Cultural Heritage List by the State Council of China.

_____

_____

(3) Now, the Mid-autumn Festival is listed as an official holiday in China. Many people use this "mini-holiday" to visit families and friends.

_____

_____

(4) Families across the land make special New Year's purchases, wrap dumplings, paste New Year's couplets on their doors, display lanterns, hold Lion Dances, set off fireworks and drink toasts to the New Year.

_____

_____

(5) The Dragon Boat Festival commemorates the poet Qu Yuan, a patriot who drowned himself to save his country 2000 years ago.

_____

_____

5. Translate the following paragraph into English.

中国饮茶的传统可以追溯到公元前3000多年，但"下午茶"的概念却是到17世纪中叶(the mid 17th century)才在英国出现的。当时那里时兴的晚餐时间是晚上8点，所以一位公爵夫人(Duchess)养成了在下午4点约朋友吃糕点的习惯。很快下午茶成为当时的社会潮流。随着东西方文化交流的加深，这个英国传统逐渐进入中国。如今，下午茶在国内日渐流行起来，尤其是在广东和福建地区。

6. Activity

Group work: In China, there are many traditional festivals. Please introduce one of the traditional Chinese festivals. Each group makes a presentation for about 8 minutes.

Writing: Farewell Speech 欢送词

1. Writing Skills

旅游行程中最后的一个环节就是致欢送词，能给游客留下一个完整的印象。导游说欢送词时要有标准的语音语调，语言要生动，还要懂得外事礼仪，尽可能使气氛轻松。旅游团的欢送词属于非正式致辞，形式结构比较宽松，语言比较随和。致辞包括称呼、讲话内容和祝愿结尾语，主要就是总结这次旅行的各项事宜，对各位团友的配合工作表示感谢，最后致祝愿词；有时，欢送词也可与祝酒词互用，即欢送宴会上表示欢送之意的致辞也可叫祝酒词。

注意以下三点。(1)欢送词措辞要注意礼貌、委婉，致欢送词应该礼貌待人，创造一个友好、亲切的气氛，表达感情要诚挚、真切。篇幅不宜过长。(2)欢送词是一种宣读体的稿件，它在特定的会议或场合使用，因此它要受会议或特定时间的限制。(3)欢送词的写作要注重以情动人，多采用带有感情色彩的词语。致辞时，演讲者可根据自己与被欢送者的关系、自己的身份和地位，向被欢送者提出勉励之词或祝愿词。

2. Useful Expressions and Sentences

(1) opportunity 机会，时机

(2) mutual 互相的，相互的

(3) draw a close 结束，结尾

(4) co-operative 合作的，协作的，配合的

(5) punctual 守时的，准时的

(6) treasure 珍惜，珍爱

(7) depart 启程，离开

(8) delegation 代表团

(9) counterparts 对应的人(物)

(10) banquet 宴会

(11) delightful 愉快的，高兴的

(12) sorrow 悲伤，伤痛，悔恨

(13) Time flies so quickly and your visit to XXX is drawing a close.

Unit 11 Traditional Chinese Culture and Festivals

(14) Firstly, I will really appreciate that you have been cooperative, friendly, punctual and understanding during the journey.

(15) First of all, I wish to thank you all for the cooperation and support you have given us in the past two and a half days.

(16) Our dinner this evening is to bid him farewell. Please allow me, on behalf of XXX travel in Shanghai, to express our warm send-off to XXX.

(17) However, this is the beginning of our friendship. We believe that this friendship will continue to grow in the future.

(18) Would you please send our best regards to your family members, your relatives, your friends, and your colleagues?

3. Sample Writing

Sample 1

Ladies and gentlemen,

Times flies so quickly and your visit to Shanxi Province is drawing a close. Before we part, I would like to say a few words. First, I thank everybody. Everybody in the group has been very co-operative, friendly, understanding and punctual. As your tour guide, I really appreciated it.

China is a developing country, and tourism is a newborn thing. The problems you have met on the trip were known to everyone, but the point is that we should treasure our friendship and experience. And we believe that this is the beginning of our friendship and this friendship will continue to grow in the future. Parting is such sweet sorrow, happy to meet, sorry to depart, and happy to meet again.

Welcome to Shanxi Province again!

Sample 2

Ladies and gentlemen,

Tomorrow Mr. Nathan will conclude his visit to our company with a great success. Our dinner this evening is to bid him farewell. Please allow me, on behalf of Master's Travel Service in Shanghai, to express our warm send-off to Mr. Nathan.

Mr. Nathan, during his brief stay in Shanghai, has given us many wonderful lectures on tourism. I take this opportunity to thank him for his instructive lectures. In order to improve our service in tourism, I sincerely hope Mr. Nathan will benefit us with his kind advice and valuable suggestions.

Mr. Nathan is leaving for America. I wish him a pleasant journey.

Now please raise your glasses and join me in a toast, to the continuing development of friendly cooperation between us.

To the health of Mr. Nathan.

To the health of all the American guests and to the health of all the ladies and gentlemen present.

4. Writing Practice

Prepare a farewell speech for a group of American tourists on behalf of Beijing International Travel Service at dinner in a hotel.

Supplementary Reading

The 12 animals of Chinese Zodiac

The Chinese Zodiac or shengxiao, has been part of Chinese mythology for years. It is calculated according to the Chinese lunar calendar and is based on a 12-year cycle. There are 12 Chinese Zodiac animals used to represent years. 2019 is the year of the Pig. Zodiac signs play an integral part in Chinese culture.

What is the Chinese Zodiac?

It is said that the zodiac originally had something to do with the worship of animals. A zodiac system has existed in Chinese culture since the Qin dynasty, more than 2,000 years ago. Over time the zodiac became more and more integrated into everyday life, with different meanings and characteristics assigned to each animal. They are rat, ox, tiger, rabbit, dragon, snake, horse, goat, monkey, rooster, dog, and pig in sequence.

What is the origin of the zodiac?

One legend says that the Jade Emperor needed to choose 12 animals as palace guards. The Cat asked his neighbor Rat to help him sign up. Rat forgot, which is why they became mortal enemies.

At the palace, Ox was first in line, but Rat secretly climbed onto Ox's back and jumped in front of him. Tiger and Dragon thought it was unfair, but they could only settle behind Ox. Rabbit found it unfair too. He wanted to race with Dragon and succeeded.

This angered Dog, who bit Rabbit in a fit and was sent to the back as punishment. Snake, Horse, Goat, Monkey and Rooster fought amongst themselves as well. Pig came late, after everything was finally settled, and could only be the last.

Of course, this is only a story. Cats didn't even exist in China when zodiac animals first came about.

Here comes the most interesting part. Different people born under each zodiac sign are believed to have different personalities that represent animals of the year, and since ancient times, these signs have been used to predict people's destinies. For example, people born in the year of the Rat like saving and collecting. They never have hard times financially and live organized lives. People born in the year of the Tiger are independent and have high self-esteem. They love justice and never back down in an argument.

Folklore and astrology are deeply rooted in the Chinese culture and have been for hundreds of years. Do you know any other interesting facts about the history of the Chinese Zodiac?

Useful words and phrases

mythology [mɪˈθɒlədʒɪ] *n.* 神话
calculate [ˈkælkjʊleɪt] *vt.* 计算，预测
integral [ˈɪntɪɡrəl] *adj.* (用于构成整体)必需的，不可缺少的
integrated [ˈɪntɪɡreɪtɪd] *adj.* 综合的，完整的
astrology [əˈstrɒlədʒɪ] *n.* 占星术，占星学
the Chinese Zodiac 十二生肖
a 12-year cycle 十二年一循环
the worship of animals 动物崇拜
assign to 分配，指派
sign up 报名参加
mortal enemies 宿敌，死敌
…bit rabbit in a fit ……冲动之下咬了兔子
predict destinies 预测命运
back down 放弃，让步
be deeply rooted in… 深深地根植于……

Read the passage and decide whether the following statements are true (T) or false(F).

1._____There are 12 Chinese zodiac animals used to represent years, and according to the

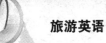

12-year cycle, 2020 will be the year of the Rat again.

2. _____ According to the order of the zodiac animals, the rabbit ranks behind the dragon.

3. _____ People born in the year of the Rat are supposed to be independent and have high self-esteem.

4. _____ Since ancient times, the animal signs have been used to predict people's destinies.

5. _____ Cats didn't even exist in China when zodiac animals first came about.

Unit 12   Chinese Arts

Learning Objectives

After learning this unit, you should:
- Understand how to introduce Chinese opera and calligraphy.
- Grasp professional English words and expressions for traditional Chinese arts and crafts.
- Get some cultural knowledge about Peking opera and calligraphy.
- Find ways to improve your writing skills about questionnaire.

Key words

Peking Opera, Chinese calligraphy, traditional Chinese

Information search

Please search some information about the topic of this unit by scanning the QR codes: (Travel Column of *China Daily*), (China Plus), (World Tourism Organization), (Travelogue of CCTV), (Ministry of Culture and Tourism of the People's Republic of China). After reading the information, please share with your classmates some information about the topic of this unit.

Warm-up

Task: In the following short video, 10 marvelous Chinese art forms are summarized by a foreign website. Discuss the following questions in groups after watching it.

1. What are the 10 marvelous Chinese art forms mentioned in the video?
2. What do you consider as the representatives of traditional Chinese arts and crafts? Why?
3. If you are going to send something as a souvenir to a foreign friend, what would you choose?

旅游英语

Passage A　Peking Opera

Peking Opera: *Drunken Beauty*

　　Known as China's national opera, Peking Opera is a form of traditional Chinese theater that originated in Beijing in the late 18th century. Compared to other types of Chinese theater, it is a relatively new style of drama, combining singing, speech, mime and acrobatics in a lively and colorful display. In Peking Opera, there are often just a table and a few chairs on the stage. The description of many situations depends on the performance of the actors and actresses. In this respect, it is quite different from modern plays of the English languages for the lack of stage manager to tell the setting, the time and overview.

　　The origins of Peking Opera date back over 200 years to the birthday celebration of a Chinese emperor. Emperor Qianlong of the Qing Dynasty (1735—1796) loved the theatre. At the time, Kunqu Opera was the most popular, but the emperor had gradually become bored with this style. The Salt Commissioner of nearby Anhui Province decided to bring the Sanqing Opera Troupe to Beijing as a birthday gift for the emperor. Sanqing was one of four main opera troupes famous for performing Anhui Opera. The occasion marked the first time regional popular theater was performed in Beijing. The four troupes later came to be known as the "four great Anhui companies", and together dominated Peking Opera for the next century.

　　Drawing on the merits of these local operas, Peking Opera came into being and became Qianlong's favorite. After becoming popular among the public, Peking Opera gradually became the most influential style of opera in China and is one of the country's greatest cultural achievements.

　　Peking Opera has four roles in general: Sheng, Dan, Jing and Chou, which are further classified by age and profession. Sheng is the main male role, which can be divided into three categories: the old, the young and the martial arts expert. Dan refers to any female role, including the young and the middle-aged, the innocent and the dissolute, girls with martial arts skills and old women. Jing is the painted-face role with distinctive temperament, character or appearance.

The color of their made-up faces can be an indication of their characters or personality. Red indicates uprightness and loyalty; white is craftiness and cunning. Blue indicates a vigorous, courageous and enterprising nature while yellow shows an intelligent character, but a less extroverted one. Black shows a sound and honest character while brown is often the symbol of a stubborn and obstinate character. Chou is a clown role with a small patch of white chalk around the nose. This character is sometimes positive, kind-hearted and humorous, but sometimes negative, crafty, malicious or silly. Each role has its fixed singing and acting styles.

The four main roles in Peking Opera

The Painted Faces in Peking Opera

Peking Opera can be divided into "civil" pieces, which focused on love, marriage, folktales, and military, which revolved around the theme of war and was known for featuring thrilling acrobatic fights.

In the early days, women were not allowed on stage so men had to take on the female roles. Peking Opera artist Mei Lanfang was famous for his skillful portrayal of female characters, with his beautifully rhymed and sweet arias and exquisite performances. In commemoration of him, China National Peking Opera Company built the Mei Lanfang Theatre, which is a perfect combination of tradition and modern art.

Peking Opera represents an important part of Chinese culture and has become a refined form of art as a result of the hard work of hundreds of artists over the past two centuries. Peking Opera has been inscribed on UNESCO's Representative List of the Intangible Cultural Heritage of Humanity on November 16th, 2010.

New words and expressions

acrobatics [ˌækrəˈbætɪks] *n.* 杂技(动作)
overview [ˈəʊvəvjuː] *n.* 概述，概要
occasion [əˈkeɪʒ(ə)n] *n.* 时机，机会，场合，理由
dominant [ˈdɒmɪnənt] *adj.* 占优势的，支配的，主导的

旅游英语

merit ['merɪt] *n.* 优点，长处
innocent ['ɪnəs(ə)nt] *adj.* 无辜的，天真的
dissolute ['dɪsəlu:t] *adj.* 放荡的，风流的
distinctive [dɪ'stɪŋ(k)tɪv] *adj.* (特征、性格或外表)独特的，与众不同的
temperament ['temp(ə)rəm(ə)nt] *n.* 气质，性情，性格，禀性
vigorous ['vɪɡ(ə)rəs] *adj.* 强健的，精力旺盛的
courageous [kə'reɪdʒəs] *adj.* 有胆量的，勇敢的
enterprising ['entəpraɪzɪŋ] *adj.* 有魄力的，有胆量的，有进取心的
intelligent [ɪn'telɪdʒ(ə)nt] *adj.* 有智慧的，聪明的
extraverted ['ekstrəvə:tɪd] *adj.* 外向的
stubborn ['stʌbən] *adj.* 顽固的，倔强的
obstinate ['ɒbstɪnət] *adj.* 顽固的，倔强的
positive ['pɒzətɪv] *adj.* 积极乐观的
negative ['neɡətɪv] *adj.* 消极的，负面的
malicious [mə'lɪʃəs] *adj.* 恶意的，恶毒的
civil ['sɪv(ə)l] *adj.* 公民的，民间的，文明的，有礼貌的
portrayal [pɔ:'treɪəl] *n.* 描绘，扮演，表现
exquisite [ɪk'skwɪzɪt] *adj.* 精致的，细腻的
refined [rɪ'faɪnd] *adj.* 优雅的，精妙的，完善的
represent [reprɪ'zent] *vt.* 代表，表现
depend on 取决于
in this respect 在这个方面
be bored with 对……感到厌倦的
draw on 利用，吸收
come into being 形成，产生
cultural achievement 文化成就
martial art 武术
craftiness and cunning 奸诈狡猾
sound and honest 诚实可靠的
a small patch of 一小块
revolve around sth. 以……为主题，围绕
take on 承担
in commemoration of 为了纪念
be inscribed on 被列入/记在……上

Notes

1. the four great Anhui companies(四大徽班): 清代乾隆年间活跃于北京剧坛的四个著名徽班，是三庆、四喜、和春、春台的合称。"四大徽班"进京，被视为京剧诞生的前奏，在京剧发展史上具有重要意义。

2. UNESCO: United Nations Educational, Scientific and Cultural Organization，联合国教育、科学及文化组织，简称联合国教科文组织，于 1946 年 11 月正式成立，总部设在法国首都巴黎，现有 195 个成员，该组织旨在通过教育、科学和文化促进各国合作，对世界和平和安全作贡献，其主要机构包括大会、执行局和秘书处。

3. Representative List of the Intangible Cultural Heritage of Humanity: 人类非物质文化遗产代表名录，是根据《保护非物质文化遗产公约》第十六条由联合国教科文组织下属的保护非物质文化遗产政府间委员会所编制的名录，用以扩大非物质文化遗产的影响，提高对非物质文化遗产重要意义的认识和从尊重文化多样性的角度促进对话。

4. Peking Opera artist Mei Lanfang was famous for his skillful portrayal of female characters, with his beautifully rhymed and sweet arias and exquisite performances. 京剧艺术大师梅兰芳以其韵律优美、悦耳动听的演唱和精湛的表演技巧，娴熟地刻画了许多女性角色，举世闻名。

5. 梅兰芳(1894－1961)，中国京剧表演艺术大师。1950 年任中国京剧院院长；1951 年，任中国戏曲研究院院长；1953 年，任中国戏剧家协会副主席。梅兰芳在 50 余年的舞台生活中，发展和提高了京剧旦角的演唱和表演艺术，形成一个具有独特风格的艺术流派，世称"梅派"。其代表作有《贵妃醉酒》《天女散花》《宇宙锋》《打渔杀家》等。

Exercises

1. Answer the following questions according to the passage.

(1) When did Peking Opera start?
_____

(2) Which opera is Peking Opera derived from?
_____

(3) Can you describe the main role types in Peking Opera?
_____

(4) What are the symbolic meanings of different colors of the Painted Faces?
_____

(5) What are the main features of Peking Opera as a performance art?
_____

(6) What is the difference between civil pieces and martial pieces in Peking Opera?
_____

(7) Can you name some famous plays of Peking Opera?
_____

(8) Is there any regional opera in your hometown? What is it?
_____

2. **Fill in the blanks with the appropriate form of the words or phrases given below in the box.**

| treasure | integrity | depend | overview | courageous |
| bored | occasion | dominant | temperament | take on |

(1) The country _____ heavily on its tourist trade.

(2) He is a man of _____. He never breaks his promises.

(3) I know sometimes you feel _____ in the class, but you have to force yourself to be concentrated.

(4) The old man always _____ the memory of the days spent with the poor but kind boy.

(5) I have a suit but I only wear it on special _____.

(6) To be a champion, skill is not enough, you have to have the right _____.

(7) He was wrong, but _____ enough to admit it.

(8) No other organization was able or willing to _____ the job.

(9) The document provides a general _____ of the bank's policies.

(10) Japan became _____ in the mass market during the 1980s.

3. **Translate the following expressions into English or Chinese.**

(1) become popular with the public _____

(2) a perfect combination of tradition and modern art _____

(3) a group of highly intelligent students _____

(4) the most exquisite craftsmanship _____

(5) an integral part to human body _____

(6) take a profound interest in _____

(7) come into existence _____

(8) intangible cultural heritage _____

(9) 国粹 _____

(10) 脸谱 _____

(11) 一个性格鲜明的角色_____
(12) 武旦_____
(13) 精力充沛的年轻人_____
(14) 对古代生活的真实描绘_____
(15) 文化传播_____
(16) 把房间装饰成红色_____

4. Translate the following sentences into English with the words or phrases given in the brackets.

(1) 京剧主要有生、旦、净、丑四大角色，这些角色还可以根据年龄和职业进行细分。(classify)
_____

(2) 中国也有一则像罗密欧与朱丽叶一样的爱情故事。故事中的恋人梁山伯和祝英台同样为爱殉情了。(die for)
_____

(3) 明晚大剧院有一出精彩的中国传统戏剧，不知道你们是否感兴趣。(wonder)
_____

(4) 如果你是一个易怒的人，你可以尝试着打太极，它可以让你变得平静。(irritable)
_____

(5) 漂亮的建筑和古老的集市是该镇的主要特色。(feature)
_____

(6) 红色在中国文化中是一种流行的颜色，象征着好运、快乐和幸福。(symbolize)
_____

Passage B Chinese Calligraphy

Calligraphy, literally "beautiful and artful writing" has been appreciated as an art form in many different cultures throughout the world, but the stature of calligraphy in Chinese culture is unmatched. In China, in a very early period, calligraphy was not just considered a form of decorative art but a supreme visual art form, and was more valued than painting and sculpture, and ranked alongside poetry as a means of self-expression and cultivation.

Five Scripts in Chinese Calligraphy

In Chinese calligraphy, characters can be written by five major styles: seal script, clerical script, regular script, cursive script and semi-cursive script.

1. Seal Script (篆书): It is the oldest style. Most people today cannot read this ancient script but it is widely used for seal engraving, hence the English name—seal script.

Orchid Pavilion Preface, Wang Xizhi (303–361), Jin Dynasty (266–420)

2. Clerical Script (隶书): It is also an archaic style but more legible than seal script. It is widely used for artistic flavor in advertisements.

3. Regular Script (楷书): It is the last major calligraphic styles, also the most easily and widely recognized style. As the name suggests, the regular script is "regular" and usually studied first by the learners of calligraphy.

4. Cursive Script (草书): It is faster to write than other styles, but difficult to read. Cursive script is always written as a work of art because of its beautiful and abstract appearance.

5. Semi-Cursive Script (行书): It's between regular and cursive: less angular and rounder than regular script, but more legible than cursive script.

Examples (龍) of these scripts:

Examples (龍) of the five scripts

Tools for Calligraphy: Brush, Ink, Paper and Ink Slab

Like painting, calligraphy employs the same tools — brush, ink, paper and ink slab(砚台), also known as the "Four Treasures of Study".

The Four Treasures of Study

- Brush—Chinese brushes are made of animal hair, being soft and flexible. By controlling the pressing or raising of the brush, the calligrapher delivers a feeling of thickness or fineness, feather-weight or heavy-strength.
- Ink—The process of ink grinding requires time and patience, thus, this process is able to make people stay calm and enter a state of mind suitable for calligraphy. Such practice of cultivation is a stage that must be gone through for studying and practicing calligraphy.
- Paper—Paper is one of the four major Chinese inventions. Paper produced in Xuan county of Anhui Province is the most famous, known as "xuan paper"(宣纸). Papers for the use of calligraphy differ in their strength of ink absorption. Thus, the selection of paper is made according to the ideas the calligrapher wants to present.
- Ink Slab—An Ink slab is an essential for ink grinding and writing. Ink slabs made from stones of the highest quality can produce ink of the best kind. Furthermore, the longer they are preserved, the higher their value is.

Related video resource: Decoding Chinese Calligraphy

All in all, differences in skills, habits, and the aesthetic tastes of calligraphers bring a difference in their dealings with strokes, structural combinations and layouts for the same character, even when identical papers, brushes, ink and ink slabs are used. Such a feature is unique to the calligraphy of Chinese characters.

New words and expressions

stature ['stætʃə] *n.* 名声，声望

unmatched [ʌn'mætʃt] *adj.* 无可比拟的，无与伦比的

supreme [suː'priːm] *adj.* 至高无上的，极度的

sculpture ['skʌlptʃə] *n.* 雕塑品，雕塑艺术

archaic [ɑː'keɪɪk] *adj.* 古代的，陈旧的，古体的

旅游英语

legible ['ledʒɪb(ə)l] *adj.* (字迹)可以辨认的，易读的
abstract ['æbstrækt] *adj.* 抽象的
angular ['æŋgjʊlə] *adj.* 有棱角的，瘦削的
flexible ['fleksəb(ə)l] *adj.* 灵活的，柔韧的
grind [ɡraɪnd] *v.* 研磨
county ['kaʊntɪ] *n.* 郡，县
absorption [əb'zɔːpʃ(ə)n] *n.* 吸收
essential [ɪ'senʃ(ə)l] *adj.* 极其重要的，本质的
stroke [strəʊk] *n.* 笔画
identical [aɪ'dentɪk(ə)l] *adj.* 完全相同的
rank alongside 并驾齐驱
self-expression 自我表达
seal engraving 印章篆刻
aesthetic taste 审美品位

Notes

1. five scripts: 指书法中的五种汉字字体，即篆书、隶书、楷书、草书、行书。

2. the Four Treasures of the Study: 文房四宝，中国古代传统文化中的书写、绘画工具，即笔、墨、纸、砚。文房四宝之名，起源于南北朝时期。

3. By controlling the pressing or raising of the brush, the calligrapher delivers a feeling of thickness or fineness, feather-weight or heavy-strength. 书法家通过控制运笔方式，下压或抬高毛笔，来实现不同的书写效果——或粗或细，或轻或重。

4. Four major Chinese inventions: 中国四大发明，是指中国古代对世界具有很大影响的四种发明：造纸术、指南针、火药及印刷术。

5. All in all, differences in skills, habits, and the aesthetic tastes of calligraphers bring a difference in their dealings with strokes, structural combinations and layouts for the same character, even when identical papers, brushes, ink and ink slabs are used. 总而言之，由于书法家的技巧、习惯和审美品位不同，即使是使用相同的纸、笔、墨、砚，书写同一个汉字，其对笔画、结构和布局的处理也不尽相同。

Exercises

1. Choose the best answer for the following questions.

(1) Calligraphy has been _____ as an art form in many different cultures throughout the world.

A. regarded   B. considered   C. remembered   D. praised

(2) The following statements introduce the main scripts of Chinese calligraphy and their features respectively, which is NOT correct? _____

    A. Seal script is the oldest style. Most people today cannot read this ancient script.

    B. Clerical script is more legible than seal script. It is widely used for artistic flavor in advertisements.

    C. Cursive script is always written as a work of art because of its beautiful and abstract appearance.

    D. Semi-cursive script is faster to write than any other styles, but extremely difficult to read.

(3) Which of the following statements about Chinese calligraphy is true according to the passage? _____

    A. Wang Xizhi was the most famous calligrapher in the Song dynasty.

    B. If you are going to learn Chinese calligraphy as a beginner, you'd better study the regular script first.

    C. The regular script is too "regular" for the self-expression of the artists.

    D. Calligraphy employs a set of tools different from painting.

(4) Which of the following statements was ranked alongside poetry as a means of self-expression and cultivation? _____

    A. Sculpture.   B. Calligraphy.   C. Painting.   D. Writing.

(5) Which of the following statements is NOT included in the "Four Treasures of Study"? _____

    A. Ink.   B. Paper.   C. Brush rack.   D. Ink slab.

(6) Which of the following statements about the "Four Treasures of Study" is NOT true? _____

    A. Chinese brushes are made of animal hair, being soft and flexible.

    B. The process of ink grinding requires time and patience, which can make people enter a state of mind suitable for calligraphy.

    C. Paper produced in Xuan county of Anhui province is the most famous.

    D. Ink slab is not so important in practicing calligraphy. A plain stone can serve as an ink slab.

(7) The longer ink slabs are _____, the higher their value is.

    A. preserved   B. made   C. produced   D. protected

2. Fill in the blanks with the appropriate form of the words given below in the box.

stroke   flexible   absorb   deliver   afar   permanent   quality   regular

(1) The drug is quickly _____ into the bloodstream.

(2) The gift itself may be light as a goose feather, but sent from _____, it conveys deep feeling.

(3) Many of the products on the market were of poor _____.

(4) He phones us every Sunday at six, _____ as clockwork.

(5) Each Chinese character consists of a group of _____ arranged in a set of order.

(6) I'm not a _____ employee. I'm working here on a fixed-term contract.

(7) The Canadians plan to _____ more food to southern Somalia.

(8) My schedule is_____. I could arrange to meet with you any day next week.

3. Translate the following expressions into English or Chinese.

(1) the cradle of Chinese civilization_____

(2) stories with a strong regional flavor_____

(3) the most easily and widely recognized style_____

(4) his growing stature as an artist_____

(5) take his words literally_____

(6) 文房四宝_____

(7) 美貌绝伦的女子_____

(8) 人物及动物石雕_____

(9) 简体与繁体_____

(10) 方块字_____

4. Translate the following sentences into Chinese.

(1) Papers for the use of calligraphy differ in their strength of ink absorption.

(2) For the experiment to be valid, it is essential to record the data accurately.

(3) The company has been successful in cultivating a very professional image.

(4) Chinese is the oldest and continuously-used language in the world.

(5) Just like English is an alphabetic language which consists of 26 letters, Chinese characters are made up of radicals and strokes.

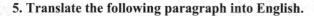

5. Translate the following paragraph into English.

灯笼(lantern)是中国传统的手工艺品(handicraft)，是中国的象征。它源于汉代(the Han Dynasty)，在唐宋时期(the Tang and Song Dynasties)最为繁盛。起初，人们在门口悬挂灯笼只是用来辟邪。后来在节假日时也悬挂灯笼以增添喜庆的气氛。灯笼的样式很多，除了圆形和方形外，还有花、鸟、鱼的形状，通常以纸和丝绸为主要制作原料。每年的元宵节(the Lantern Festival)，全国各地的人们制作出漂亮的灯笼来欢庆节日。

6. Activity

Group work: As a country with a history of more than 5,000 years, China boasts many famous traditional arts. Please introduce one of the Chinese arts with pictures or short videos. Each group makes a presentation for about 8 minutes.

Writing: Tourism Questionnaire 旅游调查问卷

1. Writing Skills

调查问卷，是调查者根据一定的调查目的和要求，按照一定的理论进行假设设计，它由一系列问题、调查项目、备选答案及说明组成，向被调查者收集资料的一种工具。

确定调查问卷的目的是问卷设计的前提条件，必须根据调查者的需求，并结合现实可行性加以确定。调查问卷中的问题类型归结起来可以分为三类：开放式问题、封闭式问题、混合型问题。(1) 开放式问题，也称自由问答题，只提问题或要求，不给具体答案，要求被调查者根据自身实际情况作答。(2) 封闭式问题：给定备选答案，要求被调查者从中做出选择；有单选和多项选择的不同设计，其中在旅游服务或者酒店服务调查问卷中，态度评比测量题很常见，这种题是将消费者态度分为多个层次进行测量，其目的在于尽可能多地了解和分析被调查者群体客观存在的态度。

设计调查问卷要注意以下几点：(1) 使调查对象回答方便；(2) 提问方式要委婉，避免采用命令性的语言，避免提出带有多种含义的问题，避免使用否定句或反意疑问句；(3) 问卷的内容不要过多，尽量简洁、清楚、避免模糊信息；(4) 回答时间不要过长；(5) 被调查者感到不好回答或不愿回答的问题，要避免提出，必要时可放在调查问卷最后；(6) 避免使用引导性语句、假设性问题、断定性语句；(7) 调查问卷最后可以简短地对被调查者的合作表示感谢。

2. Useful Expressions and Sentences

  (1) housekeeping   客房服务
  (2) check-in/check-out   登记入住/结账退房

(3) well-equipped 设施完善的

(4) concierge 礼宾服务

(5) bed linen 床品，布草

(6) punctuality 守时，准时

(7) excursion 远足，游览

(8) industry trade show 行业展销会

(9) incentive travel 奖励旅游

(10) VFR: Visiting Friends and Relatives 探亲访友

(11) resort 度假胜地

(12) cruise 邮轮

(13) We are pleased you have chosen to travel with us. In order to provide you with the best possible travel experience, we would like to know a little more about you and why you are traveling.

(14) You can help us by taking a few moments to complete this questionnaire.

(15) What is your main purpose in taking this trip?

3. Sample Writing

Sample 1: Hotel Customer Satisfaction Survey

(1) Overall, how friendly was the hotel staff? _____

 a. Extremely friendly.   b. Quite friendly.

 c. Moderately friendly.   d. Somewhat friendly. e. Not at all friendly.

(2) Overall, how polite was the hotel staff? _____

 a. Extremely polite.   b. Quite polite.

 c. Moderately polite.   d. Somewhat polite. e. Not at all polite.

(3) Overall, how professional was the hotel staff? _____

 a. Extremely professional.   b. Quite professional.

 c. Moderately professional.   d. Somewhat professional.

 e. Not at all professional.

(4) Overall, how quick was the check-in process? _____

 a. Extremely quick.   b. Quite quick.

 c. Moderately quick.   d. Somewhat quick. e. Not at all quick.

(5) Overall, how clean was your room upon arrival? _____

 a. Extremely clean.   b. Quite clean.

 c. Moderately clean.   d. Somewhat clean. e. Not at all clean.

(6) Overall, how well did the housekeeping staff clean your room? _____

a. Extremely well.   b. Quite well.   c. Moderately well.
d. Somewhat well.   e. Not at all well.   f. Not applicable.

(7) Overall, how well-equipped was your room? _____
    a. Extremely well-equipped.   b. Quite well-equipped.
    c. Moderately well-equipped.   d. Somewhat well-equipped.
    e. Not at all well-equipped.

(8) How helpful was the concierge throughout your stay? _____
    a. Extremely well-helpful.   b. Quite helpful.   c. Moderately helpful.
    d. Somewhat well-helpful.   e. Not at all helpful.

(9) How comfortable were your bed linens? _____
    a. Extremely comfortable.   b. Quite comfortable.   c. Moderately comfortable.
    d. Somewhat comfortable.   e. Not at all comfortable.

(10) Overall, how quickly did the hotel staff respond to your requests? _____
    a. Extremely quickly.   b. Quite quickly.   c. Moderately quickly.
    d. Somewhat quickly.   e. Not at all quickly.   f. Not applicable.

(11) How convenient were the hours of the food service options at our hotel? _____
    a. Extremely convenient.   b. Quite convenient.   c. Moderately convenient.
    d. Somewhat convenient.   e. Not at all convenient.   f. Not applicable.

(12) How pleased were you with the quality of the food offered at our hotel? _____
    a. Extremely pleased.   b. Quite pleased.   c. Moderately pleased.
    d. Somewhat pleased.   e. Not at all pleased.   f. Not applicable.

(13) How affordable was the hotel breakfast service? _____
    a. Extremely affordable.   b. Quite affordable.   c. Moderately affordable.
    d. Somewhat affordable.   e. Not at all affordable.   f. Not applicable.

(14) How affordable was your stay at our hotel? _____
    a. Extremely affordable.   b. Quite affordable.   c. Moderately affordable.
    d. Somewhat affordable.   e. Not at all affordable.   f. Not applicable.

(15) Overall, at what level were you satisfied with our hotel? _____
    a. Extremely satisfied.   b. Quite satisfied.   c. Somewhat satisfied.
    d. Neither satisfied nor dissatisfied.   e. Somewhat dissatisfied.
    f. Quite dissatisfied.   g. Extremely dissatisfied.

(16) How likely are you to stay at our hotel again? _____
    a. Extremely likely.   b. Quite likely.   c. Moderately likely.
    d. Somewhat likely.   e. Not at all likely.

(17) How likely are you to recommend our hotel to a friend or colleague? _____

    a. Extremely likely.   b. Quite likely.   c. Moderately likely.

    d. Somewhat likely.   e. Not at all likely.

(18) How likely are you to discourage others from staying at our hotel? _____

    a. Extremely likely.   b. Quite likely.   c. Moderately likely.

    d. Somewhat likely.   e. Not at all likely.

(19) Do you have any other comments, questions or concerns? _____

Sample 2: Guest Opinion Form

Your stay in China(Beijing)is drawing to a close. We sincerely hope that your experience has been rewarding. In order to make your future visits more enjoyable, please assist us by filling out this questionnaire.

Thank you for your co-operation and assistance.

Name of Guest: Name of Company or Tour:

Please answer the questions appropriate for your program.

As an overall experience, please rate your visit to each city.

(1) Professional meetings and site visits in this city: _____

    A. Excellent.   B. Good.   C. Average.   D. Poor.

(2) Hotel accommodations in this city: _____

    A. Excellent.   B. Good.   C. Average.   D. Poor.

(3) Quality of meals and restaurants in this city: _____

    A. Excellent.   B. Good.   C. Average.   D. Poor.

(4) Quality of local guide and interpreter in this city: _____

    A. Excellent.   B. Good.   C. Average.   D. Poor.

(5) Quality of cultural program and sightseeing in this city: _____

    A. Excellent.   B. Good.   C. Average.   D. Poor.

(6) Quality of local transportation and motor coach transfer: _____

    A. Excellent.   B. Good.   C. Average.   D. Poor.

(7) Quality of meals and restaurants in this city: _____

    A. Excellent.   B. Good.   C. Average.   D. Poor.

(8) How was your guide's ability to communicate with you? _____

    A. Excellent.   B. Good.   C. Average.   D. Poor.

(9) How would you rate your guide's knowledge of the city (country)? _____

    A. Excellent.   B. Good.   C. Average.   D. Poor.

(10) How was your guide's attitude towards group concerns? _____

    A. Excellent.   B. Good.   C. Average.   D. Poor.

(11) How was your guide' attitude towards individuals concerns? _____

    A. Excellent.   B. Good.   C. Average.   D. Poor.

(12) How would you rate your guide's friendliness? _____

    A. Excellent.   B. Good.   C. Average.   D. Poor.

(13) How would you rate your transportation service? _____

    A. Excellent.   B. Good.   C. Average.   D. Poor.

(14) How would you rate your accommodation? _____

    A. Excellent.   B. Good.   C. Average.   D. Poor.

(15) How would you rate the quality of the excursion? _____

    A. Excellent.   B. Good.   C. Average.   D. Poor.

(16) Do you have any other comments to help us make your future visits more enjoyable?

_____

_____

_____

4. Writing Practice

Work in group and design a questionnaire for a restaurant.

Supplementary Reading

Traditional Chinese Painting

    Chinese painting, commonly known as "Dan Qing" or "Guo Hua" in Chinese (meaning the national painting), is mainly drawn on the silk or paper and then framed in a scroll. It involves the use of a brush, ink, pigments, and is also known as ink and wash painting. To draw a Chinese painting, a set of fixed rules and artistic forms are to be followed, which are passed down from generation to generation.

Chinese Landscape Painting

According to subject matter, Chinese paintings can be classified as landscape paintings, figure paintings and flower-and-bird paintings. In traditional Chinese painting, Chinese landscape painting embodies a major category, depicting nature, especially mountains and bodies of water. Landscapes have traditionally been the favorite of the Chinese because they show the poetry inherent in nature. Consequently, many famous paintings are landscapes.

Meticulous Painting: Golden Pheasant and Cotton Rose Flowers with Butterflies (11th century) by Emperor Huizong of Song

When it comes to technique, there are two major categories of Chinese painting: meticulous (or the "Gongbi" school), characterized by fine brush work and close attention to detail and freehand (or the "Xieyi" school) characterized by freehand brush work and exaggerated forms. The Xieyi school of painting technique, which emphasizes the sentiments, is the basic school of thought in traditional Chinese painting.

Qi Bai-shi's freehand brushwork

Symbolism is often seen in Chinese painting. In the eyes of the artist, all the subjects could be associated with certain human personalities. For example, the Four Gentlemen, also called the

Unit 12 Chinese Arts

Four Noble Ones, in Chinese art refer to four plants: the plum blossom, the orchid, the bamboo, and the chrysanthemum. The term matches the four plants with junzi, or "gentlemen" in Confucianism, as they represent the four virtues of an ideal gentleman respectively. The stalk of the bamboo is hollow, which symbolizes tolerance, open-mindedness and unyieldingness; the plum blooming in the cold winter serves as a metaphor for inner beauty and humble display under adverse conditions; The orchid represents humility and nobility; The chrysanthemum blooms in the cold autumn air and foretells the coming of winter, which symbolizes the virtue to withstand all adversities.

Different from Western oil painting, Chinese painting has its unique aesthetic values. It lays an equal emphasis on both the artistic form and the spirit of the painted object. The drawings are not limited to time or space, but call for imagination and simplicity. These unique painting techniques not only showcase the charm of Chinese painting, but also enrich the world's art treasure trove.

Useful words and phrases

embody [ɪmˈbɒdɪ] *vt.* 包括，收录
meticulous [məˈtɪkjələs] *adj.* 一丝不苟的，小心谨慎的
freehand [ˈfriːhænd] *adj.* 徒手画的，无拘束的
exaggerated [ɪgˈzædʒəˈreɪtɪd] *adj.* 夸张的
sentiment [ˈsentɪm(ə)nt] *n.* 感情，情绪
symbolism [ˈsɪmbəlɪz(ə)m] *n.* 象征，象征主义(手法)
virtue [ˈvɜːtju] *n.* 美德，优点
hollow [ˈhɒləʊ] *adj.* 空的，中空的
tolerance [ˈtɒl(ə)r(ə)ns] *n.* 宽容
unyieldingness [ʌnˈjiːldɪŋnɪs] *n.* 不屈
framed in a scroll 装裱在卷轴中
bodies of water 水体
inherent in nature 与生俱来的
fine brush work 细腻的画风
serve as a metaphor for 是……的隐喻
humble display under adverse conditions 在逆境中表现出的谦逊
aesthetic value 审美观
the world's art treasure trove 世界艺术宝库

Read the passage and decide whether the following statements are true (T) or false(F).

1. _____It involves the use of the Four Treasures of the Study as well as pigments to draw a Chinese painting.

2. _____In terms of technique, Chinese paintings can be classified into three categories.

3. _____Like Western painting, traditional Chinese painting also stresses the scientific representation of the real world with fine nature details and exact proportion.

4. _____Symbolism is often seen in Chinese painting. For example, bamboo symbolizes tolerance, open-mindedness and unyieldingness.

5. _____Flower-and-bird paintings have traditionally been the favorite of Chinese people because they show the lively and beautiful nature.

参 考 文 献

1. 姜虹. 旅游英语[M]. 北京：经济管理出版社，2014.
2. 马飞，司爱侠. 旅游专业英语实用教程[M]. 北京：清华大学出版社，2018.
3. 王笃勤. 英语阅读教学[M]. 北京：外语教学与研究出版社，2017.
4. 于立新. 旅游英语教程[M]. 北京：北京大学出版社，2017.
5. 赵慧. 旅游英语应用文写作[M]. 北京：旅游教育出版社，2016.
6. 全国旅游职业教育教学指导委员会. 导览华夏，星耀舞台——教育部全国职业院校技能大赛高职组导游服务赛项成果展示2015[M]. 北京：旅游教育出版社，2016.
7. 中国旅游协会旅游教育分会. 导游词集锦(II)——"鼎盛诺蓝杯"第十届全国旅游院校服务技能(导游服务)大赛成果展示[M]. 北京：旅游教育出版社，2018.
8. http://www.unwto.org
9. https://www.mct.gov.cn/
10. http://www.chinadaily.com.cn/travel
11. http://chinaplus.cri.cn/
12. http://cctv.cntv.cn/lm/travelogue/